EXPLORER'S GUIDE

FINGER LAKES

FIFTH EDITION

KATHARINE DELAVAN DYSON

THE COUNTRYMAN PRESS
A division of W. W. Norton & Company
Independent Publishers Since 1923

For information about permission to reproduce selections from this book,
write to Permissions, The Countryman Press, 500 Fifth Avenue, New York, NY 10110

For information about special discounts for bulk purchases, please contact
W. W. Norton Special Sales at specialsales@wwnorton.com or 800-233-4830

Manufacturing by Versa Press
Book design by Chris Welch

The Countryman Press
www.countrymanpress.com

A division of W. W. Norton & Company
500 Fifth Avenue, New York, NY 10110
www.wwnorton.com

978-1-58157-300-8 (pbk.)

1 2 3 4 5 6 7 8 9 0

This book is dedicated to those optimistic souls who appreciate the wonder of the world around them and have the passion to discover something new each day.

EXPLORE WITH US!

This book covers the region of the Finger Lakes around or within easy driving distance of the lakes, an area that falls approximately inside the perimeter of a rough circle drawn along the New York State Thruway (Interstate 90), US 81, NY 17, and US 390 and stretching from Syracuse to Rochester and south to Ithaca. It encompasses 11 lakes (plus a few smaller lakes) in an area of about 90 miles by 60 miles.

A general history of the region is followed by an overview of the best routes into the area—by land, air, and water. The lake areas are described in five chapters: "Skaneateles, Owasco, and Otisco Lakes," "Cayuga Lake," "Seneca Lake," "Keuka Lake," and "Canandaigua Lake" (including Canadice, Conesus, Hemlock, and Honeoye). Within each of these chapters, you will find information about everything from history, lodging, and restaurants to recreation, shopping, and cultural attractions arranged under the town or area where they are located.

Find suggestions for special interests ranging from family escapes and romantic getaways to exploring wine trails and seasonal pleasures. Places to stay are geared to visitors' interests and needs. A "Wine & Beer" section in each chapter highlights a robust selection of itineraries. Features in major cities—Syracuse, Rochester, Corning, Elmira, and Cortland—are described in a separate chapter. The last chapter, "Information," gives Finger Lakes facts and figures.

In the index you will find lodging and dining facilities. Every effort has been made to place towns and villages in the chapter that covers the lake (or lakes) nearest to the place. Still, there are coin tosses on some spots that straddle an area between two lakes. In this case the index can be your best guide.

Although all information was as accurate as possible as of publication, I suggest that you call ahead before visiting. Please note that many places are open only during the warmer months, usually from mid-April through mid-October.

PRICES Since the Finger Lakes region is most active with visitors during the warmer months, you can expect prices to be higher at that time, especially for lodging. In addition to higher prices during the popular months, you may also find that some places require a two- or three-night minimum. Cabin or house rentals may require a one-week minimum. Off-season is a different story. But always ask.

BOATS ARE ALL FITTED OUT FOR JULY 4TH

A general price range is given with lodging prices per room, double occupancy, and may or may not include breakfast or other meals. Restaurant prices indicate the cost of a meal for one person including an appetizer or salad, main course, and dessert. Bar beverages are extra.

LODGING PRICE CODES:
$: Up to $75 per couple
$$: $76–$150 per couple
$$$: $151–$250 per couple
$$$$: More than $250 per couple

DINING PRICE CODES:
$: Up to $10
$$: $11–$25
$$$: $26–$40
$$$$: More than $40

I welcome your comments on the content of the book and any personal experiences you care to share. A major effort was made to include all key historic sites and attractions as well as a wide variety of lodgings, restaurants, retail establishments, and other places of interest. The purpose of this book, however, was not to include everything but to provide you with a good sense of what there is in order to entice you to explore further, and to give you contact points, typically websites, phone numbers, and addresses, so you may get more particulars as needed.

Check out my website for more information, updates, and ongoing events: www .FingerLakesInfo.com.

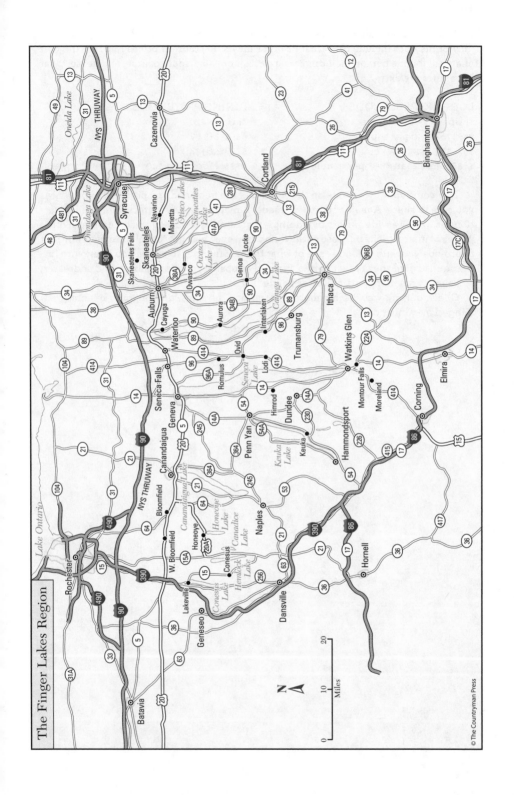

The Finger Lakes Region

© The Countryman Press

CONTENTS

MAPS

ACKNOWLEDGMENTS

In the process of researching, writing, and updating this book, I have continually met people who went out of their way to help me. I must first thank Dan Crissman, senior editor at The Countryman Press, a division of W. W. Norton & Company, publisher. I truly appreciate all the energy and insight offered by copyeditor Holly Delavan, who worked tirelessly to pull it all together. Paul Thomas, executive director of the Seneca Wine Trail, was a great help in filling me in on the wine and exploding brewery industry, while Brittany Gibbs of the Watkins Glen Chamber of Commerce was a font of knowledge about her area, as was Mike Linehan, president and CEO of the Yates County Chamber of Commerce.

A big thank you also to Meg Vanek of Cayuga County Tourism; Tara Lynn of the Skaneateles Chamber of Commerce; and Carol Eaton, vice president in marketing, and Nikita Jankowski, communications manager, both of Visit Syracuse. Valerie Knoblauch, president of the Finger Lakes Visitors Connection, whose overview of the region is astounding, along with Karen Miltner filled me on the new and exciting developments in Ontario County; while Ken McConnell, vice president of the Finger Lakes Bed & Breakfast Association, and his wife, Diane, of Barrister's B&B in Seneca Falls, shared their knowledge of the B&B scene.

I appreciated input from Cynthia Kimble of the Finger Lakes Tourism Alliance, a very savvy lady on the entire area, as well as Marybeth Hafner of Hammondsport and Kristy Mitchell of the Ithaca/Tompkins County CVB. Thanks also to Cynthia Raj of

Bonnie Gustin

BICYCLE TRAILS CIRCLE THE LAKES

Chemung County Chamber of Commerce, Rick Newman of Seneca County, and Liz Weeden of Quinn & Company.

I enjoyed touring Corning, Hammondsport, and Bath with David DeGolyer and Kevin Peterson of the Steuben County Conference and Visitors Bureau, and visiting the stunning new wing at Corning Museum of Glass (thanks also here to Kimberly Thompson, who showed us through the exhibits, and Peggy Coleman, president of the Steuben County Conference and Visitors Bureau). Claire Wysokowski of Visit Rochester and Jim Dempsey of the Cortland County Visitors Bureau also deserve my appreciation for helping with this update.

Matthew Urtz, Madison County historian, offered valuable knowledge about the history of the hops industry in Central New York, while Bill Delavan of Delavan Center filled me in on the Syracuse restaurant and art scene. Avid diners Carol and John Young, Laurel and John MacAllister, and Guy and Kathie Garnsey also contributed to the regional dining knowledge.

I loved having my grandchildren, Will and Charlie Pinckney, along on excursions to weigh in on the kid-friendly sites. And I could not have done this without the patience and support of my husband, John, who pulled together many a dinner when I was buried in notes and papers. He also did a lot of the driving on several trips, and took wonderful photos.

INTRODUCTION

As you drive through the rolling hills and valleys of the Finger Lakes, where summer brings Friday-night band concerts, acres of thriving vineyards, and sails darting across lakes, you are mindful that this region is one of the most beautiful on earth. The crystalline waters of more than 11 lakes nestle in the valleys, horses graze in meadows, corn and wheat fields create crazy-quilt patterns across the landscape, and waterfalls plunge into deep gorges.

Summer means sailboats tacking from shore to shore; endless fields of tasseled corn, alfalfa, and wheat; flashes of goldenrod, china-blue chicory, purple horsemint, and buttercups along with warm-soft evenings sparkled by the fleeting beacons of lightning bugs.

High school and college football games kick off the orange-red glow of fall, which quickly turns brisk as grapes and apples are harvested and dry bundles of corn stand like sentries in the countryside against deep lapis skies. Winter ushers in drifts of snow and ice-covered trees. Skiers take to the slopes; skaters clear snow off lakes and ponds and glide onto the ice; and snowmobiles forge new trails across pristine white fields. Spring blossoms with sweet-scented blue, pink, and white lilacs, tulips, daffodils, and clouds of forsythia, while hundreds of waterfalls burst over outcroppings of rocks, diving to icy pools below.

There are vibrant cities like Rochester, Ithaca, and Syracuse; and picture-postcard villages with expansive lawns and white-clapboard houses with front porches armed with wicker furniture and window boxes brimming over with petunias, ivy, and geraniums. There are mansions, like Sonnenberg in Canandaigua; the amazing Corning Glass Center; Watkins Glen International Raceway; and a handful of old-fashioned ice-cream parlors, wooden-floored hardware stores, and drive-in movie theaters from the '50s.

Creating a vibrant atmosphere of continual growth and cultural opportunities are Syracuse University, RIT (Rochester Institute of Technology), Cornell University, University of Rochester, Ithaca College, Wells College, Hobart and William Smith Colleges, Keuka College, and others.

Many of the original settlers in the region were farmers, and today a strong farm population still exists. Drive along country roads and you'll pass billboards promoting farm machinery, huge blue Harvestore silos, and a patchwork of plowed fields defined by tightly woven stands of trees and hedgerows. Signs along the road warn of cows or tractors crossing and advertise homemade products: stacked rows of split firewood, fruits and vegetables, cut flowers, and piles of corn.

At the end of the day as the sun melts into the horizon, you are sure to see black-and-white Holsteins crowding the gates, their udders heavy with milk, as they wait for farmers to take them into the barn and relieve them of their bounty.

In towns like Moravia, Auburn, Geneva, Aurora, Canandaigua, and Skaneateles, much of the eighteenth-century architecture has been preserved; while a reminder of our Native American heritage is found at the Ganondagan State Historic Site in Victor, a seventeenth-century Native American settlement, just outside Rochester.

Many of the pleasant little towns like Homer, Avon, and Dresden, anchored by farmland on either end, usually have shops worth browsing, a barn full of antiques piled helter-skelter, a place to eat, or a nice bed-and-breakfast. Some shops post their hours as "open by chance or appointment." This lack of commercial hype promises a few days' escape from the corporate treadmills. In the Finger Lakes, the pace is kinder. Gridlock? What gridlock?

This does not mean there isn't plenty to see and do. There are vineyards to visit, trails to hike, cruises to take, and historical sites to explore such as the Erie Canal Museum and the Women's Rights Park. There are great restaurants, festivals and fairs, beautiful villages and cities, and places to stay ranging from wonderful bed-and-breakfasts to large hotels and boutique spa resorts.

Having grown up in Skaneateles and lived in this village for more than half of my life, I can trace family roots back six generations. My father was born in Seneca Falls, and relatives live throughout the region from Rochester to Syracuse. As a travel writer I am fortunate to be able to visit places all around the world, from Africa to China to Brazil to Europe. Perhaps because of these experiences, I have a deep appreciation for the Finger Lakes, a part of our world that combines some of the best characteristics of those places I have enjoyed the most. It's good to know in America, there is such a place as the Finger Lakes.

—Katharine Dyson

WHAT'S WHERE IN THE FINGER LAKES

According to Native American legend, when the Great Spirit laid his hands on this land to bless it, the imprints left by his fingers filled with water to form lakes. Hence the "Finger Lakes." You can believe this or the geologists' explanation: More than 550 million years ago, during the Pleistocene Ice Age, glaciers crept through the area from north to south, carving deep slices in the land. The ice pushed the land and rocks southward. Gradually the ice melted and the glaciers withdrew, leaving shale-bedded valleys of water so deep in some places that their bottoms are below sea level.

As the glaciers receded, the pileup of rocks in the southern ends of lakes like Skaneateles and Cayuga produced fiord-like terrains with steep sides and deep waters, creating perfect microclimates for growing grapes. Spectacular waterfalls were formed, like the 215-foot-high Taughannock Falls off the southwestern shores of Cayuga Lake and the deep gorges of Watkins Glen at the southern end of Seneca Lake.

The glacial landscaping—the lakes, the moraines (debris fields left by glaciers), and the small "kettle lakes" (bowl-like depressions)—create a uniquely stunning landscape and fertile agricultural lands.

The clarity of the water of the Finger Lakes has gained a worldwide reputation—in places so clear, it's like looking through glass straight down to the bottom.

TAUGHANNOCK FALLS OVERLOOK IS JUST NORTH OF ITHACA

First There Were the Native Americans

There is no doubt as to the Native American heritage of the region. Names of lakes, villages, streets, restaurants, inns, and even today's families are derived from tribal languages: Taughannock, Owasco, Skaneateles, Genesee, and Cayuga.

Before the American Revolution in 1775, some twenty thousand members of the Haudenosaunee (the Six Nations of the Iroquois Confederacy) lived in the Finger Lakes region. The Mohawks were the warriors and keepers of the eastern door of the longhouse while the Onondagas were the fire keepers and the "secretaries" of the tribes. The Senecas, hunters and keepers of the western door and the largest of the nations, were the most fiercely protective of the tribes of their territory. There were also the Oneida and Cayuga, the farmers, and later the Tuscarora.

Before the first white settlers found their way here, life in the Finger Lakes was remarkably democratic. The Great Law of the Native Americans gave their people free speech, religious liberty, and the right to bear arms to protect the security of each person. Women were influential in this society, while the war chiefs were subordinate to the highly respected elected civil chiefs such as Joseph Brant, a Mohawk, and Cornplanter, a Seneca.

In 1794 the Pickering Treaty, an agreement between the United States and the Haudenosaunee, confirmed the Phelps and Gorham Purchase of 2.6 million acres east of the Genesee River for $5,000 plus an annuity of $500 in perpetuity, thereby establishing the sovereignty of the nations. Each year on November 11, the signing of the Pickering Treaty is celebrated at the county courthouse, with G. Peter Jemison and other Native Americans in attendance.

At the Wood Memorial Library in Seneca Falls, you'll find a piece of faded old parchment, the Native Americans' copy of the original Pickering Treaty, signed by Red

Genesee Country Village and Museum

THE GENESEE COUNTRY VILLAGE AND MUSEUM NEAR ROCHESTER RECALLS WHAT EARLY LIFE WAS LIKE.

Jacket, Little Beard, and Cornplanter. A boulder on the courthouse grounds in Canaan marks where the signing took place.

The eighteenth and nineteenth centuries were turbulent times. Settlers were pitted against natives; natives against settlers. Families on both sides—including women and children—were killed or taken prisoner. Some were tortured. Others, like Mary Jemison, were assimilated into the tribal community.

During the Revolutionary War, General George Washington, believing that the Native Americans were siding with the British, ordered Generals Clinton and Sullivan to wipe out Indian activity in the region around Seneca and Cayuga Lakes. In carrying out their assignment, more than five thousand men with four thousand horses torched villages and cornfields, cut down trees, and exiled the people. Not a single Indian settlement or field of corn was spared. Their wave of destruction broke the backbone of the Iroquois community.

A plaque on the west side of Cayuga Lake near Burroughs Point reads SITE OF AN INDIAN VILLAGE DESTROYED DURING THE SULLIVAN CAMPAIGN 1779. As reminders of lives past, arrowheads and bits of pottery occasionally turn up in the fields and along lakeshores.

Settlers Move In

In the late 1700s people like Job Smith and John Cuddeback settled communities like Seneca Falls and Skaneateles. Most early settlers were farmers, while some raised cattle and established dairy farms. After the Revolutionary War, when the United States government granted land to officers and soldiers who had fought for independence, the population in the region expanded rapidly.

After the opening of the Erie Canal, businesses developed along waterways. The most imposing buildings of the period were the grist and sawmills that were built along rivers and outlets. With the construction of the Seneca Turnpike in 1803 from Utica to Canandaigua, traffic increased and stagecoaches rumbled across regular routes. A long bridge built across the northern end of Cayuga Lake meant travelers on the Great Western Turnpike no longer had to go the long way around Montezuma Swamp. At either end of the bridge, taverns and general stores blossomed, creating mini boomtowns. Today the bridge is gone, and the area known as Bridgeport consists merely of a firehouse, an old cemetery, and a park.

John Dyson

BOATS TIED UP ON THE CAYUGA-SENECA CANAL IN SENECA FALLS

Following the Great Depression of 1929, many farms were abandoned. Some areas, such as the land southwest of Skaneateles Lake, were purchased in the 1930s and replanted by the Civilian Conservation Corps. Today these state forests are used for hiking, biking, and other recreational purposes.

In the early 1900s when most buildings were made of wood and firefighting equipment and transportation of water were primitive, many villages, including Seneca Falls, Skaneateles, and Geneva, were scarred by major fires. New buildings were built of brick and constructed with firewalls, very visible in the business block along Genesee St. in Skaneateles.

The Erie Canal

The Erie Canal was first derided as a major folly. Stretching from Albany to Buffalo, "the Big Ditch" took an army of laborers eight years to complete. The first ceremonial shovel of dirt was dug in Syracuse in 1817 near the spot where the Erie Canal Museum now stands. When the canal opened in 1825, sending a rush of water flowing from Lake Erie and the Hudson River, cannons spaced 5 miles apart along the 363-mile canal heralded this grand event.

The canal was an idea sparked by a man from his jail cell. As the story goes, Jesse Hawley, once a man of substance in the freight-forwarding business, found himself languishing in debtor's prison in Canandaigua after his failed attempts to transport grain from farms to mills in Seneca Falls and finally to New York City. It was too expensive and too treacherous.

During his 20 months behind bars, he wrote 14 essays, including one proposing a better way to move his products. He envisioned a man-made waterway from Lake Erie to the Mohawk River. He made sketches and wrote several articles detailing how it could be done. Eventually these materials landed in the hands of DeWitt Clinton, mayor of New York City.

Clinton became obsessed with the idea, and work began. Lacking proper engineering talent, the project became a huge on-the-job-training exercise. Special challenges included constructing locks, developing waterproof cement, blasting through rock, constructing aqueducts, and solving the problem of keeping the water from drying up in areas prone to drought.

With the canal completed, goods could be moved from Buffalo to New York City in just ten days instead of six weeks, and a ton of freight cost $10 instead of $100. Commerce thrived, encouraging immigrants to move to the area. In 1835 the canal was widened and deepened, and locks were doubled to handle the gridlock from the increasing traffic. Continual improvements over the next few years included rerouting a portion of the canal to incorporate existing rivers and lakes and building a "spur"—the Cayuga-Seneca Canal, which connected the two lakes. In 1918 the Erie Canal became the Barge Canal.

The canal brought new prosperity to the state and especially to the villages along the waterways, including Syracuse, Port Byron, and Seneca Falls. Portions of the canal are still open today, and its use as a recreational waterway has replaced its importance as a commercial conduit.

Women's Rights

A small bronze marker on a building on Fall St. in Seneca Falls marks the location where the women's rights movement all started: a convention held in 1848 at the Wesleyan Chapel in Seneca Falls. Led by the determined duo of Elizabeth Cady Stanton and Lucretia Mott, the convention dealt with such hot issues as temperance, abolition, suffrage, and dress reform. The Declaration of Sentiments and Resolutions was read to 300 people, including 40 men. One hundred people signed it.

Mennonites and Amish

Around Seneca, Keuka, and Cayuga Lakes, the horse-drawn black buggies of the more than 300 Amish and Mennonite families on the roads are a reminder that there are still those who choose to live their lives with no electricity, telephone, television, or computer. For Old Order Amish, a subgroup of the Mennonites, such things as cars, planes, and trains are seen as threats to the family unit, corrupting the values they hold dear. Mennonites, like the Amish, live a simpler life, but they are not as strict in their living habits and are more moderate toward the use of modern technology.

Because of their hard work, close-knit families, and sense of community, the Amish and Mennonites typically flourish. They own their own land, are very self-sufficient, take great joy in their children, and make strong contributions to their communities, most earning their living through farming, building, and commercial endeavors like the Weaver family's Weaver View Farm Country Store and B&B on Seneca Lake and Sauders amazing bulk food outlet in Seneca Falls.

Transportation

With the Finger Lakes region just a one-day drive (about 300 miles) from about 50 percent of the population of the United States, many visitors arrive by car. Some, however, come by rail via Amtrak, which runs from Albany to Buffalo. Airports in Syracuse, Rochester, Ithaca, Elmira/Corning, and Binghamton link the region to the rest of the world. Finally, the Greyhound and Trailways bus systems offer point-to-point service throughout all the major cities. 800-231-2222, www.greyhound.com; 800-858-8555, www.trailways.com

Approximate distance to the center of the Finger Lakes Region:
Albany: 214 miles
Buffalo: 138 miles
New York City: 295 miles
Washington, D.C.: 337 miles

Major transportation hubs include:
Syracuse: William F. Walsh Regional Transportation Center www.centro.org /syracuse.aspx
Rochester: RTS Transit Center www.myrts.com/transitcenter
Ithaca: TCAT (Tompkins Consolidated Area Transit) www.tcatbus.com

Paulette Likoudis

HORSES ARE STILL USED IN THE FIELDS BY THE AMISH

GLIDER TAKING OFF AT HARRIS HILL SOARING IN ELMIRA

BY CAR Many roads follow old Native American trails along waterways. For example, NY 5, which runs east–west through the region and becomes NY 5 and US 20 much of the way, was once a Native American footpath about 18 inches wide and blazed by hatchet notches on trees. The Great Central Trail led to the longhouses on the shores of Onondaga Lake. A cavalcade of colonial settlers, French priests, traders, explorers, adventurers, and pioneers widened the trail as their wagons rumbled along the routes.

EAST–WEST ROUTES

Major east–west routes include scenic NY 17 (being converted to Interstate 86), the New York Thruway (Interstate 90), US 20, and NY 5 and US 20. From New York City, it's about a four- or five-hour drive to the easternmost part of the Finger Lakes following these routes.

So important is the east–west Route 5 and 20 that a special committee has been declared promoting the farms, food, and fun along this "authentic American road" (www.routes5and20.com).

Interstate 86: From Jamestown to Orange County just north of New York City, this divided highway offers rest and picnic areas along the way. Although I-86 seems to be continually under repair at various points, for the most part the surface is good, and the scenery along the rivers and through the Catskills and southern tier of the state to Erie, Pennsylvania, makes it well worth going this way unless you are into high-speed driving (the speed limit is 55 mph).

The New York Thruway (I-90): This limited-access divided toll road runs along the top third of the state, from Albany to Buffalo and south to Erie. It's rather boring but efficient, with a speed limit of 65 mph in many sections.

US 20: The old route used extensively before the Thruway was built links Albany to Buffalo. It runs through the center of many of the most beautiful towns in the Finger Lakes. If you have the time—village speed limits and stoplights will slow your

THE BIKE TRIP AROUND THE OUTER PERIMETER OF KEUKA LAKE IS 46 MILES

pace—and want to capture the flavor of the region, take this route. Major towns along US 20 include Skaneateles, Auburn, Seneca Falls, Waterloo, Geneva, and Canandaigua.

NORTH–SOUTH ROUTES

Major north–south routes are I-81 bordering the eastern lakes region and US/Interstate 390 going from I-86 to Rochester.

Interstate 81: Running along the easternmost border of the region, this divided highway has fair-to-good roads (except in a snowstorm) and well-marked exits. Two lanes run each way along most of the route, and some portions allow 65 mph driving. Picnic areas and services are available along the highway.

US 15: Runs from Washington, D.C., through central Pennsylvania, Harrisburg, and through the heart of Amish country to Corning.

Interstate 390: Skirts the western part of the region from I-86 to Rochester.

BY FOOT AND BIKE The **New York State Canalway Trail** has more than 230 miles of multi-use recreational trails which crisscross the Finger Lakes region. Most are adjacent to the state's canals or run along remnants of original canals no longer in use. The typically flat terrain provides excellent biking for all skill levels. Those who want to fill in the gaps of the entire 524-mile canal system can use New York State Bike Rts. 5 and 9, which run north and west along current state roads.

BY WATER

ERIE CANAL

Running east–west from Albany to Buffalo, the New York State canal system contains 524 miles of canal and waterways connecting Albany, Utica, Syracuse, Rochester, and Buffalo. Systems include the Erie Canal, the Champlain and Oswego systems, and the Cayuga-Seneca Canal built in 1821 to connect the two lakes. Great destinations for day trips, weekend excursions, or connecting points to other waterways, the New York State canals are usually navigable April through November. Adjacent to the canals are more than 260 miles of hiking and biking trails. The system has 60 locks, making it possible for canal boats and pleasure craft to go across the entire state by water. Boat launches are located at points along the way. Two-day, ten-day, and seasonal permits are available. $5–$100; 800-4CANAL4; www.nyscanals.gov

BOATING In line with the Federal Boating Act, every boat using auxiliary power must be registered and numbered. Licenses are issued for a three-year period.

Those bringing in boats from other states do not need to get a license for 90 days, provided these boats are numbered according to federal law. If you don't have a proper registration, you need to get one. Contact the Department of Motor Vehicles, Division of Motor Vehicle Regulation, Empire State Plaza, Albany, New York 12228; www.nydmv.state.ny.us

Speed limit is 5 mph within 100 feet of shore, except on Canandaigua and Keuka Lakes, where the limit is extended to 200 feet from shore.

THE CANAL SYSTEM AND LAKES ARE POPULAR WITH KAYAKERS

Arriving in Host Cities

CORNING & ELMIRA

BY AIR Elmira/Corning Regional Airport, Exit 51 on NY 17, Corning 14830. Scheduled air services are available with American Airlines and Northwest Airlines. Corning is about equal distance from the Syracuse and Rochester airports. www .ecairport.com

BY TRAIN Corning is also about equal distance from the Rochester and Syracuse Amtrak stations, approximately 75 miles in either direction. www.amtrak.com

RENTAL CARS Avis, Hertz, and National car rentals are available at the airport.

ITHACA

BY AIR Tompkins County Airport, 72 Brown Rd., Ithaca 14850. The airport is served by Delta Airlines and American Airlines. The airport has a café, conference room, computer/fax/modem jacks, and a limousine shuttle. www.flyithaca.com

BY TRAIN Ithaca is about 47 miles from the Syracuse Amtrak station.

RENTAL CARS Avis and Hertz rental cars are available at the airport terminal.

ROCHESTER

BY AIR Greater Rochester International Airport: On the south side of Rochester, 15 minutes from downtown, the airport has one main terminal with two concourses. Airlines include Southwest Airlines, United Airlines, Air Canada, Delta Air Lines, Jet-Blue Airways, and American Airlines. On-site services include shuttles to the hotels, car rentals, taxi and bus service, sheltered parking garage, business center, meeting rooms, restaurants, and gift shops. 1200 Brooks Ave., Rochester 14624; (585-753-7000); www2.monroecounty.gov

Rochester Shuttle Express: Round-the-clock, door-to-door service between your home and the Greater Rochester International Airport. The shuttle also offers mini tours of Rochester and trips to Niagara Falls, Buffalo, and Toronto. www.rocshuttle.com

BY TRAIN Amtrak: Services include ticket sales, Quik-Trak ticketing machines, and checked baggage. The trip to New York City takes about 6.5 hours; the run from Rochester to Syracuse is 1 hour 16 minutes. www.amtrak.com

BY BUS The Regional Transit Service: A quick, convenient way to get around. Check New York State Trailways and Greyhound. www.rgta.com

BY CAR A color-coded sign system aids drivers in navigating downtown Rochester: Convention Center-red; Eastman Theatre-blue; Shopping-orange; Strong Museum—brown; War Memorial—green. Auto rentals (Alamo, Americar, Avis, Budget, Enterprise, Hertz, National, and Thrifty) are at the Greater Rochester International Airport and other outlets.

CHARTERING A CANAL BOAT

Erie Canal Cruise Lines: Half-week and full-week charters on the Erie Canal are available for up to six adults. Included in the fare are linens, fuel, housewares, lock fees, itinerary, and tax. The 42-foot custom-built canal cruisers feature two private suites with a vanity, toilet, and shower, a dinette that converts to a full-size berth, and a fully equipped galley. The boats are air-conditioned and equipped with a television/VCR and CD/cassette player. Social and lounging areas are located on aft and top decks. The curtains and knotty-pine interior of the boats have a homey feeling.

Start in Seneca Falls on the Cayuga-Seneca Canal, where you will experience the double lock, lifting you 50 feet in back-to-back lock chambers. You'll join the Erie Canal just beyond the Montezuma National Wildlife Refuge. You can also push off in Fairport, southeast of Rochester, and cruise west toward Pittsford and Lockport. 800-962-1771; www.canalcruises.com

MID-LAKES NAVIGATION COMPANY: Mid-Lakes offers two- and three-night canal cruises with accommodations at ports along the way. For example, the 42-passenger Emita II, with departures from Buffalo, Macedon, Syracuse, and Albany, has a bar, a library, an open front deck, and an upper deck.

For those who prefer to captain their own boat, Mid-Lakes charters Lockmaster canal boats ranging from 33 feet to 44 feet long and 10 feet wide, with a top speed of about 6 mph. The boats are fairly simple to operate, and you can navigate the locks in about 20 minutes. Each comes with a fully equipped galley, VHF radio, ice cooler, gas range, refrigerator, binoculars, linens, cleaning supplies, and two bicycles. Some have two cabins. Weekly charters are available. Starting at Cold Springs Harbor near Syracuse, you can choose to cruise three different canals. One of the most popular is the Cayuga-Seneca Canal; tie up in Seneca Falls for the night. Mid-Lakes also offers daily cruises on Skaneateles Lake and the Erie Canal. www.midlakesnav.com

Rent kayaks, canoes, and other human-powered watercraft for fun on the lakes and rivers through Fuzzy Guppies at 1278 Waterloo-Geneva Rd. between Seneca Falls and Geneva. The "Gups" harbor bus can also transport kayakers, campers, and guests to various locations for special outings. www.fuzzyguppies.com

BY TAXI Taxis can be found at airports, bus stations, train terminals, hotels, and on call.

SYRACUSE

BY AIR Syracuse Hancock International Airport: Airlines serving Syracuse include United Airlines, Air Canada, Delta Air Lines, JetBlue Airways, Allegiant and American Airlines. There is no regular shuttle or bus service to downtown Syracuse. Be prepared to take a taxi. www.syrairport.org

BY TRAIN William F. Walsh Regional Transportation Center: Services include ticket sales and checked baggage. www.centro.org

Amtrak: Provides rail-passenger transportation from the William F. Walsh Regional Transportation Center with frequent daily departures. The trip to New York City takes about 5.25 hours. www.amtrak.com

BY BUS Greyhound/Trailways: Located in the same transportation terminal as Amtrak. www.greyhound.com

Centro Bus: Provides public transportation in the city and to the suburbs. Onondaga Coach, Greyhound, Syracuse & Oswego, and Trailways also have intercity passenger service. www.centro.org

BY TAXI There are a number of taxi services on call in the Syracuse area including the Syracuse Taxi Service 315-488-TAXI; the Syracuse Green Taxi 315-460-0299; Dependable Taxi 315-741-5127; and Blue Star Taxi 315-437-4000

BY CAR Alamo, Avis, Budget, Enterprise, Hertz, Dollar, National, and Thrifty auto rentals are available at Hancock International Airport and other outlets. Those needing to park their car for a few days while they are away may want to overnight at the Holiday Inn Express at the airport where as guests, they can park their car for free (for a limited time), take the hotel shuttle the short way to the terminal, and pick up their car on return.

Visiting the Finger Lakes

People come to the Finger Lakes for a variety of reasons, but there is one thing for sure: The time of year when you come will determine the activities you enjoy in this four-seasons region.

June, July, and August are usually gloriously warm and sunny, perfect for water sports, hiking, biking, and outdoor markets and fairs.

Fall comes around mid-October or earlier, providing wonderful color and bright-blue skies—great football weather. Snow usually comes in November but has arrived as early as mid-October.

Winter usually delivers deep snow—blustery, huddle-around-the-fire type stuff; temperatures can plunge below zero. The lakes often freeze and sometimes are dotted with skaters and ice boaters.

The long-anticipated spring usually appears before Easter, but some years the Easter Bunny has needed snowshoes because the lakes are still frozen.

Wineries, Breweries, and Distilleries

Where just a handful of vineyards existed in the Finger Lakes in the early 1960s, today there are more than 130 vineyards and wineries neatly marching up and down the hillsides of Seneca, Cayuga, Keuka, Canandaigua, and Skaneateles Lakes and on the land in between, along with a growing number of breweries and distilleries springing up throughout the region. To get an overview of the wineries and breweries in the state, your first stop might be the New York Wine and Culinary Center in Canandaigua where there are tasting rooms, dining rooms for small private parties, a restaurant with a deck overlooking the water, a culinary kitchen where classes are taught, a gift shop, a culinary garden, and historical exhibits. It's impressive.

But it's not just the number of vineyards; it's the quality of the wines that gives cause to celebrate. After many years when regional wines were generally considered inferior to those from France and California, Finger Lakes wines are finally being recognized as standing with the best in the world. Indeed, during the past few years, the

DR. FRANK'S VINIFERA WINE CELLARS HAS BEEN A PACESETTER IN THE FINGER LAKES WINE INDUSTRY

region has produced award-winning wines including rieslings that are now touted as the finest in the country. Torrey Ridge received double gold medals for their Lucky and Diamond wines in the 2015 Florida State Fair International Wine Competition, and *Wine Enthusiast* magazine recognized New York State as its "Wine Region of the Year" in 2014.

As early as 1873, Great Western was the first champagne from the United States to win a gold prize at the Vienna Exposition. Glenora Wine Cellar's 1987 chardonnay was featured at George Bush's inaugural dinner in 1989, and wines from Dr. Frank's Vinifera Wine Cellars have been served at the White House and continue to beat French wines in blind tastings—their dry riesling has won numerous golds at competitions around the world.

Finger Lakes vineyards are typically owned and operated by families whose roots run deep here; some have been growing grapes for generations. Jerry and Elaine Hazlitt, who opened their winery in 1985 (Hazlitt 1852 Vineyards Winery), are the sixth generation in a family that has been growing grapes in the Finger Lakes since the mid-1800s; Art Hunt (Hunt Country Vineyard) is also sixth generation in the business.

Whereas the Finger Lakes region is best known for its whites, reds like Fox Run's cabernet sauvignon and Hazlitt's, Hosmer's, and Lakewood's cabernet franc are receiving accolades from outside the region. In four recent international and national wine competitions, 25 Finger Lakes wineries took gold medals for close to 60 wines, with an increasingly diverse array of wines, from grüner veltliner and syrah to teroldego and gewürztraminer.

FARM-BREW RENAISSANCE

The farm-brew renaissance is on the move in the Finger Lakes as a hot new industry in the region fueled by a resurgence in growing hops and a desire for killer beer. In the late 1800s, 80 percent of hops grown in the United States—seven million pounds—was produced in Madison County to the east of Syracuse and nearby regions, but the industry declined to a trickle. Now, thanks to the Farm Brewery Law (2013), licensed breweries are required to use at least 20 percent of New York–grown ingredients in the production of their beer, and they can serve beer in an on-site tasting room or tap house, a law that has encouraged breweries to go into business—The Lost Borough in Rochester, Nedloh in Bloomfield, Climbing Bines Hop Farm on the west side of Seneca Lake in Torrey, and Abandon Brewing in Penn Yan.

At last count there were close to 70 brewing companies clustered in areas like Rochester, Binghamton, Elmira, and Syracuse and around the lakes. Yes, there is a "beer trail," but as trails go, there seems no easy route to follow—it's more like a collection. Breweries are popping up everywhere. Look for itineraries on their website: www.fingerlakesbeertrail.com

And then we have cider. A staple beverage in Britain, hard cider is just now being discovered here, and the Finger Lakes region is at the forefront. Check out the Finger Lakes Cider House in Interlaken (www.fingerlakesciderhouse.com) and the Boathouse Beer Garden in Romulus.

Laura Kozlowski

THE FINGER LAKES CIDER HOUSE OFFERS BEER, FOOD, AND FUN

History

In 1829 Reverend William Bostwick planted Catawba and Isabella grapes in the rectory garden of St. James Episcopal Church in Hammondsport. But the good reverend was in another business, and it wouldn't be until 1860 that the first bonded Finger Lakes winery was founded, the Pleasant Valley Winery. The Urbana Wine Company was established in 1865 and renamed Gold Seal Winery in 1887, and Taylor Winery began operations in 1880. By that time there were more than 30 vineyards in the region.

One of the greatest boosts to winemaking here occurred when *Vitis vinifera* grapes were introduced in the early 1940s. Up until this time, the region had primarily concentrated on growing *Vitis labrusca* grapes like Catawba and Niagara—hardy varieties that grew very well in the cool climate. Wines produced from these grapes tended to be fruity, foxy, and grapey in taste—considered no match for the chardonnays and pinot noirs from France and California. Most area winemakers were convinced that the European grapes like chardonnay and cabernet sauvignon could not survive the region's harsh winters.

In 1934 Gold Seal's president went to Rheims, France, and persuaded Charles Fournier, chief winemaker of Cliquot Ponsardin, to come to Hammondsport and rebuild the winery's Prohibition-devastated reputation. Fournier brought with him several French-American hybrid grapes that had been developed in France to withstand diseases. These new hybrids added another dimension to the quality of the grapes grown in the Finger Lakes.

In 1943 the winery's Charles Fournier Brut was introduced, and the winery won a gold medal in 1950 for champagne at the California State Fair. By this time, interest was escalating in growing European grapes beyond the hybrids.

The industry received a major boost when Fournier brought Dr. Konstantin Frank, an immigrant from Ukraine, to Gold Seal to establish a *Vitis vinifera* nursery. His theory—graft the *Vitis vinifera* grapes to hardy rootstock to make the vines winter-proof—was convincing.

Dr. Frank eventually founded Dr. Frank's Vinifera Wine Cellars Ltd. in the hills above the west side of Keuka Lake. Today Finger Lakes wineries and vineyards are producing award-winning wines from grafted, winter-hardy chardonnays, riesling, pinot noir, cabernet franc, gamay, and other European grapes.

Today you find everything from small family-run businesses to larger, sophisticated wineries with handsome facilities including shops, restaurants, lodging, and tours. Many wineries offer wine tasting and participate in events throughout the year.

Special events incorporating several wineries along organized wine trails entice you to sample wines and food at bargain prices. Also growing in the region is the number of beer and ale breweries along with distilleries.

Wine Trails

Cayuga, Seneca, Keuka, and Canandaigua Lakes have established wine trails, with maps and listings of the participating wineries. All sponsor wine-related events.

Canandaigua Wine Trail: 877-386-4669; www.canandaiguawinetrail.com

Cayuga Lake Wine Trail: 800-684-5217; www.cayugawinetrail.com

Keuka Lake Wine Trail: 800-440-4898; www.keukawinetrail.com

Lake Ontario Wine Trail: www.lakeontariowinetrail.com

Seneca Lake Wine Trail/Seneca Lake Winery Association: 877-536-2717, 607-535-8080; www.senecalakewine.com

More information: www.fingerlakeswinecountry.com

Note: Be sure to call ahead. Some wineries, breweries, and distilleries are not open on a daily basis, and some serve food only on certain days.

Sampling the Breweries

Here is a partial list of breweries in the Finger Lakes.

The Brewery of Broken Dreams housed in a historic stone building in Hammondsport is the fulfillment of a dream by owners Doug and Shelly who creatively design

Visit Syracuse

BREWERIES LIKE EMPIRE BREWING COMPANY ARE HOT INDUSTRIES IN THE FINGER LAKES

beer using local ingredients. Try their Summer Blues wheat ales, Crying Loon pale ale, Unfinished Business, Scottish-style ale, and others. 8319 Pleasant Valley Rd., Hammondsport 14840; 607-224-4050; www.thebreweryofbrokendreams.com

Cider Creek Hard Cider House on a family farm southwest of Hammondsport produces several ciders from locally grown apples, including their original Farmhouse Cider, Cascade Hopricot and others. 6459 Cunningham Rd., Canisteo 14823; 857-400-0872; www.cidercreekhardcider.com

Climbing Bines Craft Ale Co. & Hop Farm specializes in small-batch, handcrafted ales brewed on-site. Their House Line has more than 15 kinds, like Spicer, Hefehopfen, and Stout, while their Pandemonium Line is made from estate–grown hops and organic barley harvested 4 miles down the road. Join in some games while you're there—perhaps cornhole and navigating around a nine-hole frisbee course. 511 Hansen Point Rd., Penn Yan 14527; 607-745-0221; www.climbingbineshopfarm.com

Empire Brewing Company (See "Dining Out" in the Syracuse section)

Grist Iron Brewing Company on Seneca Lake is continually adding new beer to its repertoire: Blueberry Wheat, Grizzled Skipper Smoked Vanilla Porter, and Flippeny Apple Graff. As whimsical as the names sound, these are worth trying. On the menu their "House Chews" quickly whet your appetite with items like local corn chowder and baked mac 'n cheese. The Inn at Grist Iron gives you three choices of accommodations (see "Lodging" in the Seneca Lake East Side section) 4880 NY Rt. 414, Burdett 14818; 607-882-2739; www.gristironbrewing.com

Heavily Brewing Company south of Watkins Glen is located in a 100-year-old dairy barn where you can sip Heavily beer, hang at the bar made from an old tree trunk, play games like darts and Jenga, and lounge on very comfy couches. Hungry? Try their hearty Reuben sandwich. 2471 Hayes Rd., Montour Falls 14865; 607-535-2739; www .heavilybrewingcompany.com

Iron Flamingo Brewery was established in 2013 in a former fruit market a five-minute walk from the Corning Museum of Glass. Beer choices include dark English-style ale, India pale ale, Mocha Coffee porter and red ale, plus seasonal styles. 196 Baker St., Corning 14830; 607-936-4766; www.ironflamingobrewery.com

Keuka Brewing Company on Keuka Lake is part of the Seneca Wine Trail. Named NY State's top craft brewer at the TAP New York Craft Beer and Food Festival (2014), their beer includes 607 Vienna-style Lager; bold and spicy Afterburner Habanero Ale; Hoppy Laker IPA, a light, flavorful blend of four varieties of hops; and others. 8572 Briglin Rd., Hammondsport 14840; 607-868-4648; www.keukabrewingcompany.com

Lucky Hare Brewing Company operating in a barn is a young producer with some sound products like Milk Milk, Cézanne, Falcon Punch, and London Gentleman. Their food offerings include smoked wings, pork buns, and fish and chips. 6085 Beckhorn Rd., Hector 14841; 610-613-8424; www.luckyharebrewing.com

Seneca Lake Brewing Company pours wine, cider, and spirits that you can enjoy from a deck overlooking Seneca Lake. Looking for a traditional British pub experience where you can play darts, bar billiards, and other fun things while drinking Real Cask Ale? Come on over. You just may get drawn into a game of Bubble Ball Soccer. Kinda hard to explain—you play soccer from inside a bubble while your legs poke through. Kids love it. Grownups love it (well, some do!). 4520 NY Rt. 14, Rock Stream 14878; 607-216-8369; www.senecalakebrewing.com

Two Goats Brewing in a barn overlooking Seneca Lake produces beer utilizing a seven-barrel system from Vermont. Two Goats' impressive lineup includes Dirty Butt, Danger Goat! Blonde Doppelbock, Redbeard Red Ale, and more. They serve a mean roast beef sandwich, slow-cooked "forever," with crispy chips. Live music, too. 5027 NY Rt. 414, Hector 14818; 607-546-2337; www.twogoatsbrewing.com

More information: www.fingerlakesbrewtrail.com

Distilleries

Another new thing in the Finger Lakes is the burgeoning distillery industry. Several have recently debuted, including:

Beak & Skiff Orchards, producing handcrafted hard ciders and small-batch premium vodka and gin made from apples, using the "1911" brand designating the year Beak & Skiff was founded. 2708 Lords Hill Rd., Marietta 13110; 315-696-6085; www.1911spirits.com, www.beakandskiff.com

Finger Lakes Distilling, a very large facility evoking Scottish whisky distilleries, utilizes two stills to create their range of spirits—a 300-gallon copper pot still and a 25-foot continuous still from Kentucky. It's the region's first stand-alone distillery, and everything is produced in small batches from scratch. Try their vodka, gin, whisky, brandy, and liqueurs. 4676 NY Rt. 414, Burdett 14818; 607-546-5510; www .fingerlakesdistilling.com

Hidden Marsh Distillery & the Montezuma Winery produce distilled vodkas, brandy, and liqueurs. 2981 Auburn Rd., Seneca Falls 13148; 315-568-8190; www .montezumawinery.com

Last Shot Distillery in Skaneateles is bringing back the art of liquor distilling to a facility along Skaneateles Creek where a similar distillery operated more than 100 years ago. Last Shot uses local ingredients as the base for whisky, vodka, gin, brandy, and other spirits. 4022 Mill Rd., Skaneateles 13152; 315-727-9736

THE LIVELY RUN GOAT DAIRY IN INTERLAKEN SPECIALIZES IN ARTISAN FARM PRODUCTS INCLUDING CHEESE

Myer Farm Distillers and Scottish-style tasting room features craft distilled flavored vodka, gin, bourbon, and whisky from local organic grains. 7350 NY Rt. 89, Ovid 14521; 607-532-4800; www.myerfarmdistillers.com

The O'Begley Distillery specializes in Irish-style whiskeys. NY Rt. 14, Dundee 14837; 585-750-8560; www.obegley.com

Please note: Wineries, breweries, and distilleries included in suggested itineraries in the lake chapters are meant to whet your appetite for Finger Lakes products and not to be considered as an all-inclusive listing. We suggest you pick up a wine trail map in town or at your first stop and follow the directions and map as you travel. Each trail has its own brochure.

Cheese

More than a dozen family farms, many with on-site markets, sell their homemade cheeses and produce. As there are locations throughout the Finger Lakes, it helps to have a map to find such places as Dutch Hill Creamery in Chenango Forks, selling cheese curds, fresh mozzarella, yogurt, and milk; Side Hill Acres Goat Farm in Candor, offering a variety of goat milk cheeses and other products; and Engelbert Farms in Nichols, featuring organic cheddars, beer-brined Moochego, MooVache, and organic meats and produce.

TIPS TO TRAVELING THE FINGER LAKES CHEESE TRAIL
- Check the farm's hours and call in advance.
- Plan your route and put the addresses into your GPS.
- Bring a cooler.
- Jeans, sneakers, or boots are good to wear as you are visiting farms.
- Look for the dates of trail-wide open houses on www.flcheesetrail.com.

Experiencing Farms

As you drive throughout the Finger Lakes, you cannot help but notice the beautiful farms and fields that lie between the villages and towns. Some of the finest are owned by the Amish and Mennonites. Many farms sell their produce at farm stands and regional farmers' markets as well as offer pick-your-own fruits and vegetables. There is a dramatic growth in specialty and artisan farm producers, like Bob's Maple in Waterloo, Copper Beacons Herb Farm in Trumansburg, Parker Road Organic Farm in Seneca Falls, and Lively Run Goat Farm in Interlaken.

SKANEATELES, OWASCO, AND OTISCO LAKES

lose to Syracuse and the most eastern of the Finger Lakes, Skaneateles, Owasco, and Otisco are all quite different in style and spirit.

Skaneateles

At 16 miles long and just 1 to 2 miles wide, Skaneateles Lake lives up to the meaning of its name, "long lake." Tucked in and around the lake are the small villages of Skaneateles at the north end, Mandana and New Hope on the west side, Glen Haven at the south end, and Spafford and Borodino on the east side. Because of its depth—up to 350 feet—the color of the water can change dramatically from deep cobalt to brilliant turquoise. It is the clarity of the lake, however, that most astounds. On a calm day, you can see right to the bottom.

At the northern end, Skaneateles—18 miles southwest of Syracuse—reigns as the prima donna of Finger Lakes villages. Time and wise local policies have dealt kindly with it. This pampered and prosperous place—about 2,800 in the village, 7,500 in the town—attracts affluent residents, while summer brings a constant flow of tourists.

Meticulously maintained historic homes line tree-shaded streets—some Greek Revival, some Second Empire with slate mansard roofs and cupolas, and others with wide porches furnished with wicker rockers. Former modest-size "camps" around the lake have been upgraded to full-season homes, and many are now quite grand and best seen by boat.

With its brick sidewalks and period lighting, the downtown area has many interesting boutiques, craft shops, galleries, and cafés. The Old Stone Mill, a historic landmark, occupies a prominent position on the outlet. A former grist- and sawmill, it has been thoughtfully restored and now houses condos and office spaces.

In the summer on Friday evenings, the community band plays from the lakeside gazebo in Clift Park. Sunday afternoons in July and August polo is played in a field off W. Lake Rd., and the last weekend in July is the Antique and Classic Boat Show. There are often music festivals on the side lawn of the Sherwood Inn, and in August, the Skaneateles Festival showcases world-class music under the stars with concerts held at Anyela's Vineyards on the lake and in local churches.

On Labor Day, the Skaneateles Fire Department rolls out old-fashioned field days featuring a parade, fireworks, rides, games, and a major triathlon starting with an 800-yard swim in Clift Park. At Thanksgiving the Turkey Trot offers a fun run for charity and at Christmastime, Dickens characters stroll the sidewalks, greeting shoppers; while throughout the year, pancake breakfasts rotate among area fire halls.

The village has three lakeside parks: Clift Park, Thayer Park, and Shotwell Park; as well as Austin Park on the north end of town, with tennis courts and ball fields. The Skaneateles Community Center and Allyn Arena offer amazing sports facilities, with an Olympic-size pool along plus four other pools, some with impressive water features

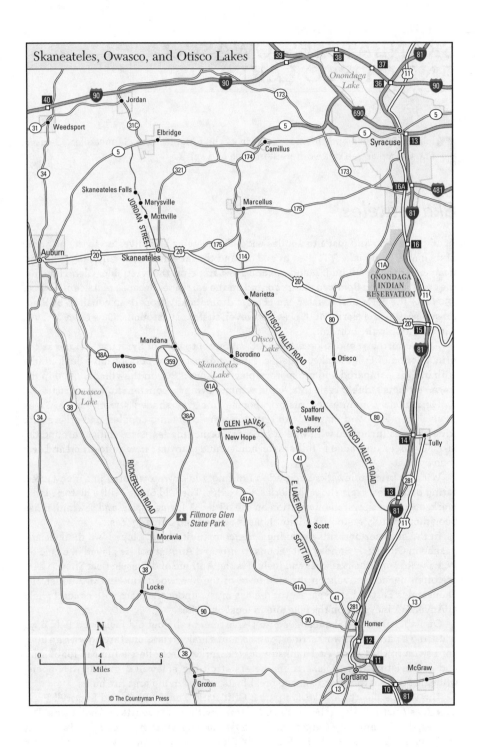

Skaneateles, Owasco, and Otisco Lakes

© The Countryman Press

including a giant slide and kinetic waterworks. There is a regulation-size ice arena, fitness center, and meeting rooms.

What industry there is in Skaneateles is located on the fringes of town. One of the most respected companies—named by *Fortune* magazine as one of the best places to work in the United States—is Welch Allyn, Inc., a medical instrument and fiber optics company and a major employer of more than 1,000 people in the area. Recently this family-owned company was sold to Chicago-based Hill-Rom Holdings.

Lodging options in Skaneateles range from the Sherwood Inn, a former stagecoach stop, and the nearby Packwood House, to small boutique hotels, motels, and bed and breakfasts. Restaurants, too, offer a huge variety of choices, from the renovated Krebs, appealing to those craving a New York City–style dining experience, and Joelle's French Bistro, located in a historic farmhouse, to the lakeside Blue Water Grill, and Doug's Fish Fry where people line up down the block to get English-style fried fish.

SKANEATELES: GROWTH AND DEVELOPMENT In 1791 Skaneateles contained 41 military lots given to Revolutionary War soldiers, surveyors, and early settlers as compensation for service. When Jedediah Sange constructed a log dam in 1797, where the outlet from the lake flowed under a bridge and the main street, the increased water flow created power to operate a grist- and sawmill.

In 1794 John Thompson settled on military lot #18, and Abraham A. Cuddeback took a 43-day wagon journey from Orange County, New York, to Skaneateles, bringing his wife, eight children, three yoke of oxen, one horse, and twelve cows. He built a log cabin on a heavily wooded piece of land on the west side of the lake, and more families followed.

THE OLD STONE MILL IS NOW RETAIL SPACE, OFFICES, AND CONDOS

An ideal location to attract settlers, Skaneateles was at the junction of east–west major routes: US 20 (the Cherry Valley Turnpike) and the Great Genesee Road, which followed the old trail from Utica and Canandaigua used by Native Americans.

The outlet to the lake provided water power for mills and other industries; the soil was fertile for corn, beans, and wheat; and not only did the lake supply settlers with water but the scenery soothed the soul. Skaneateles's first store was opened in 1803 by Winston Day, and by 1830 there were seven stores, a Masonic hall, three hotels, two sleigh and carriage factories, five flour mills, six sawmills, two iron foundries, and one brass foundry.

The sprawling blue Sherwood Inn, dominating the lakefront on the west end of the village, started life as Isaac Sherwood's Tavern in 1807, welcoming travelers arriving by stagecoach. Sherwood also owned the Old Mail Line Stagecoach Company, which made 15 stops daily in town.

Over the years the hotel expanded and changed names from Sherwood's Tavern to Lamb's Inn, Houndayaga House, Packwood's National Hotel, Packwood House, Kan-Ya-To-Inn ("beautiful view"), and back to the Sherwood Inn, thanks to Chester (Chet) Coates, one of the previous owners. Today the Sherwood Inn is owned by William Eberhardt.

Early carriage builders included Seth and James Hall, John Packwood, and former blacksmith John Legg. Boat companies founded here included the Bowdish Boat Company, the Edson Boat Company, and George Barnes's Skaneateles Boat and Canoe Company where the first Lightning Class sailboat was built.

In the late 1800s, Syracuse, 18 miles to the northeast, started tapping into the lake for its drinking water. The water in the outlet slowed down, waterwheels turned more sluggishly, and industry was curtailed.

THE COMING OF THE RAILROAD AND STEAMBOATS In 1840 a railroad with horse-drawn cars shuttled passengers back and forth between the village and Skaneateles

ANTIQUE CARS LINE UP IN FRONT OF HISTORIC SHERWOOD INN

Junction, 5 miles north of town, where they could connect to the Syracuse-Auburn Railroad. The Skaneateles Railroad, a steam line, was launched in 1865, replacing the equine version. The line was so short that when some became concerned about snow and rain, one man replied, "Hell, build a roof over it." Passenger service was discontinued in 1931, and the railroad was abandoned in 1982.

Around 1900 the Auburn and Syracuse Electric Trolley began shuttling people between cities. Both the train and later the trolley tied into the lake steamboats including the 80-foot *Independent*, the *Ben H. Porter*, and *City of Syracuse-on-the-Lake*, which carried passengers to Glen Haven at the south end of the lake, where there was a spa-style resort and small village. The hotel is gone, but a small community and lakeside restaurant remain.

Large steamboats ceased to exist in 1917, but smaller boats took up the slack for such important services as mail delivery to the lake-bound cottages. Today this practice continues on the U.S. Mailboat Cruise operated by Mid-Lakes Navigation Company.

Among the early boat operators were Mr. A. J. Hoffman, who ran the *Florence*, and the Stinsons, who ran the Stinson Boat Line from 1938 until 1968, when the boat *Pat II* was sold to Peter Wiles of Mid-Lakes (now being restored at the Finger Lakes Boating Museum in Hammondsport). Today the *Barbara S. Wiles* and the *Judge Ben Wiles*, a handsome double-decker diesel craft resembling the old steamboats, offer dining and sightseeing cruises on Skaneateles Lake.

FAMOUS VISITORS AND RESIDENTS Famous visitors to Skaneateles have included Revolutionary War hero Marquis de Lafayette as well as statesman and orator Daniel Webster, who visited in 1825. General J. W. Wainwright, hero of Bataan in WWII, had strong ties to Skaneateles and during Bill Clinton's presidency; and the Clintons vacationed here at a private home on E. Lake Rd. John Walsh of *America's Most Wanted* and Alec Baldwin, actor, have family ties to the area; and Thom Felicia, designer, author, and TV actor (*Queer Eye for the Straight Guy*) lives here.

Skaneateles was the home of several Roosevelts. Nicholas Roosevelt lived in town from 1831 to 1854. His relative, Samuel Montgomery Roosevelt, and later his son, Henry Latrobe Roosevelt, spent summers in an imposing pillared Greek Revival mansion called Roosevelt Hall. Famous guests included Theodore as well as Franklin and Eleanor Roosevelt. William H. Delavan, who purchased the home in 1942, renovated the mansion and restored a large conservatory-style greenhouse, filling it with tropical trees, flowers, and a fountain.

Delavan sold the estate in 1959 to Ken Dunning, and later Roosevelt Hall was purchased by Dennis Owen, who resided there for several years with his family. Owen deeded the property to the Catholic Diocese, and the Christian Brothers used it for some years before giving it back to Owen, who then sold it and gave the money to the Christian Brothers. Once again it is a private residence.

GONE WITH THE WIND Over the years a number of activities have come and gone, including horse racing, ice boating, roller-skating, and Microd racing. From 1954 to 1965 young boys, with help from their dads, and the Robinson family, who built the first Microd in their barn, constructed miniature automobiles made of plywood and powered by lawn-mower engines. Weekly races were held on the track where the Austin Park Pavilion now stands. If you think Little League baseball gets competitive, you should have seen this crowd.

When the Lyric Circus came to town in 1952 and erected its huge blue tent on a site just east of the village, professional actors, actresses, and musicians from New York City would perform in a summer series of musicals on a round stage. In the late '50s, attendance declined. The final blow came from a hurricane, which toppled the tent, and by 1960 the theater had shut down.

Today some of the local institutions are threatened, including the historic stone library in the center of town. As of this printing, there are rumors it may be sold and repurposed, with a new library taking its place up the street in a building yet to be built. For the past 125 years, the library has changed little and remained one of the hubs of village life as well as one of only two libraries in the state that is totally privately funded.

Over the years, the village's Historic Landmarks Preservation Committee has helped preserve the character of many structures in the downtown Historic District, so this area continues to be a thriving commercial, cultural, and retail center for the entire Finger Lakes region.

✳ Lodging

Rates during the summer are at their highest, and you should book early as hotels fill quickly, often a year ahead of time to accommodate events like weddings and the Antique Boat Show.

HISTORIC The **Sherwood Inn** just across from Clift Park was built in 1807 and was once a stagecoach stop. A rambling three-story blue building, it has an enclosed wide veranda overlooking the water, and a pub-like bar and dining room. All 24 rooms and suites are different; some overlook the lake, others the backyard and parking lot (if quiet is more important to you than water views, book these). Décor is eclectic colonial, with a bit of early American and Victorian thrown in. One of the best views is from room #28, a second-floor corner room overlooking the lake and the village. $$–$$$ 26 W. Genesee St., Skaneateles 13152; 800-3-SHERWOOD; www.thesherwoodinn.com. Also note the B&Bs, which follow.

B&BS Just outside the village, **Hummingbird's Home B&B**, a gracious, circa-1803 colonial home, has four guest rooms with private baths and original plank floors. Some rooms have fireplaces; one has a Jacuzzi. A full gourmet breakfast is served, and children are welcome. Hummingbird's is on Rt. 20 just west of town. $$–$$$ 4273 W. Genesee St., Skaneateles 13152; 315-685-5075; www.hummingbirdshomebandb.com

The mid-nineteenth-century Federal-style **Arbor House Inn & Suites** on Fennell St. may be across from a supermarket, but it's just a five-minute walk to the lake. There are 11 guest rooms, six with fireplaces and seven with Jacuzzis. A full breakfast is served. $$$ 41 Fennell St., Skaneateles 13152; 888-234-4558; www.arborhouseinn.com

The Gray House is a smartly decorated Victorian home with two large living rooms, air conditioning, two porches, and gardens. Two suites have queen-size beds and sitting rooms. A full breakfast is served. Their adjacent property, the 1840 Little Gray House, is available for weekly or monthly rental. $–$$ 47 Jordan St., Skaneateles 13152; 315-685-0131; www.gray-house.com

The Redd Rose Bed and Breakfast combines an 1850s historic home, three acres of countryside and gardens, and a home-cooked hearty breakfast. There are three rooms, each with a private bath, and all are uniquely furnished with period-piece items—quilts, straw hats, baskets, and artwork. $$ 1193 Lacy Rd., Skaneateles 13152; www.reddrosebedandbreakfast.com

Perched high on 320 hillside acres overlooking the lake five minutes from the village center, **Hobbit Hollow Farm Bed & Breakfast**, a beautifully furnished

34 STATE IS A LUXURY B&B WITH SPACIOUS, EXQUISITELY DECORATED SUITES

one-hundred-year-old colonial house, has all the amenities of a lovely private home—which it once was. Rooms overlook horses grazing in white-fenced fields and, beyond them, vineyards and the lake. Your "estate" for your stay includes gilt mirrors, oriental carpets, hand-painted murals, polished floors and matelassé and Frette linens. A full breakfast is served. $$–$$$$ 3061 W. Lake Rd., Skaneateles 13152; 877-7-HOBBIT; www.hobbithollow.com

34 State Historic Luxury Suites, just a short walk from the Historic District, is exquisitely decorated with great attention to detail. The mood is light and airy, upbeat with a bit of whimsy. Each of the two suites, of about 700 square feet, contains a bedroom, sitting room, and spacious bath. Nice extra amenities include a well-equipped guest pantry with fresh ice, a sink, and a fridge stocked with things like yogurt and milk. Breakfast can be served in the dining room, or you can be treated to breakfast in bed. $$–$$$$ 34 State St., Skaneateles 13152; 315-685-7473; www.34state.com

Located on nine acres eight miles from Skaneateles, the three-bedroom **Pine Grove B&B** offers spectacular views of the lake from its high-up perch. Each room has a queen bed with plush-top mattresses and fine linens, WiFi, Jacuzzis, and country-style furnishings. A full breakfast is served. $$–$$$ 2707 Pine Grove Rd., Borodino 13152; 315-673-2558; www.pinegrovebb.com

HOTELS AND INNS Tucked into 12 hillside acres on the edge of town, **Mirbeau Inn & Spa**'s 34 rooms, cottages, and suites are built around gardens and a pond evoking Monet's water garden at Giverney. This ochre-hued European-style inn, with its arched iron trellises, climbing roses, and wisteria, creates a romantic entry to the cottages. Guest rooms are spacious and appointed with Provence–style fabrics designed in France, linens from Italy, and duvets filled with Canadian down. Armoires with fine inlays, period pieces, antiques, and fireplaces add to the ambiance. Each room has a

patio or balcony with a wrought-iron table and chairs. There is also a 14,000-square-foot spa and outdoor Aqua Spa where, even in the winter, you can soak in the hot water pool while the snow falls and a fireplace warms. $$$$ 851 W. Genesee St., Skaneateles 13152; 877-MIRBEAU; www.mirbeau.com

Packwood House in the center of town across from the lake contains a Talbots retail outlet on the first floor (the only chain store in town) while rooms and suites are on the second level. Amenities include mini fridges, televisions, WiFi, phones with voice mail, kitchenette with microwave and refrigerator, coffeemaker, and complimentary continental breakfast. Some rooms have terraces and all feature soft, subdued colors and Arts and Crafts–style furniture. $$–$$$ 14 W. Genesee St., Skaneateles 13152; 800-374-3796; www.packwoodhouse.com

At the **Village Inn of Skaneateles** you'll enjoy total privacy and quiet. Each of the four rooms in this European-style boutique hotel in the town center has a fireplace, furnishings by Stickley, Audi & Company, whirlpool bath, and mini fridge, while the Terrace Room has a balcony with a view of the lake. A continental breakfast is served on the porch of the Sherwood Inn nearby. $$–$$$ 25 Jordan St., Skaneateles 13152; 800-374-3796; www.villageinn-ny.com

IN-TOWN DIGS In addition to the **Sherwood Inn**, **Packwood House**, **Village Inn**, and a handful of B&Bs, try **The Skaneateles Suites Boutique Hotel**, located in a fully reno-vated building on Fennell St. This 6-room inn with a wonderful porch is within walking distance of the lake, the supermarket, and the village center. Two of the guest rooms have oversized Jacuzzis, and one is handicapped accessible. All feature pillow-top queen mattresses, free WiFi, and complimentary coffee. $$–$$$ 12 Fennell St., Ska-neateles 13152; 315-685-2333; www.skaneateleshotel.com

EASY AND INEXPENSIVE MOTELS If you're looking for a clean, neat motel with TV, good towels, and a good price, try **The Bird Nest** on Rt. 20 east of the village. It's not fancy, but it does have a pool tucked between the road and parking area. $–$ 1601 E. Genesee St., Skaneateles 13152; 315-685-5641; www.thebirdsnest.com

The **Skaneateles Inn on 20** (formerly the Colonial Motel) on the west side of town on Rt. 20 has had a facelift inside and out. Rooms come with a mini fridge, microwave, air conditioning, and coffeemaker. There is also an outdoor pool. $–$ 4239 E. Genesee St., Auburn, 13021; 315-685-5751; www.skaneatelesinn.com

The recently renovated **Whispering Winds Motel** next door has a heated pool and a wooded backyard with gardens. Rooms have comfortable beds, nice linens, and air conditioning. $–$ 4223 W. Genesee Rd., Auburn, 13021; 315-685-6056; www.whisperingwindsmotel.com

SWEET SUITES **Skaneateles Suites**, motel-style bungalows just 2 miles west of the village on Rt. 20, has 12 spacious suites. Ask about the four-bedroom/two-bath house and the Treetop Suite with a full kitchen. $–$$$; 4114 E. Genesee St., Auburn 13021; 315-685-7568; www.skaneatelessuites.com

✳ Dining Out

TRADITION, TRADITION Arguably the most famous restaurant in the Finger Lakes, **The Krebs** has been long known for its eat-all-you-want multicourse prix-fixe dinners. Now owners Kim and Adam Weitsman have breathed fresh life into the historic eatery. The original sign, front porch, and exterior look have been retained but honed and polished, while inside there have been serious renovations. The new look, combining elegant, sophisticated creams, grays, and muted tones along with tapestry fabrics and beautiful wood and upholstered chairs, complements the fine cuisine. You can dine on items like duck with pear and black garlic pickles; foie gras with blood orange, rolled oats, and brioche; and chocolate soufflé with double cream and ganache. In tune with the Finger Lakes farm-to-table principle, the menu focuses on fresh, local ingredients. Whereas formerly Krebs was open only seasonally, Krebs is now open throughout the year, Thursday through Sunday. $$$–$$$$ 53 W. Genesee St., Skaneateles 13152; 315-685-1800; http://thekrebs.com

The **Sherwood Inn** gives you choices: traditional in the dining room; casual, pub-like in the Tavern; and lake views on the enclosed porch. Dining room fare is traditional, while the Tavern serves pub food like fabulous burgers and grilled chicken sandwiches. Favorite menu items drawn from classic American fare include baked scrod Christopher and Yankee pot roast. Breads from the Inn's Pâtisserie are served and available for sale in the quaint shop near the parking lot. Weekends there is often live music in the Tavern. $–$$ Tavern, $$–$$$ dining room; 26 W. Genesee St., Skaneateles 13152; 315-685-3405, 800-3-SHERWOOD; www.thesherwoodinn.com

Note: A new book by Bill Eberhardt and Denise Owen Harrigan, *The Sherwood Inn*, published in 2014, covers the 200-year history of the hostelry and contains recipes of the inn's favorite dishes. The book is available in the hotel gift shop.

ALL ABOUT THE VIEW For spectacular sunsets, reserve a table at the **1820 House** near Borodino on the east side of the lake, where the quality of the food matches the quality of the scenery. Dine on classics like palm sugar duck, scallops diablo, and lobster piccata; while in the tavern, find sandwiches, pizza, and appetizers such as Buffalo chicken wings and chicken satay. Days open vary seasonally. $–$$$ 1715 E. Lake Rd. Skaneateles 13152; 315-673-2778; www.the1820house.com

In Homer at the **Glen Haven**, arrive by boat or car and eat overlooking the lake. It's not fancy, but the food goes beyond burgers and fries—for example, wood-grilled salmon and blackened steak, along with pasta and black-bottom key-lime tarts. Call for directions; it's not easy to find. $–$$$ 7434 Fair Haven Rd., Homer 13077; 607-749-3779; www.theglenhaven.com

If you like wine, cheese & views, order a bounteous platter of cheese, fruit, and crackers, and a fine bottle of wine, and enjoy the vistas of vineyards and lake on the terrace of **Anyela's Vineyards** 4 miles south of the village. 2433 W. Lake Rd., Skaneateles 13152; 315-685-3797; www.anyelasvineyards.com

HIP BISTRO-STYLE At the **Blue Water Grill** along the outlet to the lake, portions are huge. Sit inside along the windows, on the open upper deck, or lower screened deck. Stick with good things like grilled chicken pesto wraps, ravioli, fajitas, and nachos, and expect to take home a doggie bag. Vegetarians will find plenty of tempting items, too. There is a good selection of beer and wines along with shooters from the freezer. $–$$; 11 W. Genesee St., Skaneateles 13152; 315-685-6600; www.bluewaterskaneateles.com

For upper-crust Italian cuisine head to **Rosalie's Cucina**, an adobe taverna–style restaurant and arguably the village's most go-to place, serving homemade breads (available at their bakery), succulent meats, and pizza from a wood-fired oven. Among the specialties are farfalle con pollo (bow ties, chicken, pancetta, asiago cream, red onions, and peas) and arrosto con porc (slow-roasted pork, oregano, garlic, and cannelloni beans). Prices are on the high side for an Italian eatery, and the noise level can be annoying to those looking for a quiet evening, but no one seems to care, as those who love good food keep on coming. $$$ 841 W. Genesee St., Skaneateles 13152; 315-685-2200; www.rosaliescucina.com

Gilda's, an intimate place located across from the lake, serves craft pizzas, creative appetizers, and great hamburgers. Popular are the small plates. Eat indoors or out in the summer. $–$$ 12 W. Genesee St., Skaneateles 13152; 315-685-7234; www.gildasskaneateles.com

Ed Moro, a highly respected chef in this area, has opened a second restaurant, **Moro's Kitchen**, in a nineteenth-century stone building, once a carriage factory, blacksmith shop, and garage. The décor is metro chic in grays, blacks, and whites along with white ceramic tiles and stainless-steel accessories. Food is creative and tasty in the best Italian bistro style. It's a definite plus to the local food scene. $–$$$ 28 Jordan Rd., Skaneateles 13152; 315-685-6116; www.moroskitchen.com

ULTRA ROMANTIC There is nothing more romantic on a summer's eve than sitting on the patio at **Joelle's French Bistro** overlooking gardens and fields. Owners Joelle Bollinger and Alain Castel, both born in Africa, came to Skaneateles by way of Europe and their popular Country Café in Soho, Manhattan. Bringing their exotic taste adventures to Skaneateles, Joelle creates classic French food with a Moroccan twist using local, fresh produce and herbs and vegetables from her own gardens. Alain, the maître d', is ever ready to help you with your wine selection. The charming indoor dining rooms of this former farmhouse evoke France with its flowing flowered drapes, linen-covered tables and warm colors. Come here for that special dinner, perhaps hot fois gras with caramelized apples, crispy shrimp tempura, sautéed frog legs, or escargot à la bourguignonne. Special events include Bastille Day, Greek Night, and Jazz Nights. $$–$$$$ 4423 State Street Rd., Skaneateles 13152; 315-685-0345; www.joellesfrenchbistro.com

JOELLE'S FRENCH BISTRO IS ONE OF THE MOST ROMANTIC PLACES TO DINE IN THE REGION

Mirbeau's dining room creates intimate spaces, while the gardens just outside enhance the mood. Although the menu features many steak choices, there are good seafood and fish selections as well as a lighter spa-inspired menu. Regional produce and meats are used in the farm-to-table French-influenced cuisine prepared as per classic methods. Pick a special evening, reserve a table on the terrace, and enjoy a splendid dinner. For a more casual evening, try their wine bar, where you can order small plates or tapas and use a Smart Card to tap into wines from the wine station (from $5–$20). $$$–$$$$ 851 W. Genesee St., Skaneateles 13152; 315-685-5006; www.mirbeau.com.

Also see **Elderberry Pond** in Auburn.

MAINLY FISH The **Mandana Inn**, a non-pretentious, long-established restaurant built in 1793 and a former stagecoach stop (1835), is located on the west side of the lake across from a marina. It is under new ownership with Mike Tudor as GM and Chef Chris Kuhns, who is passionate about adhering to the farm-to-table concept. "Anything else is not an option," he says. The inn is famous for its scrod prepared with a broiled crumb topping, but there are some excellent new choices like scallops, black Angus beef sirloin, and even herb-marinated frog legs, as well as hearty sandwiches. $$ 1937 W. Lake Rd., Skaneateles 13152; 315-685-7798

CASUAL FARE A line may spill into the outside, but the good news—it moves fast. Since 1982, **Doug's Fish Fry** has been the place to venture for fish, wrapped to go, English style. Eat in the dining room or take your food to the "garden," a roped-off picnic area in the parking lot. Doug's is a perennial favorite, especially for fish sandwiches big enough to share and fish dinners with fries and slaw. There is also dippin' chicken, shrimp, lobster rolls, oysters, clams, and onion rings. Top off your meal with hard or soft ice cream or even a warm apple sundae. $–$$ 8 Jordan St., Skaneateles 13152; 315-685-3288; www.dougsfishfry.com

For an inexpensive, quick breakfast with awesome home fries, join the locals at **Hilltop Restaurant** on W. Genesee. A bonus: Adjacent to the restaurant is the local Cedar House Bowling Center. $ 813 W. Genesee St., Skaneateles 13152; 315-685-0016; www.cedarhousebowlingcenter.com. Another choice locals swear by: **Valley Inn** in Marcellus. $ 315-673-7448

Stop in at **Skaneateles Bakery & Cafe** for melt-in-your-mouth doughnuts, made fresh each morning, or grab a sandwich and soup for lunch. Get there early enough to get the doughnuts still warm and fresh out of the hot oil. Wicked good. $ 19 Jordan St., Skaneateles 13152; 315-685-3538

Johnny Angel's Heavenly Burgers is the place for breakfast eggs, bacon, and a healthy stack of pancakes. For lunch and dinner, they roll out half-pound burgers, homemade soups, fish, chicken, hot sandwiches, battered fries, ice cream, beer, and wine. $–$$ 22 Jordan St., Skaneateles 13152; 315-685-0100

At the **Pâtisserie**, there are just a few tables on a patio in this delightfully small bakery tucked into a corner behind the Sherwood Inn. Savor freshly made breads, cakes, pies, and pastries, along with coffees and teas. We love the stretch and the cheese breads. $–$$ 4 Hannum St., Skaneateles 13152; 315-685-2433

The former Morris's Grill on Genesee St. has for years been a huge draw for locals, bikers, and anyone who wants some convivial conversation in a down-home pub. When owner Burt Lipe died in 2008, Morris's closed, much to the dismay of the entire town. Happily, thanks to some local investors, it has been reborn as the **Lake House Pub** and is once again everybody's watering hole. It's the place to get a quick roast beef sandwich, Reuben, nachos, and other pub-style fare along with beer, spirits, and entertainment. $ 6 W. Genesee St., Skaneateles 13152; 315-554-8194; lakehousepub.com

THE PÂTISSERIE BEHIND THE SHERWOOD INN BAKES WONDERFUL BREADS AND PASTRIES WHILE DINERS ENJOY A SMALL SEATING AREA IN THE COURTYARD

BEST OF SKANEATELES

BURGERS: Johnny Angel's Heavenly Burgers; Sherwood Inn Tavern
ROMANCE (& PROPOSING): Joelle's French Bistro; Mirbeau
FOOD: Rosalie's Cucina; The Krebs
VIEWS: 1820 House; Sherwood Inn Porch
BREAKFAST: Blue Water Grill; Skaneateles Bakery
FISH: Doug's Fish Fry; Mandana Inn
ITALIAN: Rosalie's Cucina; Moro's Kitchen
ACTION: Sherwood Inn Tavern; Lake House Pub
WINE & VIEWS: Anyela's Vineyards
ICE CREAM: Skan-Ellus Drive-In; Skaneateles Skoops
DOUGHNUTS: Tim's Pumpkin Patch on Rose Hill Rd., sadly open only around Halloween. Tim's also sells fresh-baked cookies and pumpkin fritters. The rest of the year for your doughnut fix, go as early as possible to the Skaneateles Bakery.
HIGH-END BUZZ: The Krebs
FARM-TO-TABLE: Elderberry Pond (Auburn)
BREAD: Stretch bread from the Pâtisserie

ICE CREAM Going strong for more than 40 years, **Skan-Ellus Drive-In** on Rt. 20 at 1659 E. Genesee St., 13152 sells ice cream, deli sandwiches, burgers, hot dogs, and fries. 315-685-8280. **Doug's Fish Fry** on Jordan St. has soft and hard ice cream, while the new **Skaneateles Skoops** serves American frosty favorites at 22 Jordan St. 315-685-3915

✳ To See

In August the **Skaneateles Festival** fills the air with Mozart, Bach, Tchaikovsky, Bartok, Prokofiev, and other great composers in concerts overlooking the lake and vineyards at the new pavilion at Anyela's Vineyards at 2433 W. Lake Rd., Skaneateles. Listen to music under the stars (bring a picnic, lawn chairs, blankets, and flashlights) or, on some nights, in the First Presbyterian Church. Enjoy new music groups, like the Grammy-winning Roomful of Teeth and folk music programs. FamilyFest performances such as Aesop's Fables and Krazy Klezmer are free. 315-685-7418; www.skanfest.org

John D. Barrow Art Gallery located in a separate wing of the village library contains the life's work of one of the area's most prolific nineteenth-century poets and painters. See numerous oil portraits and early scenes of the area. John D. Barrow was a Hudson River School–style painter. 49 E. Genesee St., Skaneateles 13152; 315-685-5135; www.barrowgallery.com

The Creamery Museum is situated in a 100-year-plus building where farmers used to sell their milk, cream, butter, and other dairy products. Today The Creamery houses a boat museum, carriages, the original Lightning Sailboat, sleighs, and industry memorabilia. The Skaneateles Historical Society is located in the building as well as hundreds of artifacts, a research and archives department, gift shop, and meeting room. Call for hours. 28 Hannum St., Skaneateles 13152; 315-685-1360; www.skaneateleshistoricalsociety.org

SKARTS (Skaneateles Area Arts Council) celebrates the visual and performing arts in the community, sponsoring a variety of cultural programming and free concerts and issuing grants to artists and arts organizations in the area. Fundraisers have included an artists' studio tour and evenings with top entertainers. 315-685-3540; www.skarts.org

Antique boats are showcased (usually last weekend in July) at the **Skaneateles Antique and Classic Boat Show** set up on the grounds of Clift Park and at boat slips along the Village Pier. See mahogany runabouts by Chris Craft, Hacker, and Gar Wood along with sailboats, canoes, rowing craft, and race boats, many beautifully restored and operable. 315-685-0552; www.skaneateles.com/boatshow

✳ To Do

The 11,000-square-foot **Skaneateles YMCA Community Center** houses the W. G. Allyn Arena (a full-size heated ice arena); the Mary H. Soderberg Aquatic Center, with five pools including a plunge pool, an eight-lane competition pool, and a 12-person hot tub; a fitness facility; a pro shop; locker rooms; a track; a viewing area; and other multipurpose rooms. Also on the property is Austin Park Pavilion (the original ice rink), now utilized for special events. 97 State Street Rd., Skaneateles 13152; www.skaneateles communitycenter.com

BIKING **Skaneateles Lake Loop** (40 miles): Starting from the village, go south on W. Lake Rd., then continue on NY 41A to Glen Haven Rd. Return to the village by cycling north on NY 41. Key stops along the way include New Hope Mills (just south of Mandana on NY 41A), Glen Haven at the end of the lake, and Borodino on NY 41.

BOATING **Skaneateles Sailing Club**, on the east side of the lake in a protected cove, holds informal races weekly and other sailing events. There is a membership fee and fee for boat storage or mooring; members can use the clubhouse and dock facilities. 2745 E. Lake Rd., Skaneateles 13152; 315-685-7542

For sailboat and canoe rentals, go to the **Sailboat Shop**. 315-685-7558. Also cruise the lake on the Sherwood Inn's restored classic antique Chris Craft, The *Stephanie*. 315-685-3405, 800-374-3796

Cruise the canals and locks of the Erie Canal aboard a chartered, fully furnished boat from **Mid-Lakes Navigation**. 315-685-4318; www.midlakesnav.com

FISHING Skaneateles Lake is popular with anglers who fish for perch, trout, bass, and other fish. Winter brings out the ice fishermen.

CRUISES Tour the canals of the Finger Lakes aboard the *Emita II* at the astounding speed of about 7 mph. **Mid-Lakes Navigation Company** offers a variety of cruises through New York State's canal system as well as on Skaneateles Lake, where two boats—the double-decker *Judge Ben Wiles* and the *Barbara S. Wiles*, a smaller classic wooden craft—feature lunch, dinner, sightseeing cruises, and special-interest cruises including a three-and-a-half-hour US Mail Cruise delivering snail mail to camps around the lake. Theme cruises include a DJ Dinosaur Dinner, a Full Moon Cruise, Pirate Day, and music cruise.

Mid-Lakes also offers cruises departing Syracuse, Albany, and Buffalo on the Erie Canal and drive-your-own canal boats for charter. 11 Jordan St., Skaneateles 13152; 315-685-8500; www.midlakesnav.com

MARINAS AND LAUNCHES If you want access to the lake, several marinas have public launch and docking facilities including **Glen Haven** (607-749-3779) in Homer; **New**

York State Launch 3 miles from the village on W. Lake Rd.; the full-service **Skaneateles Marina** at 1938 W. Lake Rd. in Mandana—also a good place to rent pontoon boats (315-685-5095); and the **Town of Skaneateles Boat Launch** (315-685-3473) in Mandana.

GOLF **Skaneateles Country Club** has a fine 18-hole course but is private; however, several other golf facilities are open to the public in the area.

    Dutch Hollow Country Club (See listing in Auburn)

    Highland Park Golf Club (See listing in Auburn)

    Pearl Lakes Golf Course in Skaneateles is a laid-back place to warm up your game and take the family. 1441 Old Seneca Tpke., Skaneateles 13152; 315-685-6799

    Finger Lakes Driving Range on Rt. 20 just east of the village has several grass driving stations and marked targets. 1485 E. Genesee St., Skaneateles 13152

    Golf courses are open from about mid-April through October. www.pga.com; also check www.nygolftrail.com

HELI TOURS CNY Helicopters, an FAA-certified, locally owned and operated service with tours and instruction takes place out of Skaneateles Aerodrome, 2984 Benson Rd., Skaneateles 13152; 315-406-2555

HIKING The trail in the 25-acre **Bahar Nature Preserve** on the west side of Skaneateles Lake brushes by a 65-foot crescent of lakeshore, a good spot to beach a canoe or kayak before hiking up the ridge. Catch dramatic views of the 100-foot-deep Bear Swamp Creek Ravine. 3800 Apple Tree Point Rd., New Hope 13118; 607-275-9487; www.fllt.org/preserves/bahar-preserve

Baltimore Woods has several loop trails from 0.25 to 0.7 miles laced throughout this 170-acre area site. Moderately difficult trails go up and down hills, across brooks and flood plains, and through woods and fields. The Violet Trail contains a 0.3-mile maze with labeled gardens of wildflowers and plants. Summer nature camp programs are offered. 4007 Bishop Hill Rd., Marcellus 13108; 315-673-1350; www.baltimorewoods.org

Bear Swamp State Forest, off the southeast end of Skaneateles Lake, occupies 3,280 acres with 13 miles of well-marked trails. It's great for hunting, hiking, fishing, bird watching, trapping, cross-country skiing, mountain biking, and horseback riding. Take the rather difficult 3.4-mile loop, or the longer and also difficult 7.8-mile loop. www.cnyhiking.com/BearSwampStateForest

Cayuga County Erie Canal Trail starts just east of Port Byron off NY 31 at Randolph J. Schassel Village

THE CHARLIE MAJOR TRAIL FOLLOWS THE OLD RAIL BED

Park. Walk 9.3 miles along the former towpath and abandoned canal bed, and tie into a 14.8-mile trek through Erie Canal Park in Camillus for a 20-mile walk. www.cnyhiking .com/OleErieCanalTrail

An easy, short trail if you have young kids in tow is the **Charlie Major Nature Trail** off Fennell St. Look for a parking area and nature trail sign just after Old Seneca Turnpike. The 1.6-mile trail follows an abandoned rail line. Partway down, look for the falls on your right, and take the path that goes across some large foundation stones to the falls. 315-685-3473

SKIING Area ski facilities are located in **Song Mountain** in Tully 315-696-5711; www .songmountain.com; and **Greek Peak** near Cortland with 32 trails and a vertical drop of more than 900 feet. 800-955-2754; www.greekpeak.net. Cross-country skiing is great most of the winter throughout the region.

SWIMMING Public swimming is available across from the Sherwood Inn at Clift Park. There are stone steps leading into the water and a raft close to shore. Swimming is free to Skaneateles residents, while non-residents pay a nominal fee.

FAMILY FUN At **Beak & Skiff Apple Orchards** in Lafayette, apple trees hang heavy with several varieties of apples from late summer through October. Ride to the orchards on a tractor-drawn wagon and pick your own apples. Children enjoy a giant pumpkin blow-up and live pony rides. Weekends are jammed, but the orchard handles the crowds well. There are picnic tables, a colorful retail store, home-baked pies, doughnuts, candy apples, and a snack stand. 2708 Lords Hill Rd., Lafayette 13084; 315-696-6085; www .beakandskiff.com

Beaver Lake Nature Center (see "Discovering Nature" in the Syracuse section)

At **Carpenter's Brook Fish Hatchery** in Elbridge, see where thousands of brown, rainbow, and brook trout eggs are hatched and put into ponds to grow. There are picnic tables, workshops (by reservation), and fishing programs for senior citizens and special needs groups. NY Rt. 321, Elbridge 13060; 315-689-9367; cbfh@ongov.net

The Erie Canal Museum (see "Family Fun" in the Syracuse section)

There are more than 450 craft booths along with pie contests, a demo cider mill, food and apple stands, and entertainment at the **Lafayette Apple Festival**, the largest craft show in the northeast. Held on the grounds and in barns and buildings of a former dairy farm in early October, the festival is located at the junction of NY Rts. 11 and 20. www .lafayetteapplefest.org

MOST: Milton J. Rubenstein Museum of Science and Technology (see "Performing & Visual Arts" in the Syracuse section)

Rosamond Gifford Zoo (see "Discovering Nature" in the Syracuse section)

The fields are covered with pumpkins come fall at **Tim's Pumpkin Patch**. Pick your own pumpkins, explore the hay maze, and watch the goats in the animal barn. Try their amazing pumpkin fritters,

TIM'S PUMPKIN PATCH SELLS PUMPKINS, SQUASH, FALL GIFTS, AND BAKED SWEETS INCLUDING DOUGHNUTS

GRADUATES FROM SKANEATELES HIGH SCHOOL TAKE A LEAP INTO THE LAKE AFTER THE CEREMONY HELD IN THE GAZEBO.

homemade pumpkin doughnuts, and other goodies. 2901 Rose Hill, Marietta 13110; 315-673-9209; www.timspumpkinpatch.com

✳ Shopping

The main shopping streets—Genesee, Jordan, and Fennell—are lined by attractive boutiques, art and craft galleries, restaurants, and specialty shops. The shopping experience is enhanced by attractive brick sidewalks, hanging baskets of flowers, and period lighting.

ANTIQUES Call before you go as some of these shops have flexible hours.

Start in town at the **Skaneateles Antique Center** and browse through the antiques and collectibles of more than 30 dealers located on two floors. Find furniture, pottery, books, jewelry, linens, lighting, primitives, militaria, coins, decorative arts and crafts, and accessories. 12 E. Genesee St., Skaneateles 13152; 315-685-0752

For mostly high-end items, stop at **White & White Antiques & Interiors**. Stephen and Beverly White continually look for unique antiques, both furniture pieces and collectibles. 18 E. Genesee St., Skaneateles 13152; 315-685-7733

Eight miles south of the village on NY Rt. 41A, **Brown Dog Antiques** has a large collection of troll beads, antiques, collectibles, memorabilia, furnishings, and vintage jewelry. Call for hours. 4669 W. Lake Rd., Skaneateles 13152; 315-263-8189; www .browndogantiques.com

THE ARTS The number of retailers selling art and original crafts is growing to the point where if this is the only thing you are interested in, Skaneateles is worth a special trip. On **First Friday Art Night**, a monthly happening from May to December, you are invited to visit participating galleries, meet the artists, and enjoy refreshments and music. 315-685-858; www.skaneatelesartisans.com

Imagine sells fine arts and fine craft jewelry—including art glass, ceramics, woodworking, fabric designs, hand-woven scarves by Laurel Morenz, paintings, printmaking, and puzzle boxes—from more than 30 artists, including ceramics by gallery director Sarah Panzarella. 38 E. Genesee St., Skaneateles 13152; 315-685-6263; www.imagineskaneateles.com

Gallery 54 sells original work of more than 15 area artists with a wide range of media—paintings, mosaics, quilts, jewelry, basketry, pottery, mixed-media collages, silk wearables, photography, stained glass, woodwork, handbags, and scarves. 54 E. Genesee St., Skaneateles 13152; 315-685-5470; www.gallery54cny.com

BALLOONS ARE PART OF THE FUN AT SIDEWALK SALE DAYS IN SKANEATELES

Many of the items in **Love Skaneateles** come from local artists and craftsmen. From jewelry to baby art and painted furniture, these unique pieces reveal the talent in the region. 3 W. Genesee St., Skaneateles 13152; 315-554-8216; www.loveskan@aol.com

One of the newest additions to the unique gift shop scene is **Nest 58**, where you will find clever, one-of-a-kind items, many created by local artists. Owners Susan Gorman and Amy Burns have a keen eye for finding the unusual, often with a rustic flair like the "farmpunk" furniture and accessories crafted by Unite Two Design made from recycled wood and metal parts. 58 E. Genesee St., Skaneateles 13152; 315-685-5888; www.nest58.com

On Fennell St. on the ground floor of the Old Stone Mill, **Skaneateles Artisans** showcases work of many local artists who contribute to this cooperative's success. Find paintings, photographs, jewelry, fiber arts, weavings, baskets, sculpture, ceramics, furniture, glass pieces, faux finishing, and other fine arts and crafts. 3 Fennell St. #2, Skaneateles 13152; 315-685-8580; www.skaneatelesartisans.com

Come to the **Snake Oil Glassworks** studio on Jordan Rd. to find unique glass art pieces. 4251 Jordan Rd., Skaneateles 13152; 315-685-5091; www.snakeoilglassworks.com

BOOKS **McCarthy's Finger Lakes Photography and Gallery** on Jordan St. contains an excellent selection of regional books, posters, notes, prints, and gifts by acclaimed photographer John McCarthy. 9 Jordan St., Skaneateles 13152; 315-685-9099; www.johnfrancismccarthy.com

CLOTHING AND ACCESSORIES For chic, sassy, and sophisticated women's apparel, go to **cate & sally** on Genesee St., where notable lines include Eileen Fisher, Babette, Hanky Panky, Saint James, Fresh Produce, Angela Moore jewelry, and Harshita scarves. 4 E. Genesee St., Skaneateles 13152; 315-685-1105; www.cateandsally.com

Irish goods like thick wool sweaters, linens, and themed gifts are found at **The Irish Store**. 5 Jordan St., Skaneateles 13152; 315-685-6230; www.theirishstore.us

For down-home basics like tees, jeans, gloves, Smartwool socks, and woolies, **Roland's** has been the place to go for more than 50 years. 14 E. Genesee St., Skaneateles 13152; 315-685-7389

Shoes, Frye boots, MZ Wallace bags, Citizens of Humanity jeans, Sonya Renee jewelry, and other hip items can be found at **Skaneateles 300** on the corner of Genesee St. and Jordan. 2 W. Genesee St., Skaneateles 13152; 315-685-1133; www.skaneateles300.com

A mix of fashionable furs and designer women's items is available at **Skaneateles Furs** (36 E. Genesee St., Skaneateles 13152; 315-707-8601); while **Country Ewe** offers fun, funky, and classic women's clothing, outerwear, and jewelry including Clara Sunwoo, Dansko, Tribal Sportswear, and Veronica M. 18 E. Genesee St., Skaneateles 13152; 315-685-9580; www.countryewe.com

Talbots—the only chain store in town—sells classic women's clothing and accessories. 14 W. Genesee St., Skaneateles 13152; 315-685-1479; www.talbots.com

Village Choices has an insane selection of Vera Bradley bags and purses along with other items. 12 E. Genesee St., Skaneateles 13152; www.villagechoices.com

FARMERS' MARKETS AND SPECIALTY FOODS During the summer and fall, the **Farmers' Market** sets up booths near the Allyn Arena just off Austin St. Thursdays and Saturdays. Farmers and other vendors sell vegetables, fruit, flowers, herbs, cheese, meats, eggs, breads, and other items in this colorful open marketplace. www.skaneateles.com

F. Oliver's sells top-shelf imported olive oils, wonderfully aged balsamic vinegars bottled on-site, and other products guaranteed to tempt those who love to cook. Many items are available to taste. Also check out stores in Canandaigua, Rochester, and Ithaca. 4 Jordan St., Skaneateles 13152; 315-685-7585; www.folivers.com

Goat Hill Farm in Manlius, off US 20 east of Skaneateles, sells goat cheese produced from milk of more than 150 goats. The 57-acre farm is owned by Steven and Jennie Mueller. 315 Fayette St., Manlius 13104; 315-655-3014

SEVERAL ORGANIC FARMS SELL THEIR PRODUCE AT THE SKANEATELES FARMERS' MARKET

Infused! is sure to have just the thing to pep up your food, from their artisan olive oils to Ma Poole's Chutney and spices and seasonings. Their Skaneateles Fire Dept. 2 Alarm Chipotle Hot Sauce will rev your taste buds into high gear. 37 Fennell St., Skaneateles 13152; 315-685-9260; www.infused.com

Stone-ground unbleached, unenriched grain products, such as whole-wheat and buckwheat flours and blended pancake mixes, have been produced at **New Hope Mills** near Mandana for decades. Today they are located in Auburn. Enjoy their products prepared at their café, or purchase them in their store, both located on the premises. Their buttermilk pancake mix is justifiably popular. And you can't beat the prices. 181 York St., Auburn 13021; 315-252-2676; www.newhopemills.com

Rhubarb Kitchen and Garden Shop, located in a former bookstore, is a treasure for those who love to cook. It contains all kinds of kitchen gadgets, cookbooks, gourmet foods, cutlery, aprons, espresso makers, cookware, and salsas. 59 E. Genesee St., Skaneateles 13152; 315-685-5803

The aroma of freshly baked bone bread and biscotti draws you to **Rosalie's Bakery** in the back of Rosalie's Cucina. They also make desserts, wedding cakes, Hawaiian fruit bread, and other goodies. 841 W. Genesee St., Skaneateles 13152; 315-685-2200

Pick your own strawberries from convenient "towers" at **Strawberry Fields Hydroponic Farm & Store** on Route 20 as well as find fresh vegetables, condiments, chutneys, and other local foods. 4240 E. Genesee Street Rd., Auburn 13021; 315-751-5657; www.strawberryfieldsupick.com

Vernak Farms Country Store in Borodino sells everything from pizza and ice cream to Amish food and groceries. 1889 E. Lake Rd., Skaneateles 13152; 315-673-9327; www.vernakfarms.com

I dare you to come to the **Vermont Green Mountain Specialty Company** and leave empty-handed. There are just too many good things here: handmade chocolates, gourmet coffees and foods, old-fashioned lollipops, cookies, cakes, and other pastries, gift baskets, and novelties. 50 E. Genesee St., Skaneateles 13152; 315-685-1500

GIFTS Pet lovers will need to stop at **Aristocats and Dogs** for leashes, collars, toys, treats, and other pet products. 62 E. Genesee St., Skaneateles 13152; 315-685-4849; www.aristocatsanddogs.com

General gifts and a wealth of Christmas ornaments and seasonal items are found in the rambling rooms of **Chestnut Cottage.** 75 E. Genesee St., Skaneateles 13152; 315-685-8082

Housed in a former bank, **1st National Gifts** is a popular stop for any kind of special gift or greeting card, with hot lines like Brighton, Caswell-Massey, Ahava, and Portmeirion. 2 E. Genesee St., Skaneateles 13152; 315-685-5454; www.firstnationalgifts.com

Pomodoro is a treasure trove for primitive art, candles, ornaments, candies, cards, and other unique gifts along with brand-name collectibles such as Mary Engelbreit, Land and Wise, and Portmeirion. 61 E. Genesee St., Skaneateles 13152; 315-685-8658; www.pomodoro.com

The White Sleigh sells everything for Christmas: Dickens' Villages, Byers' Carolers, old-world santas, trees full of ornaments, and candles as well as soaps and much more. 24 E. Genesee St., Skaneateles 13152; 315-685-8414

KIDS' THINGS **HABA USA**, a German company, distributes high-quality children's wood products including trains, carts, and games. It originated from the former Skaneateles Handicrafters that made wooden blocks and the popular maple pull-train and tracks. This factory outlet on Jordan Rd. offers great toys at discounted prices. 4407 Jordan St., Skaneateles 13152; 315-685-6660; www.habausa.com

Hobby House Toys has a good selection of toys for all ages. 7 Jordan St., Skaneateles 13152; 315-291-7012

The Kinder Garden has lovely children's clothes and toys, including stuffed animals, jewelry, and games as well as books, blankets, and keepsakes. 3 E. Genesee St., Skaneateles 13152; 315-685-2721; www.kindergardenkid.com

Pride & Joy is a parent's and grandparent's promised land with high-end clothing for babies and tots along with items like dining sets, carriages, special toys, and accessories. 22 Jordan St., Skaneateles 13152; 315-685-7576; www.prideandjoyshop.com

WINES AND SPIRITS **Anyela's Vineyards** on W. Lake Rd. just outside Skaneateles sits on top of a hill overlooking their vineyards and the lake. Taste their wines, like their Curvee Blanc and Blush, while watching the sailboats streak across the water. 2433 W. Lake Rd., Skaneateles 13152; 315-685-3797; www.anyelasvineyards.com

Last Shot Distillery (see "Distilleries" in What's Where in Finger Lakes)

White Birch Vineyards is Skaneateles's newest entry into the wine world. A portion of the grapes used in the wine is grown on W. Lake Rd. while the tasting room is on Genesee St. across from the lake. White Birch offers wine, whisky, and champagne flights and wines for sale. Call for tasting hours. 18 W. Genesee St., Skaneateles 13152; 315-685-9483; www.whitebirchvineyards.com

Owasco Lake and Auburn

Auburn, 2.5 miles north of Owasco Lake and established in 1793, once manufactured products such as shoes, rope, and farm machinery. In the last 50 years most of these companies have moved out, leaving behind a much different town but still one with a great deal of charm. Owasco Lake is surrounded by rolling farmland, lakeside homes, and camps. At the southern end is Moravia, a small village of nineteenth-century homes and the birthplace of our 13th president, Millard Fillmore, as well as the childhood home of John D. Rockefeller. One of the area's biggest assets, Fillmore Glen State Park, is also in Moravia and is blessed with nature trails, picnic areas, deep gorges, and waterfalls.

In the past few years a number of restaurants have opened along with outdoor dining in cozy sidewalk enclaves, one reason Auburn is starting to catch the eye of foodies. There is even a handsome corner bar dedicated to whiskies and a new Sweet Treat Trail leading you to some enticing goodies like honey and candy.

Auburn has exceptional art and historical museums, including the Seward House, and more than two hundred homes and buildings of architectural significance, particularly in the South St. area, a National Register Historic District.

In July and August, usually on Tuesday evenings, concerts and a movie take place in Hoopes Park—the concert at 6:30, the movie when it gets dark. In Emerson Park, the Merry-Go-Round Playhouse stages professional musical productions in a building that formerly housed a fabulous carousel (now in Hershey Park, PA). The amusement park and games arcade, once a source of family fun in the park, is gone, but the large pavilion—formerly the scene of many a big-band cotillion—still exists and has been revived as a venue for weddings and other large parties and events.

Auburn's shopping activity has to some extent moved from Genesee St. west on Rt. 20 to the Fingerlakes Mall, home to Bass Pro Shops, and east along the Grant Ave. strip outside the city center. Still, some retailers are starting up shops in the city center.

Those passing through town along Rt. 20 don't get a peek at the 11-mile-long deep-blue lake, so reward yourself with some magnificent views of the water by taking a detour via Lake Ave. to Emerson Park.

✳ Lodging

HISTORIC **Springside Inn**, a four-story mid-1800s inn, believed to have once harbored runaway slaves, is graced by hanging flower baskets on the porch, perennial gardens, and a sunny breakfast room. Rooms are traditionally decorated, many with toile and Waverly-style flowered wallpapers and fabrics, and come with four-poster canopy beds, wet bars, and Jacuzzis for two. Springside has a pretty dining room and is popular for weddings. $$–$$$ 6141 W. Lake Rd., Auburn 13021; 315-252-7247; www.springsideinn.com

B&BS **A Wicher Garden** in a country setting in Auburn has four guest rooms, two sharing a second-story porch. All are beautifully decorated and furnished with king or queen beds along with pillow-top mattresses, fine linens, flat-screen TVs, and en-suite baths. The four-course breakfast is worth waking for. $$–$$$ 5831 Dunning Avenue Rd., Auburn 13021; 315-252-1187; www.wichergardeninn.com

10 Fitch, an exquisitely decorated colonial house located in the historic district, has three guest suites, five fireplaces, a library, a sunroom, and a beautiful garden. Each room is decorated with rich designer fabrics, traditional antiques, and

SPRINGSIDE INN HAS LONG SERVED OVERNIGHT AND DINNER GUESTS

BEST OF AUBURN

HISTORY: Springside Inn; Hunter's Dinerant
BURGERS: Green Shutters; Parker's Grille
ROMANCE: Elderberry Pond
FOOD: Moro's Table
VIEWS: Elderberry Pond terrace

ITALIAN: Osteria Salina; Michael's
MEETING PLACE: A.T. Walley & Co.
POWER LUNCH: Parker's Grille and Tap House
MEXICAN: Tres Primos

reproduction furniture. Enjoy wonderful mattresses, high-thread-count linens, rain-head showers, and chandeliers. For adults only, this is a serene place to end a busy day with plenty of space to spread out and extras like a guest fridge and nightly turndown. A full breakfast is served. $$$–$$$$ 10 Fitch Ave., Auburn 13021; www.10fitch.com

HOTELS AND INNS The new 92-room **Hilton Garden Inn**, in the middle of town and 35 miles from the Syracuse Hancock Airport, offers modern accommodations, a business center, Internet, four meeting rooms, room service, two restaurants, and a bar. BeauVine Chophouse, the fine-dining restaurant, serves exceptional cuisine in contemporary surroundings where you can eat inside or in the outdoor courtyard. 74 State St., Auburn 13021; 315-252-5511; www.hiltongardeninn3.hilton.com

Centrally located, the 165-room **Holiday Inn** caters to those on the road. Rooms are comfortable; some come with Jacuzzis, and some overlook the courtyard. There is a nice indoor pool and courtyard along with a fitness center, business center, restaurant, game room, and lounge. McMurphy's Irish Pub and Restaurant offers lunch and dinner daily, while the Falls Room is open for breakfast. $$ 75 North St., Auburn 13021; 315-253-4531; www.hiauburn.com

A modest hotel with extras, the **Inn at the Finger Lakes**'s amenities are modern and efficient, and rooms are furnished with luxury pillow-top sleep sets. Among the amenities are WiFi and a fitness center. A deluxe continental breakfast is served. $–$$ 12 Seminary Ave., Auburn 13021; www.innatthefingerlakes.com

✳ Dining Out

From dependable chains like Applebee's to small bistros, Auburn has just about anything you might be looking for, often at more reasonable prices than Skaneateles. Several places from the early '30s continue to thrive as generations of families keep the good food and magic going.

TRADITION, TRADITION **Balloons Restaurant**, a small steak house in the shadow of the Auburn prison, has been delivering good food at reasonable prices for more than 50 years. Many of the waiters have been here long enough to seem like family. Specialties include prime rib, steaks of all kinds, and salads, along with pasta dishes. Bring your appetite. $–$$ 65 Washington St., Auburn 13021; 315-252-9761; www.balloonsrestaurant.net

Michael's Restaurant is a third-generation establishment serving delicious home-cooked Italian food. Start with their amazing greens and beans appetizer, then order veal saltimbocco—or any veal dish for that matter. All good. Ask Duffy, the owner and

AUBURN PRISON

Looming in a corner of the city, the gray walls of the Auburn Correctional Facility, a maximum-security prison, continue to draw curious onlookers. Site of the first electric chair (now a museum piece) and the place Chester Gillette, immortalized in the film, *An American Tragedy*, was put to death, the prison is an important part of Auburn's history and is still in operation.

cook, to prepare his spectacular bananas flambé. 196 Clark St., Auburn 13020; 315-252-349

At **Springside Inn**, dine in the Oak & Vine, where seasonal produce and meats are used to prepare fare like tequila honey house wings, sweet potato fries with maple syrup, citrus salmon, and butcher steak. Pub plates are available and additional dining venues are suitable for larger groups. $$–$$$ 6141 W. Lake Rd., Auburn 13021; 315-252-7247; www.springsideinn.com

A longtime winner among locals for Italian food, pub fare, steaks, and seafood, **Curley's Restaurant** has been serving food and drink to patrons since 1934. Lunch is big here. $$–$$$ 96 State St., Auburn 13021; 315-252-5224

HIP BISTRO-STYLE **A. T. Walley & Co.** is the place to come for music, wine, and spirits. The brick and mellow-wood paneling and bar set the mood for drinks and food like slow-roasted beef and hot pastrami sandwiches. And yes, you can stash your own bottle of premium whisky in a private niche. Discover rare brands like Green Spot, Midleton Very Rare Irish Whiskey, and Jameson Black Barrel. 119 Genesee St., Auburn 13021; 315-282-7314; www.atwalley.com

Bambino's Bistro serves "Oh my God, great" Italian cuisine, says foodie Dimitris Dimopoulos. Bring your own bottle of wine and dig into homemade pasta and chargrilled pizza. Open for lunch and dinner. 105 Genesee St., Auburn 13021; 315-255-3385; www.bambinosbistro.com

BeauVine Chophouse & Wine Bar in the new Hilton Garden Inn treats its patrons to dinner in a sophisticated setting. We particularly love the tomahawk rib eye steak, paired with local vegetables and house-made tots or hand-cut sea salt fries. Also try the roasted guinea hen or pistachio-encrusted salmon. 74 State St., Auburn 13021; 315-515-3162; www.beauvinechophouse.com

Chef Edward Moro and his wife, Beth, have brought a bit of California to Auburn with **Moro's Table**. It's a class act with beautiful presentations and reasonable, not overkill, portions. Décor is smart with a zinc bar punctuating the white, eggplant, and silver theme. One of the big pluses here, besides the superb food, is that you can order half portions for most items. If you love mussels—wow. 1 E. Genesee St., Auburn 13021; 315-282-7772; www.morostable.com

Osteria Salina, tucked into a side street with an outdoor café, is a cozy, European-style eatery with brick walls, a long bar, and an adjacent bakery and créperie. Serving traditional Sicilian cuisine, along with organic rotisserie meats, steaks, wood-fired brick-oven pizzas, and a nightly raw bar, Osteria Salina has quickly become a popular local spot. And wait till you see their martini menu! 20 State St., Auburn 13021; 315-258-9070; osteriasalinaauburn.com

Parker's Grille and Tap House, one of the few restaurants in the heart of the business district, is packed at lunchtime. In addition to a long bar, there are regular tables, high-top tables, and booths, plus Tiffany-style lamps and lots of wood trim. Food is good pub style—finger food, hamburgers, Philly steak sandwiches, pita pockets, and

soups—plus several brews on tap. 129 Genesee St., Auburn 13021; 315-252-6884; www
.parkersgrille.com

Prison City Pub & Brewery plays off the reputation of Auburn's huge, hulking
prison. But prison food was never this good. With an on-site brewery and a kitchen
focused on friendly comfort food like a ploughman's platter good enough to make a
Brit's heart beat faster, shepherd's pie and shrimp & grits washed down with the house
Mug Club beer, this is one brick-walled "prison" you'll be happy to visit. 28 State St.,
Auburn 13021; 315-604-1277; www.prisoncitybrewery.com

COUNTRY FARM **Elderberry Pond**, an Arts and Crafts–style building in a bucolic
setting of gardens, fields, and lawns, looks like it's been here forever. It is, in fact,
relatively new. A member of Finger Lakes Culinary Bounty, Elderberry Pond specializes in dishes made from organic foods grown in the restaurant's own gardens. Eat
in the dining room or on the small patio in season. Hours can vary. A farm store is
open in season. $$–$$$ 3728 Center Street Rd., Auburn 13021; 315-252-6062; www
.elderberrypond.com

PIZZA AND PASTA When you come to **Lasca's**, bring your heartiest appetite—
some come for the leftovers. Specialties include shrimp scampi, gramp's eggplant
parmigiana, and chicken piccata. For an appetizer, try the antipasto Nicholas or
deep-fried mushrooms. $$–$$$ 252-258 Grant Ave., Auburn 13041; 315-253-4885;
www.lascas.com

Also try **Balloons**, **Bambino's**, and **Michael's** (above).

OSTERIA SALINA SERVES TRADITIONAL SICILIAN FOOD

MEXICAN Locals are quickly discovering **Tres Primos** ("three cousins"), west of Auburn in Elbridge on Rt. 5, is the place to come for authentic Mexican fare and killer margaritas. Family-owned and -operated, the cuisine is perfectly seasoned and prepared from scratch. Dishes like enchilada poblanas topped with their own cream sauce, a killer chimichanga, and hearty 3 primo burrito are served on giant Fiestaware platters accompanied by tasty sides like beans, Mexican rice, and avocado salad. Portions are huge and prices are very reasonable. Service is superb and friendly. No wonder Tres Primos is already enjoying a lot of repeat business—it's the real deal. $–$$ 1099 NY Rt. 5, Elbridge 13060; 315-277-5508.

HUNTER'S DINERANT IS AN ICONIC AUBURN RESTAURANT

CASUAL FARE You've gotta know a place named **McMurphy's Authentic Irish Pub & Restaurant** at the Holiday Inn serves Irish food and beer, burgers, sandwiches, steak, and seafood. And you'd be right. Try the shepherd's pie or Cousin Katie's Guinness stew. 76 North St., Auburn 13021; 315-253-4531

For a yummy, quick burger and a dose of nostalgia, pull into **Green Shutters Drive-In** across from Emerson Park. Remember car hops? They still have them, except the servers don't wear roller skates anymore. There is a counter and a picnic area out back as well as a small dining room. Go for the burgers. Ice cream is a hot seller as well. $ 6933 Owasco Rd., Auburn 13021; 315-253-6154

Reese's Dairy Bar on NY 5 and US 20, west of Auburn, is a candy-colored dairy bar selling ice cream, hamburgers, and other foods-to-go. 1422 Clark St., Auburn 13021; 315-252-7323

Eat overlooking the lake on the open deck or inside at **The Lake Side Grill and Bar** in Moravia. Pull up by boat, or come by car for hamburgers, sandwiches, chicken, and salads. Live entertainment through the summer. $–$$ 2846 Fire Lane 1, Moravia 13118; 315-497-1602; www.lakesidegrillandbar.com

For eats 24/7, **Hunter's Dinerant**, at the entrance to Auburn's downtown, is one of the last of its kind. Hunter's has been serving customers for more than 50 years, dishing out homemade pies and puddings, meatloaf, mashed potatoes, and other comfort foods. Don't expect gourmet. 18 E. Genesee St., Auburn 13021; 315-255-2282

Another vintage model, **The Auburn Diner** (from the 1920s) has been rescued from abandonment. Come here for diner burgers and other typical diner fare. 64 Columbus St., Auburn 13021; 315-253-7375

In addition to a selection of ready-to-go foods, **Wegman's** has a cappuccino and latte bar in their full-service grocery store. Buy a dessert, bagel, or sub, and head to the seating area. 40-60 Genesee St., Auburn 13021; 315-255-2231

Sweet Treat Trail invites you to visit locally made delights from more than 20 vendors in Cayuga County. Satisfy your sweet tooth by stopping at places like Strawberry Fields Hydroponic Farm, Reese's Dairy Bar, Karen's Country Confections, Dorie's Bakery, and Fly by Night Cookie Company. Find honey, jams, chocolates, apples, sweet wines, fresh baked goods, fruits, syrups, and many other delicious things. 800-499-9615; www.tourcayuga.com

✳ To See

MUSEUMS, EXHIBITIONS, AND HISTORIC SITES The **Cayuga Museum of History and Art** contains exhibits about life in Cayuga County and Native American art attractively displayed in the Willard Case mansion (circa 1840). Behind the mansion is the **Case Research Laboratory**, where Theodore Case, an important inventor of his time, perfected the tube that made sound movies possible. 203 Genesee St., Auburn 13021; 315-253-8051; www.cayugamuseum.org

The **Cayuga-Owasco Lakes Historical Society Museum** in Moravia—the "History House"—is a treasure trove of more than five hundred items, focusing on local history and genealogy. 14 W. Cayuga St., Auburn 13118; 315-497-3906

Fort Hill Cemetery was used as a fortress by the Iroquois and Cayuga tribes around 1100. The remains of the last fortifications are still evident. Chief Logan, one of the great Native American leaders, is buried here, along with William H. Seward and Harriet Tubman. 19 Fort St., Auburn 13021; 315-253-8132

A visitor center on the grounds of **Harriet Tubman's home** pays tribute to this heroic woman and former slave from Maryland often called "the Moses of her people." A Union spy, scout, and nurse, she made 19 dangerous trips south to rescue more than 300 slaves. The house she built is open and contains Tubman's sewing machine, her coal stove, a number of pieces of furniture, and other memorabilia. 180 South St., Auburn 13021; 315-252-2081; www.harriethouse.org

The extensive **Schweinfurth Memorial Art Center** displays changing contemporary art exhibits like *Quilts=Art=Quilts*, *Made in New York*, *Both Ends of the Rainbow* (children's and seniors' artwork), and others. The museum has an excellent gift shop and offers a number of classes, lectures, and trips. 205 Genesee St., Auburn 13021; 315-255-1553; www.schweinfurthartcenter.org

CAYUGA MUSEUM OF HISTORY AND ART

The **Seward House Museum** is the early nineteeth-century home of William H. Seward, New York governor, U.S. senator, and secretary of state under Presidents Lincoln and Johnson. Seward was instrumental in the purchase of Alaska and was one of the founders of the Republican Party. The museum contains period and Civil War pieces, has a lovely garden and gazebo, and is the venue for various special events throughout the year. 33 South St., Auburn 13021; 315-252-1283; www.sewardhouse.org

The **Ward W. O'Hara Agricultural Museum** contains farm implements and tools circa 1800–1930 along with a blacksmith shop, general store, woodworking shop, cooperage, 1900s country kitchen, and veterinarian's office. Events include a draft horse show, antique tractor rodeo, miniature horse show, Old Threads Days, Victorian Doll House Day, and Old Ways Days. Also on the grounds is a **Disc Golf** facility. Throw discs (for sale at park) into designated "baskets." 6880 E. Lake Rd., Auburn 13021; 315-252-7644; www.cayugacounty.us/community/parks-and-trails/ag-museum

The Romanesque Revival **Willard Memorial Chapel** is the only complete and unaltered Tiffany chapel in the country. The interior contains a rose window, opalescent nave windows, leaded glass chandeliers, a jeweled pulpit, and gold-stenciled furniture and ceiling. Simply dazzling. 17 Nelson St., Auburn 13021; www.willard-chapel.org

Follow the **Auburn Public Art Trail** to discover creative work like the Exchange Street Plaza Murals, the Boyle Center Mosaic, "Wheel to Reel" sculpture, and many more expressions of art throughout the city. 315-252-7674; www.auburnarttrail.com

The Finger Lakes Art Cooperative is filled with one-of-a-kind items by area artists ranging from paintings, jewelry, fiber art, ceramics, and to much more. Be sure to check out monthly First Fridays and the painting parties offered throughout the year. 101 Genesee St., Auburn 13021; 315-406-0097; www.flartcoop.org

PERFORMING ARTS The **Finger Lakes Musical Theatre Festival** showcases "Broadway in the Finger Lakes" at three venues. **Merry-Go-Round Playhouse** brings six professionally-produced musicals to the Finger Lakes each summer such as *West Side Story*, *The Light in the Piazza*, and *Saturday Night Fever* staged in the carousel pavilion in Emerson Park. 315-255-1785; www.merry-go-round.com

The Auburn Public Theater is an innovative center for theatrical productions, a 75-seat movie theater featuring independent and foreign films, and a venue for edgy cultural offerings. 8 Exchange St., Auburn 13021; 315-253-6669; www.auburn publictheater.org

At **Pitch**, the next generation of musical theater writers, directors, and actors present their new work in process. Following the performance, the audience is asked for their comments. You sit around tables in the intimate Theater Mack housed in a historic former carriage house at Cayuga Museum of History and Art. 800-457-8897; fingerlakesmtf.com

The **Auburn Players Community Theater** draws from local talent, offering four productions a year. 197 Franklin St., Auburn 13021; 315-258-8275; www.auburnplayers.org

The **Finger Lakes Drive-In** is one of the few remaining outdoor movie theaters left in the region. It's so old, each year you fully expect it to be gone, but it seems to be hanging in there. Open seasonally. 3969 Clark St., Auburn 13021; www.fingerlakesdrivein .com

Catch the performances of the **Kaleidoscope Dance Theatre**, a professional modern dance company. 315-252-4420; www.nyide.com and www.kaleidoscopedancetheatre.com

✳ To Do

BIKING **Owasco Lake Loop:** A 32-mile loop around the lake starting at Emerson Park, going south on NY 38 along the west side of the lake to Moravia and Fillmore Glen, and returning north on NY 38A. Bring your suits for a swim in Emerson Park at the end of your trip.

BOATING For boat sales and service as well as boat rentals contact **Owasco Marine** in Auburn, 315-258-9096; www.owascomarine.net; or South Shore Marina in Moravia, 315-497-3006

GOLF **Dutch Hollow Country Club:** With a large dairy farm just across the street, Dutch Hollow in Owasco's hilly rural landscape doesn't let you forget you're in the country. Water comes into play on eight holes as the course climbs up and down hills and jumps across creeks and wetlands creating some interesting, quirky holes. It's a fun play, with plenty of challenges, and popular for local outings. 1839 County Rd. 117, Auburn 13021; 315-784-5052; www.dutchhollow.com

Highland Park Golf Club: Brushing up against groves of apple trees, Highland Park in Auburn has its share of eccentric holes. The front nine was built in 1925 while the back nine, designed by Geoffrey Cornish, was added in 1969 and features some tricky rolling greens as well as a few ups and downs. Still, it's not a hard course to walk, and many do. 3068 Franklin Street Rd., Auburn 13021; 315-253-3381; www.highlandparkgolf.com

Lakeview Golf & Country Club is aptly named—you get water views from many holes on this 6,564-yard course. The expansive clubhouse is often the scene of events and golf outings. 6642 E. Lake Rd., Auburn 13021; 315-253-3152; www.lakeviewgolfcc .com

For a basic just-get-out-and-have-some-fun course, **Fillmore Golf Club** in Locke is a pretty layout overlooking Owasco Lake. Its green fees are also a good deal—in the $20 range. 315-497-3145; www.fillmoregolfclub.com

The nine-hole **Indian Head** course on Rts. 5 and 20 in Cayuga is another option for warm-up golf at a good price. 315-253-6812

Millstone Golf Course east of Auburn has no bunkers, nor a fancy clubhouse, but it's a really neat little course with some clever holes and smart routing,

MILLSTONE IS A NEAT, INEXPENSIVE 18-HOLE PUBLIC COURSE

BIG DOINGS IN SKANEATELES

We haven't had this much excitement since Banjo Greenfield's son, Dozer, towed his double-wide through town, and all the streetlights had to be raised." (Skaneateles recreation director Matt Major referring to the impending arrival of President Bill Clinton and first lady, Hillary, who came to vacation on the lake in 1999.)

especially after the second hole when you start climbing an incline up into the woods. 354 Rt. 5 W., Elbridge 13060; 315-689-3600; www.millstonegolfcourse.com

HIKING There are several marked trails in and around Owasco Lake: the **Auburn-Fleming Trail**, a straight 2-mile dirt-and-stone up-and-back trail is an easy walk along an old tree-lined railroad bed just west of the northern end of Owasco Lake. www.cnyhiking.com

Fillmore Glen State Park south of Moravia has three 1.8-mile moderately difficult dirt trails. The trails start in the valley and rise 349 feet to a dam. The North and South Rim Trails follow the rims of the gorge; the Gorge Trail (perfect for kids) goes along Dry Creek (which is actually not dry at all). At the turning point of the trails is a two-level dam. The lower pool of water is great for swimming. Check out the Cowsheds, a cavern carved out of rock by a tumbling waterfall. 1686 NY Rt. 38, Moravia 13118; 315-497-0130; www.nysparks.com

PARKS, NATURE PRESERVES, AND CAMPING **Emerson Park**, on the north shore of Owasco Lake, has long been a favorite place for picnicking, swimming, and entertainment. It has a sprawling grassy park, swimming, beaches, boat launches, picnic facilities, playgrounds, a bathhouse, and a restored pavilion. Also on the grounds is Auburn's Merry-Go-Round Playhouse located in the former carousel building and the Ward W. O'Hara Agricultural Museum. 6914 E. Lake Rd., Auburn 13021; 315-2553-5611

Fillmore Glen State Park (See listing in Hiking)

Casey Park is a multipurpose sports and recreation facility with tennis courts, an ice rink, an Olympic-size swimming pool, trails for biking and walking, picnic areas, playgrounds, horseshoe pits, and bocce courts. 150 N. Division St., Auburn 13021; 315-253-4247

The **Dorothy Mcilroy Bird Sanctuary**, a 157-acre preserve along Lake Como outlet, features a number of plants uncommon to the area and various species of birds. Walk the pleasant 1.4-mile trail. Lane A off Lake Como Rd., Summerhill 13077; 607-275-9487

Montezuma National Wildlife Refuge off Rt. 20 in Seneca Falls is a rich ecological environment and haven for birds and other wildlife. Trails, roads, an observation tower, and a visitor center make this exceptional resource easily accessible. 3395 Auburn Rd., Seneca Falls 13148; 315-568-5987

SCUBA **Finger Lake Scuba** is a full-service snorkeling and scuba center offering all levels of scuba certification in addition to local diving trips throughout the Finger Lakes. 11 Dill St., Auburn 13021; 800-764-3483, 315-252-8638; www.fingerlakesscuba.com

FAMILY FUN Hit the dirt at **Rolling Wheels** on the Cayuga County Fairgrounds, a venue for fairs, dirt-track motor races, demolition derbies, monster-truck competitions, agricultural exhibits, horse shows, concerts, and home of **Dirt Motorsports Hall of Fame and Classic Car Museum**. 8310 Grant Ave., Weedsport 13166; 315-834-6606; www.dirtmotorsports.com

Watch super baseball action of the **Abner Doubledays**, a Class A farm team for the Toronto Blue Jays, and enjoy a hot dog in a 2,044-seat baseball stadium throughout the summer at **Falcon Park** in Auburn. Abner Doubleday, baseball's legendary founder, spent much of his life in Auburn. 130 N. Division St., Auburn 13021; 315-255-2489; www.minorleaguebaseball.com

Pick your own strawberries, blueberries, raspberries, apples, cherries, vegetables, and pumpkins, and cut your own Christmas trees at **Grisamore Farms** off US 90 between Locke and Genoa south of Moravia. In the fall there are hayrides, a Halloween maze, and a working cider press. Little kids should get a charge out of the farm animals including Penelope the donkey and Silver, a miniature horse. 749 Cowan Rd., Locke 13092; 315-497-1347; www.grisamorefarms.com

The Gorge Trail is perfect for young hikers at **Fillmore Glen State Park**. Cool off in the pool at the base of the hill and later have a picnic. All in all, it makes for a fun day the kids will remember. (See listing in Hiking)

WELLNESS/SPA **The Center**, housed in a historic gray stone church, offers a variety of holistic treatments and services including massages, Mayan stone massages, drum circles, acupuncture, ear candling, shirodhara, aromatherapy, vibrational medicine, yoga, and more. 1 Hoffman St., Auburn 13021; 315-704-0319; www.thecenter4wellness .com

✳ Shopping

ANTIQUES **Auburn Antiques** is packed with all sorts of stuff from surprise finds to junk, from antique hockey sticks, jewelry, and glass to memorabilia and furniture. Dig in and see what hidden treasures you can discover. 7 Arterial E., Auburn 13021; 315-252-9701

MARKETS AND SPECIALTY FOODS **3 Leaf Tea** on Genesee St., Auburn, sells handblended all-natural teas sourced by the store's owner, Luciana Torous, from all over the world, along with hot chocolate, many flavors of matcha (the peach matcha is great), raw organic cacao, and unique tea-themed gifts. The cheerful shop has tables where you can sit down and enjoy tea and light fare including Thai cucumber salad, parfaits, waffles, refreshing matcha lemonade, and frozen hot chocolate. 25 E. Genesee St., Auburn 13021; 315-255-1022; www.threeleaftea.com

FARMERS' MARKETS **Auburn Farmers Co-op Market** on State St. (Curley's parking lot) is open Tuesday, Thursday, and Saturday 7 a.m.–2 p.m. June–October. 315-704-8609

Niles Farmers' Market at Niles Town Hall on New Hope Rd., Moravia, is open Saturday from 10 a.m.–1 p.m. June–October. 315-497-0142

CAMPING/SPORTS **Bass Pro Shops** is the main game in town at the Fingerlakes Mall in Auburn. This super sprawling store is filled with things for camping, fishing, sportswear, cooking, hunting, recreation—just about everything for the outdoors, including a huge boat showroom. 1579 Clark St., Auburn 13021; 315-258-2700; www .basspro.com

Otisco Lake

The easternmost lake, Otisco, just 6 miles long, is quiet and surrounded by wooded hills. The largest village, Amber, on the east side, has only a few stores and homes. At the northern end water spills over a dam into a river. If you have a canoe in tow, it's a perfect lake for paddling.

✳ Dining Out

CASUAL FARE Just north of Otisco Lake, **Marietta House**, a large restaurant with a beautiful brick patio and gazebo set in gardens, is a perfect setting for a wedding or special occasion. $–$$ 2819 Rt. 174, Marietta 13110; 315-636-8299; www.mariettahouse.com

For a casual bite in the summer, the **Lake Drive-Inn**, corner of Otisco Valley Rd. and Otisco Rd., Marietta, has picnic tables and a small indoor area serving ice cream, hot dogs, hamburgers, fries, pizza, and other quick food. 1644 Otisco Valley Rd., Marietta 13110; 315-636-8557

✳ To See

The Otisco Lake County Park has no swimming access, but you can picnic and hand launch your canoe or kayak there. You can also hand launch on the west side of the Otisco Lake Causeway on the southern end of the lake, also a park.

PRETTY OTISCO LAKE IS IDEAL FOR SMALL BOATS

CHIEF LOGAN

Auburn was once a Native American village, the home of Logan (Tah-gah-jute). A sachem of the Shamokins and Cayuga tribes, Logan was known as a peaceful and wise man. Because of his great oratorical skills and good sense, he often represented the Six Nations at powwows with whites. This all changed when his entire family was brutally slaughtered by a renegade band of settlers. Lashing out in retribution, he took the lives of several white families, although it is said he did not allow his warriors to torture the victims, a common practice at that time among his people. Logan is buried in Fort Hill Cemetery in Auburn, where his grave is marked with a limestone obelisk.

MORE INFORMATION **Cayuga County Office of Tourism:** 315-255-1658, 800-499-9615; www.tourcayuga.com

City of Auburn Historic Sites Commission: 315-255-1658, 800-499-9615; www.historyshometown.com

Finger Lakes Travel: 888-408-1693; Nicole@fingerlakestravelny.com; fingerlakes travelny.com

Finger Lakes Tourism Alliance: 315-536-7488, 800-530-7499; www.fingerlakes.org

Skaneateles Area Chamber of Commerce: 315-685-0552; www.skaneateles.com

PHOTO OPS **Skaneateles Lake:** One of the best views of the deep blue lake is from a spot about 2.8 miles north of Scott on NY 41.

Carpenter's Falls: The National Audubon Society has identified this area as one of the state's important bird spots. To find the 100-foot falls near New Hope, go 11 miles south on the west side of Skaneateles Lake to Apple Tree Rd. (mile marker 14), bear left at the fork, and cross over the falls at the east–west escarpment. There is a quasi trail—not maintained but well worn—to the bottom where you'll find a wonderful level place to picnic with the falls around the corner. To preserve this valuable asset, the Ithaca-based Finger Lakes Land Trust purchased 30 forested acres including the primary access to the falls and half the waterfall itself. 607-275-9487

New Hope Mills: Hardly a blink in the road along the west side of Rt. 41A—watch for a small sign, just past Mandana going south. The old mill wheel still turns, although the grinding of grains has been curtailed. A factory in Auburn produces the flour products.

Skaneateles, Owasco, and Otisco Lakes

❋ What's Happening

SPRING **Memorial Day Parades** in Skaneateles and Auburn bring out veterans, scouts, local dignitaries, floats, bands, and candy for the kids.

The first Saturday of May, a **Wildlife Festival** is held at the Montezuma Audubon Center, 10 miles north of the refuge on Rt. 89 in the town of Savannah. Enjoy food; live music; children's activities; canoe trips; hikes; and guided interaction with birds, small mammals, or reptiles. 2295 NY Rt.89, Savannah 13146; 315-365-3580

SUMMER **Auburn Doubledays home games**, Falcon Park, Auburn. Class A professional baseball games. 315-255-2489

Book Sale, by the Skaneateles Library, usually the second weekend of July. Lots of books, old and new, sold in the old firehouse on Fennell St. 315-685-5135

Cayuga County Fair, Cayuga County Fairgrounds, Weedsport. Farm animals, monster trucks, food concessions, midway games, live entertainment, and a demolition derby (July). 315-575-6219

Concerts in Clift Park, Skaneateles. Every Friday evening at 7:30 in the park—or indoors at the Allyn Pavilion if it rains.

Concerts at Emerson Park Pavilion, Emerson Park, Auburn. Live entertainment with everything from rock 'n' roll to Irish step dancers. 315-253-5611

Concert series, Ethel Fuller Park, Moravia. Free concerts at 7 p.m.

Curbstone Festival and Sidewalk Sale Days, Skaneateles: In addition to all the great bargains, there is food and entertainment, too.

Finger Lakes Lavender Festival, Lockwood Lavender Farm, Skaneateles. U-pick lavender, lavender products, and honey. 315-685-5369; www.lockwoodfarm.blog spot.com

Labor Day celebration & Firemen's Field Days, Austin Park, Skaneateles. The town's largest parade is followed by barbecues, games, rides, and fireworks.

Made in NY, Schweinfurth Memorial Art Center, Auburn. Juried show of artwork by New York State artists. 315-255-1553

Pancake breakfasts in several towns, typically held on Sundays in fire halls. Ask around. There is one somewhere almost every week.

Polo matches, Skaneateles. Sundays at 3 p.m.

Skaneateles Classic and Antique Boat Show, Clift Park and pier, Skaneateles. Antique and classic boats in and out of the water. Concerts, boat parade, and shopping (last weekend in July). 315-685-0552

Skaneateles Festival, Skaneateles. Twenty or so chamber music, jazz, and other concerts are scheduled throughout August and September. These are held under the

THE LAVENDER FESTIVAL TAKES PLACE AT THE LOCKWOOD LAVENDER FARM ON W. LAKE RD., SKANEATELES, SELLING LAVENDER PRODUCTS AND CRAFTS

DICKENS CHARACTERS STROLL THE STREETS OF SKANEATELES AT CHRISTMASTIME

stars at Anyela's Vineyards on Saturdays, and at the First Presbyterian Church on Thursdays and Fridays. There are music purists who prefer the acoustics of the church, while others love the outdoor ambiance. 315-685-7418; www.skanfest.org

Skaneateles United Methodist Church Antique Show: Browse items from more than 70 antique dealers and 40 artisans. Austin Park Arena; www.skanantique show.com

Summer Arts and Crafts Show, Marcellus. Sale and exhibit of artwork by area artisans.

Tomato Fest, Auburn. Tomatoes become the star attraction at this village festival in September.

FALL/WINTER **Dickens Days**, Skaneateles. In December, the town is dressed for the holidays, and the townspeople are dressed as Dickens characters as they stroll Genesee St. Very festive.

Polar Bear Plunge in late January raises money for local charities as brave souls take a dip in the icy waters off Clift Park in Skaneateles. It's all part of **WinterFest**, a project of the Sunrise Rotary Club, which includes ice sculpture contests, food sampling, wine tasting, and a scavenger hunt.

Turkey Trot, Skaneateles: Run/walk for all ages on Thanksgiving morning leaving from Sherwood Inn.

Winter Adventures at Baltimore Woods Nature Center: Look for Winter Family Play Days inviting you to come with the kids, strap on some snowshoes and head out into the woods for some fun. Afterward it's back at the campfire for hot cocoa and a snowball fight. Biking and hiking trails free. 4007 Bishop Hill Rd., Marcellus, 13108 315-673-1350; www.baltimorewoods.org

CAYUGA LAKE

Anchored on the southern end by Ithaca and on the north by Seneca Falls, Cayuga Lake is the longest of the Finger Lakes (40 miles) and the second deepest (435 feet). Cayuga means "boat landing" in Native American.

Driving around the lake you'll pass through small villages like Union Springs, Aurora, Cayuga, and Ludlowville on the east side, and Trumansburg, Interlaken, Sheldrake, and Canoga on the west.

Many of the lake's hills are embossed with vineyards marching down to the water's edge. Dramatic waterfalls spill over rugged cliffs, and rivers gush through gorges carved by ancient glaciers. Hikers, bikers, and all those who appreciate nature can enjoy these spectacular natural assets in the parks that lie around the lake, particularly near the southern end.

Ithaca

Ithaca is energized by its colleges, yet its neighborhoods evoke a small-town ambiance for its close to 30,000 full-time residents.

Much of the action takes place in the center of the city, known as Ithaca Commons or "the Commons," a pedestrian-only shopping area along with Aurora St. at the end and nearby Dewitt Mall housed in a historic building. A mix of boutiques, specialty shops, art studios, restaurants, bars, and cafés add up to a very upbeat, hip area worth exploring.

In Ithaca, something seems to be going on every night—a play, a concert, a poetry reading, or an opening of a new art exhibit.

Four major state parks and 150 waterfalls and dramatic gorges are all within a 10-mile radius of town. There are plenty of biking and hiking trails and great fishing. Ithaca is known for its fall-run trout.

The area is served by Ithaca/Tompkins Regional Airport.

ITHACA'S BEGINNINGS AND GROWTH In 1779, when General Sullivan swept through to destroy Native American villages, his men were impressed by the vast, fertile fields of corn and fruit groves. Some of Sullivan's men returned and built log cabins.

Mills were constructed, and by 1800 the area was buzzing with activity—so much so that some referred to it as "Sin City." Simeon DeWitt, the state surveyor general, drew up a town plan and in 1804 named it Ithaca because of its location within the town of Ulysses—the name of the ancient Greek hero who had come from the island of Ithaca.

By 1810 the town had 250 residents, 38 houses, a post office, a hotel, a

THE ITHACA FARMERS' MARKET OFFERS FLOWERS, VEGETABLES, CHEESES, BREADS, MEAT, AND MUCH MORE

HISTORIC BUILDINGS GRACE THE CORNELL CAMPUS

schoolhouse, stores, and a library. In 1817, Ithaca became the seat of a new county—Tompkins—and the freewheeling town sobered up and knuckled down to serious business. As a county leader, it had a new image to uphold.

Steamboats like the *Enterprise, Telemachus, Frontenac,* and *DeWitt* helped Ithaca develop a strong commercial base. By 1830 the population had swelled to 3,592. Railroads arrived in 1842, and an electric street railway system was established in 1884, linking the hills and the flats.

EDUCATION Ezra Cornell, who had made a fortune in the telegraph industry, established **Cornell University** in 1868. Cornell is, today, an educational leader, particularly in the fields of engineering, veterinary medicine, hotel management, biotechnology and agriculture, and life sciences.

In 1892, when violin teacher William Grant Egbert rented four rooms and arranged to teach eight students, the Ithaca Conservatory of Music was founded. Chartered as a private college in 1931, it changed its name to **Ithaca College** and is now the largest private residential college in the state, offering studies in the Schools of Music, Humanities and Sciences, Business, Communications, and Health Sciences and Human Performance. 800-429-4274; www.ithaca .edu. Other schools in Ithaca include **Tompkins Cortland Community College** and a branch of **Finger Lakes School of Massage.**

RENEWAL AND PRESERVATION In the '50s and '60s, the business district deteriorated, but by the end of the '60s, a massive urban-renewal program brought new life into the inner city.

In 1974, Ithaca Commons was created, a pedestrian zone of shops, offices, restaurants, and other commercial businesses. Older structures were rehabilitated, including the Clinton House and the DeWitt Mall.

TRUMANSBURG About 10 miles north of Ithaca on the west side of Cayuga Lake, the pleasant, leafy village of Trumansburg was founded in 1792 by Abner Truman. With a population of about 1,600 people, it is adjacent to the spectacular Taughannock Falls State Park and is home to a number of historic houses and buildings.

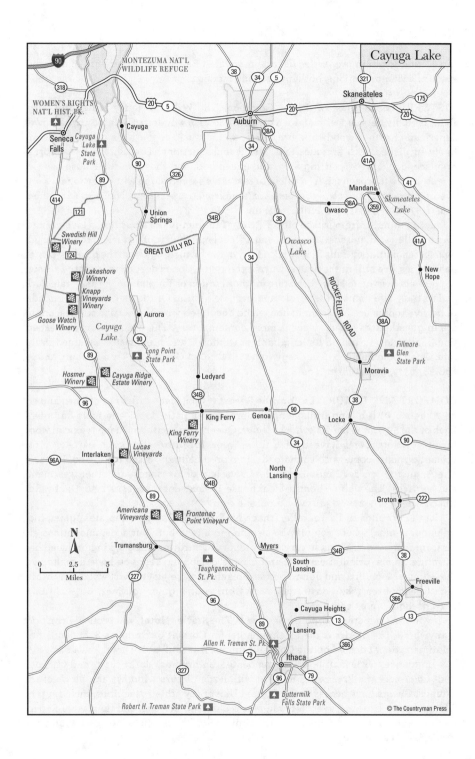

Cayuga Lake

MONTEZUMA NAT'L
WILDLIFE REFUGE

WOMEN'S RIGHTS
NAT'L HIST. PK.

Seneca
Falls

Cayuga
Lake
State
Park

Cayuga

Auburn

Skaneateles

Skaneateles
Lake

Union
Springs

GREAT GULLY RD.

Mandana

Owasco

New
Hope

Owasco
Lake

Swedish Hill
Winery

Lakeshore
Winery

Knapp
Vineyards
Winery

Goose Watch
Winery

Cayuga
Lake

Aurora

Long Point
State Park

ROCKEFELLER ROAD

Fillmore
Glen
State Park

Hosmer
Winery

Cayuga Ridge
Estate Winery

Ledyard

Moravia

King Ferry
Winery

King Ferry

Genoa

Locke

Lucas
Vineyards

Interlaken

North
Lansing

Groton

Americana
Vineyards

Frontenac
Point Vineyard

Trumansburg

Myers

South
Lansing

Freeville

Taughgannock
St. Pk.

Cayuga Heights

Lansing

N

0   2.5   5
Miles

Allen H. Treman St. Pk.

Ithaca

Robert H. Treman State Park

Buttermilk
Falls State Park

© The Countryman Press

✳ Lodging

In addition to chain properties like the renovated Ramada Inn, there are many other kinds of accommodations, both historic and modern.

HISTORIC Located just off Ithaca Commons, the **William Henry Miller Inn** (circa 1880) is richly detailed with stained glass windows, a wonderful pointed corner tower, American chestnut woodwork, fireplaces, and a music room. Nine guest rooms are finely furnished with antiques and period reproductions. The Library has a corner fireplace, bookshelves, sitting area, and queen bed, and the Carriage House has two rooms, one with a Jacuzzi. A candlelit breakfast is served along with afternoon tea and evening dessert. And, oh yes, sheets are hand ironed. $$–$$$ 303 N. Aurora St., Ithaca 14850; 877-256-4553; www.millerinn.com

Just 12 minutes from Ithaca off NY Rt. 89, **Taughannock Farms Inn**, a lovely Victorian building with porches, cupolas, and a steeply pitched roof, is tucked into a hillside next to Taughannock Falls State Park. Many of the furnishings from the original owner, John Jones, are still in the house. During the 1930s, Jones deeded most of the sprawling 600-acre estate to New York State for the creation of Taughannock Falls State Park, and in 1945, the mansion was sold and became an inn. Of the 22 guest accommodations, five rooms are in the main house and decorated with Victorian antiques; others are in guesthouses where décor is more contemporary. The dining room has exceptional lake views through its long bank of windows, and breakfast is included in the rate. Open from Easter to Thanksgiving. $$–$$$ 2030 Gorge Rd., Trumansburg 14886; 888-387-7711; www.t-farms.com

COMFORT AND LUXURY **La Tourelle Resort & Spa**, just 3 miles out of town and set on 70 acres, with hiking trails, tennis courts, and a patio, looks and feels European. Each of the 55 rooms has its own character. Queen-size bedrooms have Mexican wood furniture; king rooms have light Haitian wood furniture and peach carpets. More romantic rooms come with round beds, mirrored ceilings, disco balls, and Jacuzzis. The August Moon destination spa offers a variety of massages and other treatments and services. The John Thomas Steakhouse is next door. $$–$$$$ 1150 Danby Rd., Ithaca 14850; 607-273-2734; www.latourelle.com

On the grounds of La Tourelle, **Ithaca by Firelight Camps** celebrates "glamping" (glamour camps) where you may be sleeping in a tent, but your accommodations are far from roughing it. Think luxury safari tent with hardwood floors, king or queen bed with fine linens, oriental carpets, and private balconies. Lest you have a meltdown, the August Moon Spa and John Thomas Steakhouse are just a short walk away, while nightly campfires take you worlds away from your regular routines. 607-229-1644; www.firelightcamps.com

If you can't get spit-and-polish service at **The Statler Hotel**, you probably can't get it anywhere: The Statler is the teaching hotel for Cornell University's School of Hotel Administration. Located on the Cornell campus, this multistory hotel has a businesslike ambiance, with marble floors, renovated bathrooms, dark wood, and "Cornell Red" color accents. Rooms are modern with large picture windows and views of the campus. Guests have access to the Cornell University athletic facilities, including the Olympic pool. Dine at Taverna Banfi, Mac's Café and Terrace, and the casual Regent Lounge. $$$–$$$$ 11 East Ave., Cornell University, Ithaca 14850; 800-541-2501; www.statlerhotel.cornell.edu

B&BS IN ITHACA Near Cornell the **Coddington Guest House** has three suites, all with private baths. One suite is an intact apartment with three beds and a full kitchen, perfect for families. 130 Coddington Rd., Ithaca 14850; 607-275-0021; www.thecoddington.com

Dewitt Park Inn, a restored historic B&B in downtown Ithaca, is but a short walk to the Commons. Simply but comfortably furnished, each room has its own bath, WiFi, and air conditioning, while on-site massages are available. Start your day with a homemade vegetarian breakfast. 308 N. Cayuga St., Ithaca 14850; 607-272-1122; www.dewittparkinn.com

The **Hound & Hare B&B**, a white brick colonial deeded by General George Washington in 1793, is graciously decorated with Victorian antiques, laces, and family heirlooms along with Queen Anne wing-backed chairs, fresh flowers, and glittering chandeliers. Bedrooms feature fine linens and fluffy duvets, and you can start your day with a homemade breakfast. Grounds are beautifully landscaped and contain herb gardens, rose beds, and an old-fashioned lily pond and fountain. 1031 Hanshaw Rd., Ithaca 14850; 607-257-2821; www.houndandhare.com

(Also see **William Henry Miller Inn**)

City Lights Inn is located in an 1860s restored Greek Revival farmhouse, surrounded by gardens, trails, and sweeping views of the countryside. Recently renovated rooms, some with kitchenettes, are comfy and homelike with quilts and upbeat colors, while breakfasts by the owners (twin brothers) are delicious. 1319 Mecklenburg Rd., Ithaca 14850; 607-227-3003; www.citylightsinn.com

Rustic in looks, with soaring cathedral ceilings, massive log walls, and fireplaces, yet containing every modern amenity, the **Log Country Inn B&B** is set at the edge of a 7,000-acre forest. It should appeal to those with a love of the outdoors. A full European--style breakfast may include blintzes or Russian pancakes and home-baked breads, pastries, and jams. Enjoy the sauna, fireplaces, Jacuzzi, and afternoon tea. 4 Larue Rd., Spencer 14883; 800-274-4771; www.logtv.com/inn

ECOVILLAGE Sitting atop 175 acres, EcoVillage is all about sustainability, organic foods, fresh air, and quiet. Hike the trails, swim in a pond, and soak up the good sense of an environmentally-oriented community. At **Frog's Way B&B** rooms are clean, cheerful and spacious. Rent separate rooms or the entire house. 211 Rachel Carson Way, Ithaca 14850; 607-275-0249; www.frogsway-bnb.com.

Also check out **Wild Goose B&B** in EcoVillage. It's inexpensive (less than $100) and simply but tastefully furnished. Two bedrooms share a bath, so booking the full house is an attractive option for families, where you get a kitchen and living room. Vegan and wheat-free breakfasts are available. 111 Rachel Carson Way, Ithaca 14850; 607-272-0953; www.wildgoose-bb.com

At **Farm Stay**, wake up to fresh air, a home-cooked breakfast bounty, and the sound of chickens and horses welcoming the day. When you stay at RoseBarb Farm, you are staying on a working organic vegetable and horse farm where caring for animals and the gardens is ongoing with owners Rita Rosenberg and Don Barber. When you are not out discovering the countryside, you can take a horse-drawn wagon ride, visit the animals, and relax in your own farm cottage that sleeps six. There is also a pool. $$ 108 Landon Rd., Ithaca 14850; 607-539-6928

B&BS NEAR ITHACA In Groton, northeast of Ithaca, the nine-bedroom **Benn Conger Inn**, a Colonial Revival mansion, evokes a time when the quaint village was in its heyday as a key stop on the Lehigh Valley Railroad and the home of the manufacturing company, Smith-Corona. Built in 1921 by Conger, a state senator, this house was once used as a hideaway for notorious bootlegger Dutch Shultz. Today guests enjoy the beautifully appointed rooms in the main house and adjacent cottage. There are four dining options including a glass-enclosed conservatory. Hosts Peter Zon and Douglas Yurubi rate high marks for their service, food, and ambiance. $$–$$$ 206 W. Cortland St., Groton 13073; 607-898-5817; www.benncongerinn.com

The historic circa-1825 **Federal House B&B**, 6 miles north of Ithaca, is one of the more romantic bed-and-breakfasts in the area. Rooms are exquisitely furnished with antiques and artwork, and you can relax on the porches, or steal some privacy in the gazebo or gardens. A full breakfast is served. 175 Ludlowville Rd., Lansing 14882; 800-533-7362; www.federalhouse.com

Northeast of Ithaca in Freeville, **Foxglove B&B**, a pretty Victorian (circa 1900) surrounded by gardens and nature trails, is a special place for artists, actors, writers, and nature lovers. Performances are often staged in the gardens, and there is a labyrinth in the back. An eight-person Jacuzzi awaits on the outside deck. $–$$ 28 Main St., Freeville 13068; 607-844-9602; www.foxglovebnb.com

Halsey House Bed and Breakfast in Trumansburg is a stately home built in 1829 with five spacious bedrooms and coveted amenities like pillow-top mattresses, flat-screen HDTVs, private baths with whirlpool tubs or walk-in showers, bathrobes, and rich fabrics. Enjoy a full breakfast, the wicker-furnished porch, and the lovely lawns as well as the library game room. $$–$$$ 2057 NY Rt. 96, Trumansburg 14886; 607-387-5429; www.halseyhouse.com

Eight rooms and suites are located in two buildings at **The Inn at Gothic Eves B&B** in the historic area of Trumansburg. Both Potter House and The Inn are elegantly furnished with antiques and pillow-top beds. Rooms are quite large, some have fireplaces, and all have private baths. Relax in the wood-fired hot tub and the lovely gardens or get a massage in their on-site spa. A generous breakfast created from locally grown, organic ingredients is served. $$–$$$ 112 E. Main St., Trumansburg 14886; 800-387-7712; www.gothiceves.com

Elegance and luxury prevail at **Juniper Hill B&B** in Trumansburg. Furnished with antiques and fine art evoking masters like Mary Cassett and Picasso, décor is light, upbeat with whimsical touches. This 1920s restored Colonial Revival mansion is perfect for that special romantic getaway. Extremely comfortable beds are sumptuously dressed in fine linens, some rooms have fireplaces, and baths are modern and spacious. $$–$$$ 16 Elm St., Trumansburg 14886; 888-809-3167; www .atjuniperhill.com

From the master spa suite with a tub for two to the family room with a full bed and a set of bunks, guests can spread out when staying at **Tenwood Lodge** in Danby, where several bedroom configurations make it a good choice for families and friends traveling together. But brace yourself for some quirks, like their large trophy room displaying animal mounts, limited Internet, and no TV. Still, the peace of the surroundings, the scrumptious home-cooked breakfasts and the comfy beds make guests want to return. 986 Steam Mill Rd., Ithaca 14850; 607-273-9546; www .tenwoodlodge.com

QUIRKY AND PRIVATE The **Climbing Vine Cottage**, an ecologically friendly yurt set in discovery gardens in Newfield, 12 minutes from Ithaca, sleeps six. It comes with a full kitchen, a loft, and acres of fields and forests to explore. It's fun. $$$ 257 Piper Rd., Newfield 14867; 607-564-7140; www.climbingvinecottage.com

Escape to your private log cabin with views of Cayuga Lake—**Buttonwood Grove Winery & Cabins** in Romulus. Four cabins have mini kitchens, porches and sitting

JUNIPER HILL B&B COMBINES ELEGANCE, COMFORT, AND ART

rooms along with satellite TV. The winery is within walking distance. $$ 5986 NY Rt. 89, Romulus 14541; 607-869-9760; www.buttonwoodgrove.com

(Also see **Ithaca by Firelight Camps** under Comfort and Luxury)

SPA In Sanskrit, *rasa* means "true essence." And that's what you get when you book a spa treatment at **rasaspa** at the Island Health Center in Ithaca. You'll find a whole menu of spa services including massages, facials, scrubs, wraps, saunas, Shiatsu, hot stone, reflexology, and more. 310 Old Taughannock Blvd. #2A, Ithaca 14850; 607-273-1740; www.rasaspa.com

✳ Dining Out

With arguably more places to eat per capita than New York City, Ithaca was described by the *New York Times* as "the state's best culinary outpost outside the Big Apple." Outdoor dining has blossomed along Ithaca Commons and on Aurora Street, known as "Restaurant Row." Another cluster of restaurants is up on the hill in Collegetown.

TRADITION, TRADITION **John Thomas Steakhouse,** a 150-year-old farmhouse, is set in meadows and gardens with five dining rooms, an enclosed porch, an outside deck, and upstairs a pub-like room with beams, a bar, and a fireplace. Mike Kelly, owner, not only ages all the prime beef himself, he cuts it. Also enjoy superb lobster and chicken dishes served with French-style sauces. Priced at the high end of the Ithaca food chain, this is the place to bring your best clients or to celebrate that special occasion. $$–$$$ 1152 Danby Rd., Ithaca 14850; 607-273-3464; www.johnthomassteakhouse.net

Sitting on the crest of a hill across from a grassy lakeside park, the **Taughannock Farms Inn** just north of Ithaca has been an area fixture since 1873 when it was a private home. Dine in the enclosed lake-view room and order from a menu of traditional favorites where the price of the entrée includes appetizer, salad, vegetable, starch, and dessert. (Open seasonally) $$–$$$ 2030 Gorge Rd., Trumansburg 14886; 888-387-7711; www.t-farms.com

HIP BISTRO-STYLE Boats pull up to the docks of the trendy **Boatyard Grill** on the southern tip of Cayuga Lake. Great bar, great deck, great seafood, great steaks. It's a happening place on the water. $–$$ 525 Old Taughannock Blvd., Ithaca 14850; 607-256-2628; www.boatyardgrill.com

The farm-to-table movement is the foundation for the cuisine at **Coltivare**. Here the menu changes with the seasons as fresh ingredients become available. The accomplished chef draws from the local TC3 farm and other local producers for dishes like apple fennel salad and spinach lasagna. 235 S. Cayuga St., Ithaca 14850; 607-882-2333; www.coltivareithaca.com

If you like to order something for yourself and taste a bit of everyone else's meal, head to **Just a Taste Wine & Tapas Bar** for appetizer-size dishes. The menu is so long, you probably should have it e-mailed to you before you arrive. Order unusual items like tortilla española, deep fried salt cod fritters with garlic aioli, and borscht with sour cream. They don't take reservations, so be prepared to enjoy the convivial crowd at the bar—and don't forget to try the chocolate soufflé. $–$$ 116 N. Aurora St., Ithaca 14850; 607-277-9463; www.just-a-taste.com

Madeline's Restaurant & Bar, an upbeat, stylish bistro decorated with bold artwork features many Asian-style items like fresh chilled Asian edamame, wasabi herb-encrusted salmon filet with mango salsa served with Asian black beans, and seared marinated sushi-grade tuna over green-tea rice. Eat inside or out, and save room for dessert. $$–$$$ 215 The Commons, corner N. Aurora & E. State St., Ithaca 14850; 607-277-2253; www.madelines-restaurant.com

Authentic Thai dishes like lettuce wraps, beef pad see eew, and pad kra pao get rave reviews from patrons at **Taste of Thai** on The Commons, another locally owned and operated eatery. $$ 216 E. State St., Ithaca 14850; 607-256-5487; www.tasteofthaiithaca.com

The **Rongovian Embassy** is eclectic and casual, with a lot of brick and wood along with mismatched furniture and memorabilia like vintage chalkboards. Recently renovated, it also has one of the best beer lists around. If you can't find anything you like at the bar, you don't like drinking. $–$$ 1 W. Main St., Trumansburg 14886; 607-387-3334; www.therongo.com

CASUAL FARE **Glenwood Pines Restaurant** is the home of the Pinesburger, a 6-ounce loaded cheeseburger on French bread. Glenwood's windows and screened-in porch afford super views of the lake. Owned and run by the Hohwald family for more than 30 years, Glenwood is known for its generous portions of American staples. $–$$ 1213 Taughannock Blvd., Ithaca 14850; 607-273-3709; www.glenwoodpines.com

Ithaca Bakery, with five locations in town, is the place to come for a serious sandwich or salad along with great bagels, artisan breads, pastries and, of course, coffee. $ www.ithacabakery.com

LOCAL WATERING HOLES For lots of good Irish-inspired food and a good selection of beer and ale, try **Kilpatrick's Publick House**. Head to the Irish-Victorian dining room or a more rural cottage-style setting with a huge stone fireplace. 130 E. Seneca St., Ithaca 14850; 607-273-2632; www.kilpatrickspub.com

With more than 20 beers on tap, good hearty food, and a killer cheeseburger, **Ithaca Ale House** is a favorite watering hole for area residents. 111 N. Aurora St., Ithaca 14850; 607-256-7977; www.ithacaalehouse.com

The Nines, located in the old Number 9 firehouse in Collegetown, is buzzing with the young and hip who come here for staples like pizzas, tuna melts, burgers, and beer. Service, though, can be casual. 311 College Ave., Ithaca 14850; 607-272-1888; www.theninesithacany.com

SOUTHERN COMFORT AND SEAFOOD If you're craving some good ole soul-satisfying Southern comfort food such as jambalaya, gumbo, Cajun popcorn or crayfish, try **Maxie's Supper Club and Oyster Bar**. It's a casual, high-energy restaurant, and all the dishes are made from scratch. Especially popular are the raw oysters, clams, and peel-and-eat shrimp. There are several microbrews on tap and a long wine list. Raw oysters and clams are half price from 4–6 p.m. Free music is rolled out on Sunday nights. No reservations. $$–$$$ 635 W. State St., Ithaca 14850; 607-272-4136; www.maxies.com

VEGETARIAN AND ORGANIC The **Moosewood Restaurant** celebrates healthy, low-fat vegetarian food like grains, fresh vegetables, and fruits, drawing inspiration from regional American cooking as well as ethnic cuisines such as Mediterranean lentil salad, Mexican tomato lime soup, Thai noodle salad, and a tasty orange-based soup. Eat indoors or outdoors in season but beware, the patio can be truck-noisy and hot in the summer. $–$$ 215 N. Cayuga St., Ithaca 14850; 607-273-9610; www.moosewoodrestaurant.com

RESTAURANT COURIER SERVICES **Ithaca to Go** (www.ithacatogo.com) or **Grub-Hub** (www.grubhub.com) can provide your meals from a selection of participating eateries to be delivered to your picnic spot or wherever else you want it. You can order online and pay by credit card. Most of the time the services run smoothly, but due to restaurant backups, wait times can sometimes test your patience.

✳ To See

ARCHITECTURE Ithaca's buildings span more than two hundred years. The **Clinton House** (circa 1830), once a grand hotel, has survived several remodelings and a fire. Now this landmark has been restored and is the home of New Roots School, a charter school with a sustainable curriculum. 116 N. Cayuga St., Ithaca 14850; 607-882-9220; www.newrootsschool.org

The State Theatre, in a historic brick building (1915), was once the Ithaca Security Company Garage, with copper-clad windows along the façade, many of which still exist. In 1928, the interior was extensively remodeled, turning it into a fantasy movie palace with gargoyles, tapestries, stained glass, ornate columns, faux painted stone, and an illuminated celestial ceiling. In 1998 Historic Ithaca restored the building, and today it serves as a venue for big-name concerts and events. 107 W. State St., Ithaca 14850; 607-277-8283; www.stateofithaca.com

Cornell's **Sage Chapel**, with its rose window, painted ceiling, and brass chandelier, is worth seeing. When you walk across the center of the older campus, you may notice messages written on the sidewalks in chalk—it's a student tradition. Guided tours are given daily. 147 Hoplaza Tower Rd., Cornell University, Ithaca 14850; 607-255-2000; www.cornell.edu

WINE & BEER TASTING TOUR

START: Ithaca

TRAVEL: North on NY Rt. 89

1ST STOP: Ithaca Bakery for coffee and bagels.

2ND STOP: Bellwether, Interlaken. Challenge your taste buds with hard cider from the first cider producer in the Finger Lakes. Bellweather also makes single-vineyard wines like riesling and pinot noir. 888-862-4337; 607-387-9464; www.cidery.com

3RD STOP: Lively Run Goat Dairy, Interlaken. Sample cheeses and browse the gift shop. (See "Family Fun" in the Cayuga Lake West Side section)

Lively Run Goat Dairy

THE LIVELY RUN GOAT DAIRY IS FUN FOR KIDS OF ALL AGES

4TH STOP: The **Finger Lakes Cider House** operates out of a carefully crafted new facility at Good Life Farm in Interlaken (4017 Hickok Rd.). Their tasting room is rustic chic and locally sourced cheese, meats, and bread can be paired with artisan ciders from select regional producers. (See "Winery and Brewery Restaurants" in the Cayuga Lake West section)

Optional: Ice cream fix: **Cayuga Lake Creamery,** Interlaken, where they make their own ice cream. (See "Ice Cream" in the Cayuga Lake West Side section)

5TH STOP: Myer Farm Distillers in Ovid (See "Distilleries" in the What's Where in the Finger Lakes chapter)

6TH STOP: Boathouse Beer Garden in Romulus, in a former Amish marketplace, brings in locally produced craft beer like Hopshire Brewers, Ithaca Beer Co., and CB Craft Brewers all under one roof, inviting visitors to relax and try their beer on tap. Views of Cayuga Lake are magnificent. Food trucks and vendors are on-site Saturdays and many nights in season. Also music kicks in some Thursdays and Fridays. 607-280-0064; www.boathousebeergarden.com

LAST STOP (OVERNIGHT): Check into your private log cabin next door to the Boathouse Beer Garden, overlooking Cayuga Lake at **Buttonwood Grove Winery** in Romulus. The winery is within walking distance. (See "Quirky and Private" in the Ithaca Section)

ITHACA'S DISCOVERY TRAIL Explore eight key attractions on Ithaca's Discovery Trail (www.discoverytrail.com), starting with the **Cayuga Nature Center**, where you learn about our natural environment and landscape. Kids should particularly enjoy the summer Butterfly House, the six-story TreeTops Tower, animal feedings, night hikes, and guided fossil-hunting expeditions. 1420 Taughannock Blvd., Ithaca 14850; 607-273-6260; www.cayuganaturecenter.org

Hit the Paleontological Research Institution and its **Museum of the Earth** if you are curious about fossils, how the glaciers formed the gorges, or what kind of animal and plant life once existed here. Find hands-on science and art exhibitions; work with fossils at the Discovery Labs; see a Tyrannosaurus Rex skull more than four feet long,

Dinner: Go next door to the **Boathouse Beer Garden** (open seasonally with food vendors) or drive north to Seneca Falls and stop at **Wolffy's Grill & Marina**, long a local favorite. (See "Water Views" in the Seneca Falls section)

The next day: Starting at Buttonwood, go north on NY Rt. 89 and stop at **Varick Winery and Vineyard** where you can taste their wines and linger in their 1800s country store, which sells preserves, salsas, dipping oils, and more. Then continue to **Eleven Lakes Winery** where their wines pay homage to the 11 Finger Lakes with names like Boat Landing White and Moonglorious. (315-549-8702; www.elevenlakeswinery.com). Go east on NY Rt. 20 to the crossroads of Rts. 5 and 20 and Rt. 89; stopping at the **Montezuma Winery & Hidden Marsh Distillery** specializing in honey mead; grape and fruit wines such as Big Timber White with hints of pear, lemon, and melon; Blue Moon, a blueberry wine—and a cabernet franc—plus distilled vodkas, brandy, and liqueurs. The gift shop sells beeswax candles, honey, wine accessories, and gift baskets along with mead, the first alcoholic beverage ever consumed. (See "Distilleries" in the What's Where in the Finger Lakes chapter)

Spend some time in Seneca Falls visiting **Sauders Market**, historic sites, and museums, and dine at the **Gould Hotel** in the center of town. (See Seneca Falls section)

CABINS ARE AVAILABLE FOR RENT AT BUTTONWOOD GROVE WINERY AND CABINS IN ROMULUS

Steggy the Stegosaurus, and the 44-foot skeleton of a right whale. Get down and dirty by taking an exciting fossil-collecting excursion. 1259 Trumansburg Rd., Ithaca 14850; 607-273-6623; www.museumoftheearth.org

Stop at the **Sciencenter** to see more than 250 hands-on exhibits, a boa constrictor, water flume, two-story kinetic ball, and a walk-in camera. Whisper into a giant dish, navigate through the outdoor Emerson Science Park, discover the solar system on the Sagan Planet Walk, and play through the science-themed Galaxy Golf course. 601 First St., Ithaca 14850; 607-272-0600; www.sciencenter.org

The **Johnson Museum of Art**, designed by I. M. Pei, is a dramatic contemporary structure where you have 360-degree views of the countryside from galleries and patios. See permanent collections as well as revolving exhibits of European, American, and Asian art spanning 40 centuries and six continents. Free. 114 Central Ave., Cornell University, Ithaca 14850; 607-255-6464; www.museum.cornell.edu

The **Cornell Lab of Ornithology** is a 220-acre bird paradise with more than 4 miles of nature trails winding through wildlife habitats in the Sapsucker Woods Sanctuary. Inside the observatory, you can look out to a bird-feeding garden, learn about birds, hear sounds of just about every wild creature that exists with the push of a button, and have some fun with the interactive exhibits. 159 Sapsucker Woods Rd., Ithaca 14850; 607-254-BIRD; www.birds.cornell.edu

Cornell Plantations, a 3,000-acre museum of living plants, encompasses an arboretum, botanical garden, 14 specialty gardens, and natural areas. There are woodlands, gorges, and lakeside trails that go along the central campus, while orchids are displayed in a solarium. Free. 1 Plantations Rd., Cornell University, Ithaca 14850; 607-255-2400; www.cornellplantations.org

THE CAYUGA NATURE CENTER OFFERS A VARIETY OF EXPERIENCES, INCLUDING A FOSSIL GATHERING EXPEDITION

The History Center invites you to dig deep into the history of Tompkins County with thousands of historic photographs, documents, diaries, scrapbooks, genealogies, maps, and a self-guided walking tour of Ithaca. 401 E. State St., Ithaca 14850; 607-273-8284; www.thehistorycenter.net. **The Tompkins County Public Library** provides vast resources for just about everything. Free. 101 E. Green St., Ithaca 14850; 607-272-4557; www.tcpl.org

GREATER ITHACA ART TRAIL Follow the **Greater Ithaca Art Trail** and visit more than 40 studios and artists. See paintings, ceramics, fine crafts, furniture, sculpture, and more. Check for hours as some are open by appointment, while most open their doors on Saturdays almost every month. www.arttrail.com

PERFORMING ARTS The **Trumansburg Conservatory of Fine Arts** provides educational opportunities for all ages, including musical instruments, art, home crafts, and dance. 5 McLallen St., Trumansburg 14886; 607-387-5939; www.tburgconservatory.org

MUSIC Free outdoor summer concerts are held in **Taughannock Park** (Saturdays 7 p.m.); **Cornell Arts Quad** (Fridays 7:30 p.m.); **Myers Point Park** (Lansing/Thursdays 6:30 p.m.); **Ellis Hollow** (Tuesdays 6 p.m.); **Wagner Vineyards** (Lodi/Fridays 8 p.m.); **Six Mile Creek Vineyards** (Thursdays 7:30 p.m.); **Ithaca Commons** (Thursdays 6 p.m.); and **Montgomery Park** (Dryden/Wednesdays 6:30 p.m.).

The **Cayuga Chamber Orchestra** holds a fall–winter chamber music series in various locations along with other performances such as *Caroling by Candlelight* and the *Messiah*. 607-273-8981; www.ccithaca.org

THEATER Since 1975, the **Hangar Theatre** has been producing superb professional summer productions like *The Hound of the Baskervilles*, *Spring Awakening*, and *Talley's Folly*, the Pulitzer Prize-winning romantic comedy. Recent plays for KIDDSTUFF have included *The Emperor's New Clothes* and *Charlotte's Web*. 801 Taughannock Blvd., Ithaca 14850; 607-273-2787; www.hangartheatre.org

Go to **Ithaca College Theatre** for drama, comedy, musicals, opera, and dance performances at the George R. Hoerner and Richard M. Clark theaters from September to May, while the School of Music features concerts throughout the year. 201 Dillingham Center, Ithaca College, Ithaca 14850; 607-274-3920; www.ithaca.edu

A bold mix of plays and musicals are showcased by the **Kitchen Theatre Company** for those who appreciate groundbreaking performances up close and personal. This year-round theater draws talent from local colleges and regional artists, and some productions are devoted to the work of area playwrights. 116 N. Cayuga St., Ithaca 14850; 607-273-4497; www.kitchentheatre.com

The Schwartz Center for the Performing Arts is home to Cornell's Department of Theatre, Film, and Dance. Each year, a number of excellent concerts and dance and theatrical performances are staged. 430 College Ave., Cornell University, Ithaca 14850; 607-254-ARTS; www.pma.cornell.edu/schwartz-center

ART OUTINGS More than 53 regional artists participate in a self-guided tour on the **Greater Ithaca Art Trail**. Watch artists working and see their finished work in painting, sculpture, printing, ceramics, woodworking, jewelry making, stained glass, furniture making, and more. The trail is in full operation during October but functions as an ongoing activity throughout the year; call individual artists for hours. www.arttrail.com

Watch movies in **Stuart Park** in the summer,

PHOTO OPS **Covered Bridge**: NY Rt. 13, 8 miles southwest of Ithaca in Newfield. The only covered bridge in the Finger Lakes on a public road.

Ithaca Falls, Aurora St.

Taughannock Falls

Top of **Cornell Stadium**: Great views of the countryside.

Sunset Park: Spectacular views of the valley from the south end of the lake.

The **suspension bridge** between Cayuga Heights and the Cornell campus spans the river that cuts through rocks, and, just below, a trail winds down to the water—a great place for a picnic or to catch some sun on a ledge.

✳ Shopping

Historic downtown Ithaca and the pedestrian mall "the Commons" have many unique specialty shops, cafés, craft shops, art galleries, florists, children's toys, and other retail outlets.

ART AND ANTIQUES **Found in Ithaca**, a large multi-dealer antique and vintage marketplace, sells items from the nineteenth-century to midcentury modern. Also check out **Found Flea** every third Sunday from May through October in the parking

WINE & BEER TASTING TOUR

Start: Ithaca

Travel: North on NY Rt. 13, to 34, to 34B, to NY Rt. 90

1st Stop: Rogues' Harbor Brewing Company located next to the nine-room Rogues Harbor Inn, restaurant, and pub. Try their cream ales, and beer selections like White Dog Wig, Brewer's Choice, and even their root beer. (See "Dining Out" in Cayuga Lake East Side section)

2nd Stop: Treleaven Wines at King Ferry Winery, owned and operated by Tacie and Peter Saltonstall, produces a fine reserve cabernet franc, treleaven chardonnays, treleaven rieslings, pinot noir, a sweet red wine named Mystere, and a late-harvest Golden Iris.

John Dyson

KING FERRY WINERY SPECIALIZES IN TRELEAVEN WINES

Their semidry riesling 2012 is a top seller while Melange 2013 red blend is also popular. Wine tasting is offered in the tasting room, live music is played on some summer evenings, and pic-

John Dyson

BET THE FARM IN AURORA SELLS REGIONALLY PRODUCED FOODS AND WINES

lot of Found in Ithaca, and the **Gallery.** 227 Cherry St., Ithaca 14850; 607-319-5078; www.foundinithaca.com/flea-market

Ithaca Antique Center brings more than one hundred dealers under one roof selling a full range of antiques from fine art and books to eighteenth- to twentieth-century furniture. 1607 Trumansburg Rd., Ithaca 14850; 607-272-3611.

THE AURORA INN

nic tables are available. 800-439-5271; www.treleavenwines.com. (We also suggest a short detour to **Finger Lakes Dexter Creamery** on the Cheese Trail in King Ferry where you can get both farmstead kefir cheese and grass-fed Dexter beef. 315-364-3581; kefircheese.com)

3RD STOP: Long Point Winery south of Aurora features dry reds like merlot and syrah. Hungry? Grab a piled-high sandwich at **Amelia's Deli** on weekends. 315-364-6713; www.longpointwinery.com

4TH STOP (LUNCH OPTION): If you prefer a long, leisurely lunch, go to **Pumpkin Hill Bistro**, a charming historic farmhouse overlooking the lake, offering creative cuisine. Dine on the porch, patio, or inside where many of the old beams have been exposed. (See "Country Charm" in the Aurora section)

5TH STOP: Aurora, home of Wells College and home décor brand MacKenzie-Childs, is a good place to browse some of the unique stores like **Bet the Farm** where you can purchase regional gourmet foods like Ma Poole's Chutney and wines. For ice cream and super lunches stop at **Dorie's Cafe and Bakery**. Farther up the highway, it's fantasy overload at **MacKenzie-Childs**.

6TH STOP: Overnight at one of the historic and beautifully restored **Inns of Aurora** (Aurora Inn; Rowland House, E.B. Morgan House) or an intimate B&B, **Annie's Guest House**. For a casual dinner try **Fargos** on Main Street near the Opera House, or for more romantic surroundings, book a table at the **Aurora Inn**. (See Aurora in Cayuga section)

Juniper Hill sells American Impressionist works in its gallery along with other artwork and furnishings in the house itself. 16 Elm St., Trumansburg 14886; 607-387-3044; www.atjuniperhill.com

Mimi's Attic offers unique, stylish, and useful items for the home. 430 W. State St., Ithaca 14850; 607-882-9038; www.mimisatticithaca.com

Solá Gallery in Ithaca's Dewitt Mall specializes in Japanese prints. 215 N. Cayuga St., Ithaca 14850; 607-272-6552; www.solagallery.com

More than 40 designers and artists display and sell their work in **Handwork**, an exceptional cooperative of working artisans. Find baskets, accessories, glass, metals, home décor, jewelry, pottery, paper, wood, and clothing. 102 W. State St., Ithaca 14850; 607-273-9400; www.handwork.coop

Toko Imports in Ithaca's Dewitt Mall has a huge collection of drums from Africa, Asia, and elsewhere, along with other ethnic items. 215 N. Cayuga St., Ithaca 14850; 607-277-3780; www.toko-imports.com

In Trumansburg, **Salmon Pottery** is the studio and gallery for Mary Ellen Salmon, featuring textured ceramics and art from other local craftsmen. She also offers pottery lessons. 79 E. Main St., Trumansburg 14886; 607-387-3331; www.salmonpottery.com

BOOKS AND MUSIC For old and new books, head to the **Bookery** and **Bookery II** in Ithaca. The original Bookery specializes in selling and obtaining out-of-print books. If they don't have it, they try to locate it for you. Bookery II offers a large selection of new books. 215 N. Cayuga St., Ithaca 14850; 607-273-5055; www.thebookery.com

Browse through two floors of merchandise in the **Cornell Store**. Find everything from Cornell shirts, gifts, and logo items to an excellent selection of books and magazines. 135 Ho Plaza, Cornell University, Ithaca 14853; 607-255-4111; www.store .cornell.edu

Also find new and used books as well as college-related items in the **Ithaca College Bookstore**. 140 Phillips Hall, Ithaca College, Ithaca 14850; 607-274-3210; www.ithaca .edu/bookstore2

SPORTING SUPPLIES A full array of clothing and equipment for skiing, hiking, tennis, and other sports can be found at **Eastern Mountain Sports**. 722 S. Meadow St., Ithaca 14850; 607-272-1935; www.ems.com

For good prices on gently-used sports stuff head to the **Old Goat Gear Exchange**. Want to buy or sell bikes, skis, paddle boards, that golf shirt you can't wear? You name it, they make it happen. 320 E. State St., Ithaca 14850; 607-319-4388; www .oldgoatgearexchange.com

FARMERS' MARKETS **Ithaca Farmers' Market** is all abuzz selling local produce, plants, baked goods, meats and cheeses, crafts, clothing, and furniture sourced within a 30-mile radius. Third St. off NY Rt. 13, Ithaca 14850; 607-273-7109; www .ithacamarket.com

Ludgate Farms market offers local and imported fruits, vegetables, maple syrup, honey, preserves, salsa, fresh baked goods, flowers, and cider. 1552 Hanshaw Rd., Ithaca 14850; 607-257-1765; www.ludgatefarms.com

Seneca Falls

Seneca Falls, a quiet, modest-size village at the top of Cayuga Lake, is home of the first pump, the first fire engine, and site of the first women's rights convention.

Seneca Falls is often called the "real Bedford Falls," as it was the venue for the 1946 Frank Capra movie *It's a Wonderful Life*. The restored **Gould Hotel** in the town's center is thriving under new ownership, and events like the Empire Farms Days bring lots of visitors to town. The Cayuga-Seneca Canal that opened in 1817 (eight years before the completion of the Erie Canal) runs behind the stores. Visit the Seneca Museum of Waterways and Industry (also the location of the Seneca Falls Visitor Center) and other historical sites, parks, and art galleries including the new R Dixon Gallery for contemporary art.

NATIVES, SETTLERS, AND ENTREPRENEURS On the hunting grounds of the once-powerful Haudenosaunee (six nations of the Iroquois Confederacy), Seneca Falls was the first town to be settled in the wilderness between Utica and Buffalo. Then it was called Sha-se-onse, meaning "swift waters." And, indeed, the rapids running in the Seneca River created the waterpower for the mills and other businesses, shaping the growth and character of Seneca Falls.

The first "official" white settler, Job Smith, came to the area in 1787, followed by Lawrence Van Cleef, who was with General Sullivan on his mission to destroy the Native American villages. Van Cleef was so taken by the area's beauty, he planted his poplar staff in the ground, vowing to return. When he came back 10 years later in 1799, the staff had grown into a tree.

Van Cleef settled with his family near that tree, which stood for more than one hundred years before it was felled in a storm. A piece of it is preserved in the **Seneca Falls Historical Museum**. Van Cleef partnered with Smith in assisting travelers over the falls. He kept the first tavern in his log home, built boats, and constructed the first frame house.

The first sawmill was built about 1794, and a log schoolhouse was built in 1801. Colonel Wilhelmus Mynderse built the Upper (1795) and Lower (1807) Red Mills, and his company was known as the Bayard Company.

In 1828 the Cayuga-Seneca Canal was tied into the Erie Canal, opening vast transportation possibilities for goods originating in Seneca Falls. Additional businesses

PUMP EXHIBIT AT THE SENECA FALLS MUSEUM OF WATERWAYS AND INDUSTRY

developed, mostly along the river, but because the Bayard Company controlled the waterpower in Seneca Falls, rival villages were established nearby.

During his time with the Bayard Company, Colonel Mynderse amassed great wealth, and in 1832 he donated land to build the Seneca Falls Academy.

Early businesses included the successful Seneca Knitting Mills, and in 1855 Birdsall Holly received a patent for his rotary pump and engine, which would gain a worldwide reputation for its use in building steam fire engines.

WOMEN'S RIGHTS A convention dealing with women's rights was held in 1848 at the Wesleyan Chapel in Seneca Falls, organized by Elizabeth Cady Stanton and Lucretia Mott. The Declaration of Sentiments and Resolutions, based on the Declaration of Independence, was read to the assembly, asserting that women and men should be treated equally and that women should have the right to vote. This site and Elizabeth Cady Stanton's Greek Revival home are part of the Women's Rights National Historical Park.

FIRE AND GROWTH A devastating fire took place in the summer of 1890 leaving half of Main Street in ashes—a cruel irony, as it occurred in the town that had given the world its first fire engine. Buildings were rebuilt, and Seneca Falls continued to grow, its population swelling to four thousand in 1860.

During the early twentieth century, vessels such as the *Kate D. Morgan,* the *T. D. Wilcox,* and the grand *Frontenac* plied the waters between Ithaca and Cayuga. On July 26, 1907, encountering stormy weather, the *Frontenac* caught fire. The captain steered the ship toward shore, running it aground about three-quarters of a mile north of Levanna. Panic set in, and eight people drowned. The charred remains of the ship still show just above the lake's surface, a grim reminder of the tragedy.

In 1915 the old Cayuga-Seneca Canal was widened, smaller locks were replaced with two larger locks, and the area known as "The Flats" was flooded, becoming Van Cleef Lake, to be used as a reservoir for the locks. In the process, more than 115 industrial buildings and 60 homes were wiped out.

✳ Lodging

HISTORIC In the center of town, **The Gould Hotel** has been totally renovated and now has 48 rooms decorated in a muted palette of grays and browns with chic purple/silver touches. Enjoy plush headboards and modern conveniences like WiFi, Keurig coffee makers, iPod docking station radio/alarm and HD flat-screen TV. Sleep on pillow-top mattresses with down pillows and duvets. 108 Fall St., Seneca Falls 13148; 877-788-4010; www .thegouldhotel.com

B&BS Barristers, an 1888 Colonial Revival home in the Seneca Falls historic district, is graced by carved fireplaces and stained glass windows. Five guest

BARRISTERS IS A LOVELY B&B NEAR THE VILLAGE CENTER

rooms are furnished with queen or king beds and period furniture. Eat breakfast in the dining room, or have a continental breakfast delivered to your door. $-$$ 56 Cayuga St., Seneca Falls 13148; 800-914-0145; www.sleepbarristers.com

Set in parklike grounds on more than five acres, **John Morris Manor** was built in 1838 in the Greek Revival farmhouse style. Each of the five guest rooms is uniquely decorated. Go spacey with a circa-1950s décor of pale-blue silvery wallpaper with Saturn and other starry things in the Jetson Room, or book the Pool Room, decorated in burgundy and gold and featuring a private entrance to the pool deck, a king bed, and a Jacuzzi. This country-style 11-room house has several public areas, including a screened porch, an in-ground pool with a patio, and a TV room. Breakfasts are lavish. John Morris is gay-, pet-, and child-friendly. $$-$$$ 2138 NY Rt. 89, Seneca Falls 13148; 315-568-9057; www.johnmorrismanor.com

Vancleef Homestead B&B, an 1825 Federal-style home built by Lawrence Van Cleef and later the residence of Wilhemus Mynderse, opened as a bed-and-breakfast in 1996. Close to the center of town, the three guest rooms and one suite are attractively furnished with antiques and period reproductions, and each has a private bath. A full, hearty breakfast made from scratch is served and there is an in-ground pool. $$-$$$ 86 Cayuga St., Seneca Falls 13148; 315-568-2275; www.vancleefhomestead.com

Dining Out

HIP BISTRO-STYLE **The DiVINE Kitchen & Bar** in The Gould Hotel has an excellent chef who prefers to use locally produced fruits, vegetables, meats, and herbs in his dishes. The sophistication of the menu matches the clean, muted décor of gunmetal gray and wood. The menu features creative dishes like spring potato leek soup, grilled vegetable napoleon, and a 10-ounce. Angus reserve sirloin with bordelaise sauce. $$-$$$ 108 Fall St., Seneca Falls 13148; 315-712-4010; www.thegouldhotel.com

CASUAL FARE Casual, friendly—come to **Antonino's Italian Restaurant** for Italian and American dishes served family style. $-$$ 23 Bridge St., Seneca Falls 13148; 315-568-5107

Avicolli's, a no-nonsense Italian restaurant, serves everything from sandwiches and pizza to full dinners. 170 Fall St., Seneca Falls 13148; 315-568-2233; www.avicollisrestaurant.com

Whether they're stopping for breakfast, lunch or dinner, fans keep coming to **Magee Country Diner**. Everything is good. Good burgers, good sweet potato fries, good eggs, good wings, good service. $-$$ 1303 NY Rt. 414, Waterloo 13162; 315-539-0214

LAKE VIEWS Located next to Cayuga Lake State Park, at **Deerhead Inn** you can enjoy lake views while eating American classics on a glass-enclosed porch. Here you get a good meal at a fair price. Arrive by boat and dock just across the street. $-$$ 2554 Lower Lake Rd., Seneca Falls 13148; 315-568-2950; www.deerheadlakeside.com

Family-owned and-operated, **Marina's Restaurant** allows you to pull up in your boat and go in for some good home-cooked food. You'll love the soups. $-$$$ 2945 Lower Lake Rd., Seneca Falls 13148; 315-568-0200

Wolffy's Grill & Marina has long been a local favorite for those who want a casual meal sitting on a deck by the water (or inside if you must). Food is usually good, with lots of seafood and fish on the menu plus the usual suspects. $-$$ 2943 Lower Lake Rd., Seneca Falls 13148; 315-257-0077; www.wolffysgrillandmarina.com

❋ To See

MUSEUMS, EXHIBITS, AND HISTORIC SITES Seneca Falls Visitor Center is a good place to start your Seneca Falls visit. Ask about the detailed brochure highlighting stops on a new Seneca Falls Museum Trail. 89 Fall St., Seneca Falls 13148; www.senecafalls.com

Seneca Falls Historical Society, a 23-room Queen Anne mansion, contains furnishings from the Becker family, who lived in the house for more than 50 years. Custom-designed wallpapers, carpets from France, paintings, original lighting fixtures, stained glass windows, carved golden oak woodwork, glassware, and antique kitchen utensils give visitors a good sense of what life was like during the Victorian era. Be sure to check out the landmark Seth Thomas clock and a Gothic Revival toolshed, now called the Beehive and used as a country store exhibit. Throughout the year many events are offered celebrating earlier times. 55 Cayuga St., Seneca Falls 13148; 315-568-8412; www.sfhistoricalsociety.org

Seneca Museum of Waterways and Industry, housed in an early 1900s masonry-and-brick structure on the Cayuga-Seneca Canal, shows the importance of water and pumps in the region's development. A 35-foot mural depicts the canal, along with original drawings, engineers' plans, and photographs. Learn how a pump and a lock work, and how the Erie Canal was built, and see the first fire engines. There are a number of hands-on activities for children, like how to work simple machines and how to wash the "old-fashioned" way. 89 Fall St., Seneca Falls 13148; 315-568-1510; www.senecamuseum.com

WOMEN'S RIGHTS Women's Rights National Historical Park, near the northwestern tip of the lake, commemorates the first Women's Rights Convention held here in 1848. See exhibits relating to women's rights and Elizabeth Cady Stanton's house. A 25-minute film, Dreams of Equality, gives a good overview of the women's rights movement. A display of bronze figures honors those prominent in the effort. 76 Fall St., Seneca Falls 13148; 315-568-2991; www.nps.gov/wori

The **Elizabeth Cady Stanton House** (1815–1902), a leader in the women's rights movement, contains memorabilia from her life and work. She organized the first Women's Rights Convention in Seneca Falls in 1848 and often worked with Susan B. Anthony, coauthoring *History of Woman Suffrage*. Washington St., Seneca Falls 13148; 315-568-2991

National Women's Hall of Fame contains displays focusing on women in history who have been inducted into the National Women's Hall of Fame. Women honored include Eleanor Roosevelt, Pearl Buck, Rosa Parks, and Eileen Collins. 76 Fall St., Seneca Falls 13148; 315-568-2936; www.greatwomen.org

PHOTO OP Cayuga-Seneca Canal: Behind the main business block on NY Rts. 5 and 20, with the canal boats tied up along the pier.

❋ Shopping

ANTIQUES Mary Ann's Treasure, Waterloo, sells all sorts of things including antiques, glass, china, memorabilia, and Victorian-era items. 209 W. Main St., Waterloo 13165; 315-589-3889

FARMERS' MARKETS AND SPECIALTY FOODS **Bodine Farms** sells sweet corn and other fruits and vegetables as well as ice cream. E. Bayard St., Seneca Falls 13148; 315-568-9529

Owned and operated by Mennonites, **Sauders Market & Store** in Seneca Falls is one incredible place. Here you'll find everything from handmade garden furniture, sheds and gazebos, to a huge array of fresh produce, bulk products, Pennsylvania German meats and cooking essentials, plus a farmers' market on Fridays. Find unusual stuff, too, like ham hocks, gummy candies, sanding sugars, cards, quilts, candles, and gifts, all at great prices. 2146 River Rd., Seneca Falls 13148; 315-563-2673

GIFTS **Christina's Silver Gallery** in Seneca Falls has wonderful silver jewelry, ceramics, cards, and other unique gift items. 51 Fall St., Seneca Falls 13148; 315-568-8826; www.christinasilvercreations.com

THE ARTS **R Dixon Gallery** features juried contemporary art from across the country with exhibits such as *By & About Women: Celebrating the Female Spirit* and *It's a Wonderful Life*. Call for hours. 102 Fall St., Seneca Falls 13148; 607-279-3868; www.rdixongallery.com

Seneca County Arts Council and Gallery features locally crafted paintings, jewelry, photographs, and other items. 108 Falls St., Seneca Falls 13148; 315-730-8892; www.artsinseneca.org

Sherry's Bear and Frame Shop Unique handmade teddy bears, old and new artwork, antiques, and custom framing. 67 Fall St., Seneca Falls 13148; 315-568-5541

Aurora

Founded on the site of the Cayuga village Deawendote, which means "village of constant dawn," Aurora is on the eastern shore of the lake. Many of the buildings, including Wells College, one of the oldest private liberal arts educational institutions in the country, are listed in the National Register of Historic Places.

In addition to the fantasy-filled pottery, furniture, and glass studios of MacKenzie-Childs just north of the village center, the Aurora Arts & Design Center contains a wonderful group of vendors selling fine art, antiques, photographs, and crafts.

The Aurora Inn, a village landmark, has been brought back to its original 1833 Federalist design, much of the work funded by the Pleasant T. Rowland Foundation. Pleasant Rowland, a Wells College graduate and former owner of MacKenzie-Childs and the American Girl doll franchise, also owns the Fargo Bar & Grill, the E. B. Morgan House, Dorie's Bakery, the Old Post Office, the Taylor House, and other buildings and businesses in Aurora.

✳ Lodging

Its location within walking distance of everything in town makes **Annie's Guest House** all the more desirable. Colors are light and soft; décor traditional, simple, not cluttered. $$–$$$ 444 Main St., Aurora 13026; 315-406-6501; www.aghaurora.com

Inns of Aurora: The impeccably restored **Aurora Inn**, a historic landmark hotel on the shores of Cayuga Lake, is a gracious Federalist-style inn with double verandas and eight working fireplaces. Many of the 10 guest rooms have fireplaces, balconies, marble

WINE & BEER TASTING TOUR

Start: Seneca Falls

Stay: In one of Seneca Falls' B&Bs such as **Barristers**, **John Morris Manor**, or **The Gould Hotel**.

Travel: South on Rt. 89 down west side of lake

1st Stop: Swedish Hill Winery in Romulus, winner of the 2010 Governor's Cup for their riesling cuvée, produces wine from European varieties as well as labrusca and French-American hybrids. Notable are their rieslings, Optimus (a bordeaux-style blend), Cynthia Marie vintage port, and Eaux-De-Vie grape brandy. Set on 35 acres, the winery is

KNAPP RESTAURANT SERVES CREATIVE DISHES.

housed in a rustic red barn with a deck overlooking a pond. There are three separate tasting bars and a shop selling Amish-baked breads and gift wine packs. 315-549-8326, 888-549-WINE; www.swedishhill.com

2nd Stop (early lunch): Knapp Winery & Vineyard Restaurant in Romulus on Rt. 128 just off Rt. 89 is a stylish modern winery set on 99 acres of gardens and vineyards. In addition to wine tastings, there is an excellent restaurant where you can eat indoors or on the outdoor garden patio. Knapp specializes in classic European wines such as barrel reserve chardonnay and cabernet franc. Knapp also produces Superstition, a grapey, juicy wine, and concocts brandy in a hand-hammered copper onion-dome distillery. Ask about their Wine Dinners. 800-869-9271; 607-869-9271; www.knappwine.com

3rd Stop: Goose Watch Winery on NY Rt. 89, just five minutes south, is graced by a beautiful goose sculpture in flight on the top of the hill. The winery is in a restored one-hundred-year-old barn set in a grove of chestnut trees. Wines include classic premium European-style wines such as merlot, brut rosé champagne, their award-winning Pinot Grigio and white blend Snow Goose, their Gold winning riesling gewürztraminer, and Traminette, a Double Gold winner. Goose Watch has a picnic area and boat dock, offers agricultural tram tours, and sells a selection of cheeses, smoked trout, and other gourmet items. 888-549-9463; 315-549-2599, www.goosewatch.com

4th Stop (lunch): Thirsty Owl Wine Company in Ovid is a good place to enjoy lunch in the Bistro serving specialty

GOOSE WATCH WINERY SITS HIGH ON A CREST OVERLOOKING THE LAKE

AMERICANA VINEYARDS HAS ONE OF THE BEST GIFT SHOPS IN THE AREA

soups, salads, sandwiches, small plates, flatbread pizzas, and homemade desserts along with wines at house prices. Dine on the deck or indoors overlooking the lake and vineyards. In addition to their popular rieslings, they produce syrah, chardonnay, vidal blanc, Blushing Moon, Red Moon, pinot noir, Lot 99, meritage, and merlot. 866-869-5851; www.thirstyowl.com

5TH STOP: Sheldrake Point Vineyard and Café in Ovid is set on the edge of the lake. Their highly rated wines include riesling, gewürztraminer, dry rosé, pinot gris, chardonnay, cabernet franc, and gamay along with dessert wines. 866-743-5372, 607-532-9401; www.sheldrakepoint.com

6TH STOP: Lucas Vineyards in Interlaken, the oldest winery (1980) on Cayuga Lake, reveals beautiful views of the water from their tasting room where you can sample vinifera, French-American varietals, sparkling wines including their popular Tugboat and Nautie wines, and ice wines. 800-682-WINE, 607-532-4825; www.lucasvineyards.com

7TH STOP: Americana Vineyards and **Crystal Lake Café** just off NY Rt. 89 in Interlaken (East Covert Rd.) is housed in an 1820s swing-beam barn, moved from another location after being taken apart piece by piece. Taste their double-gold medal–winning riesling and baco noir, cabernet franc, and Barn Raising Red. The Crystal Lake Café (call first as days and hours vary) gives you yet another choice for a tasty meal where the chef uses fresh, seasonal ingredients and makes most things in-house like breads, smoked meats, even relishes and ice creams, along with items like Asian flank steak and lamb burgers. Americana also has a great gift shop selling handcrafted items and homemade fudge. 888-600-8067, 607-387-6801; www.americanavineyards.com

8TH STOP: Follow the signs up the road on the right to **Taughannock Falls Overlook** for a superb (free) look at the falls.

9TH STOP: Frontenac Point Vineyard & Estate Winery in Trumansburg specializes in dry wines like Stay Sail rosé and Frontenac Red. Of interest is the 10 foot "Stay Sail" kinetic sound sculpture on the bow of the winery deck overlooking the lake. 607-387-9619; www.frontenacpoint.com

LAST STOP (DINNER): For traditional fare in an old inn go to **Taughannock Farms Inn** or drive on to Ithaca and try one of the small boutique restaurants on Aurora Street or the Commons like **Taste of Thai** (love the lettuce wraps) or **John Thomas Steakhouse** for killer steaks. (See Ithaca section)

OVERNIGHT: Check the Ithaca "Lodging" section in Ithaca area for places like **La Tourelle Resort & Spa**, **The Hound & Hare B&B**, and **Log Country Inn**.

NEXT DAY: Explore Ithaca's **Discovery Trail**; hit the breweries and distilleries on the west side of Cayuga Lake; or head north up the east side of the lake. Or take a short detour east of Ithaca to the **Hopshire Farm & Brewery** in Freeville (NY Rt. 366 to NY Rt. 13) where they grow hops and produce Near Varna IPA (India pale ale), Scottish-style Shire Ale, and Blossom Cherry Wheat.

ROWLAND HOUSE

baths, kitchenettes, sitting areas, flat-screen televisions, and whirlpools. There is a lakeview dining room and terrace, where artwork that once hung in the inn has been found and restored and hidden fiber-optic lighting casts a romantic twinkle. Décor is fresh and light yet rich, using Audubon-style etched print fabrics and wallpaper and jewellike colors. Fresh-baked muffins and coffee are delivered outside your door each morning. In the summer cocktail cruises depart from the Aurora Inn's dock. $$$–$$$$ 391 Main St., Aurora 13026; 866-364-8888; www.innsofaurora.com

The **E. B. Morgan House**, with seven rooms, is a grand mansion on the lake often used for special events and executive retreats. Rooms are furnished with period pieces, sumptuous fabrics, and a fine private modern art collection. Some have fireplaces, some lake views. $$$–$$$$ 431 Main St., Aurora 13026; 866-364-8808; www.innsofaurora.com

Rowland House, another gracious restored former estate on Cayuga Lake, is now part of the Aurora Inns collection. After undergoing an extensive renovation, the house has 10 guest rooms—many decorated in the distinctive whimsical style of MacKenzie-Childs—private dining room, library, a two-story boathouse, gardens, expansive lawns, and even a small Grecian temple that makes a lovely wedding venue. $$$–$$$$ 453 Main St., Aurora 13026; 866-364-8808; www.innsofaurora.com

A recent addition to the Inns of Aurora family, **Wallcourt Hall** once housed Wells College students. This Colonial Revival building has been beautifully restored and now has 17 guest rooms. 391 Main St., Aurora; 13026 315-364-8888; www.innsofaurora.com

✳ Dining Out

TRADITION, TRADITION If you are a Sunday brunch fan, you have to try the **Aurora Inn**. It is simply the best, with a smorgasbord of colors and flavors from homemade pastries, fruits, and cheeses to eggs and meats. Dine on the lakeside terrace in the warmer

BEST OF AURORA

BURGERS: Fargo Bar & Grill
ROMANCE: Pumpkin Hill Bistro
BRUNCH: Aurora Inn

VIEWS: Aurora Inn
ICE CREAM: Dorie's Cafe & Bakery

weather or in the dining room. $$–$$$ 391 Main St., Aurora 13026; 866-364-8888; www .aurora-inn.com

COUNTRY CHARM Charm and romance are alive and well at the **Pumpkin Hill Bistro** south of Aurora. Located in an 1820s farmhouse (Sellen House) and moved to this hilltop from another location, Pumpkin Hill has a wonderful menu with comfort food like shepherd's pie, farmhouse pork roast, and maple duck breast with a spicy three-berry sauce. Then there's el Cubanito, a Cuban-style roasted pork sandwich with all the fixin's, and a goat cheese tartlet. Top it all off with a "Fat Chance Pop"—don't ask. Enjoy lunch or dinner in one of the cozy rooms or on the porch overlooking fields and the lake. This is one of our favorites. $–$$ 2051 NY Rt. 90, Aurora 13026; 315-364-7091; www.pumpkinhill.com

CASUAL FARE **Dorie's Cafe & Bakery** is a restored old-fashioned coffee shop and ice cream parlor serving lunch, fresh-baked breads, pastries, and desserts. Also find a selection of children's toys and books. Eat inside or on the open deck overlooking Cayuga Lake. 283 Main St., Aurora 13026; 315-364-8818

Fargo Bar & Grill serves tavern-style fare like burgers on a yummy bun, soups, wings, killer sandwiches, and homemade fries. The fried fish is a Friday night staple. Fargo's has an Irish bar–style ambiance with a great selection of beer. Warm up by the fireplace in cold weather, cool off on the patio or deck in the summer, and challenge some pals to a game of pool or horseshoes in the backyard pit. $–$$ 384 Main St., Aurora 13026; 315-364-8006; www.innsofaurora.com

Cream at the Top south of Aurora in King Ferry is good for a quick meal. Run by the Wilcox family, who also own a local grocery store, the place sells good ice cream and sandwiches. 1253 NY Rt. 34B, King Ferry 13081; 315-364-7504

✴ To See

PERFORMING ARTS Located on the second floor of the Aurora Free Library, the Tudor-style **Morgan Opera House** offers a variety of entertainment—puppet shows, concerts, theater productions, variety

PUMPKIN HILL BISTRO OVERLOOKS CAYUGA LAKE

shows, children's theater, and readings. NY Rt. 90, Aurora 13026; 315-364-5437; www.morganoperahouse.org

MUSEUMS Exhibits in the **Rural Life Museum** in King Ferry describe local agricultural life and traditions. Annual events include the Old Time Wheat Harvest Festival, with wagon rides, wheat cutting, a parade, and demonstrations of harvesting. NY Rt. 34B, King Ferry 13081; 315-364-8202

AURORA ARTS AND DESIGN CENTER FEATURES A NUMBER OF ARTISTS

John Dyson

✱ Shopping

ANTIQUES **Black Sheep Fine Antiques**, housed in a wonderful old barn off NY Rt. 34B in Aurora, sells high-quality furniture, mirrors, china, glassware, artwork, and all kinds of unique items. 2863 NY Rt. 34B, Aurora 13026; 315-729-2776; www.blacksheepfineantiques.com

ART Antique seekers should definitely stop at the **Arts & Design Center**. This renovated brick building, home to **Alexander Millen**, has an attractively displayed collection of art, antiques, and gifts; **Trillium Gallery** presents some exceptional local photography, books, and notecards; and the **Artisans Collective** features Finger Lakes

DURING THE HOLIDAYS, HORSE-DRAWN RIDES ARE OFFERED TO SHOPPERS IN AURORA

artists' crafts, books, and art. 347 Main St., Aurora 13026; 315-364-5408; www.auroraartsanddesign.com

CLOTHING AND ACCESSORIES **Jane Morgan's Little House** sells fine women's fashions and accessories, including Austin Reed, Carol Anderson, Barry Bricken, and Sigrid Olsen. 378 Main St., Aurora 13026; 315-364-7715; www.janemorganslittlehouse.com

SPECIALTY FOODS For fresh breads, fresh fruits and vegetables, jams and jellies, and other food items including picnic items, go to the **Village Market**. Presentation is great, perfect for gift baskets. 385 Main St., Aurora 13026; 315-364-8803

Bet the Farm, a small, neat shop on the main street, offers wine tastings and sells handcrafted wines by Nancy Tisch. Also find a selection of cheeses, Ma Poole's Chutney, gourmet foods, and gift baskets. 381 Main St., Aurora 13026; 315-294-5643; www.betthefarmny.com

WHIMISCAL ITEMS FROM MACKENZIE-CHILDS

GIFTS **MacKenzie-Childs** is a fantasy world of whimsically adorned pottery, glass, ceramic vanity bowls, lamps, and amazing furniture items. Tour the art studio and check out the bird aviary—colorful and captivating. You'll probably leave with a few packages of loot, but beware: Though bargains can be found on the seconds tables, this is not your factory outlet kind of place. Once a year, usually in July, a giant sale packs people in from all over the country. 315-364-7123; www.mackenzie-childs.com

Shakelton Hardware on Main Street is an old-fashioned hardware store with wonderful wood floors and an eclectic mix of goods. 286 Main St., Aurora 13026; 315-364-8211

Other Places: Cayuga Lake East Side

✲ Dining Out

Rogues' Harbor Inn, built in the 1830s, is decorated with antiques and local memorabilia. In summer, eat on the porch; in winter, warm up by the fireplaces. Dine on hand-cut USDA choice beef, local wines, microbrew drafts, and fresh seafood and fish—everything made in-house. The chowder is great. Upstairs is Rogues' Harbor B&B. 2079 E. Shore Dr., Lansing 14882; 607-533-3535; www.roguesharbor.com

For a sweet respite, **Pete's Treats** in Union Springs sells hard and soft ice cream, sundaes, and other ice cream treats, plus barbecued duck, chicken tenders, and hamburgers. Take out or sit at one of the picnic tables. US Rt. 90, Union Springs 13160; 315-889-7636

✳ Lodging

BARNS, TIPIS, CAMPFIRES, AND STORYTELLING Take a renovated barn and six lovely acres, then add four huge tipis (27 feet across), storytelling around a campfire, music fests with a didjeridoo, hammocks, and gardens, and you have the makings for a way cool and groovy adventure. At **Turtle Dreams** in Groton, six rooms in the barn operate as a bed-and-breakfast with bounteous breakfasts, while the tipis can each sleep 16 people. Bring your own sleeping bags, kick off your shoes, and grab a spot on the raised platform. Owner Paul Speight, who has spent a lot of time living in the bush in Australia, offers programs in primitive skills such as making bows and surviving in the wilderness. $–$$ 481 Lafayette Rd., Groton 13073; 607-838-3492; www .dreamingturtles.com

Other Places: Cayuga Lake West Side

Interlaken's former names—McCall's Tavern, Farmer Village, and Farmer—tell the tale of its origins: a simple community with a strong farming population. Incorporated in 1904 as Interlaken, the village has grown along NY Rt. 96 on the western side of the Cayuga Lake north of Trumansburg. Ovid, a small, sleepy town just north of Interlaken lies in the heart of the wine region—it even has a nine-hole golf course, **Bonavista State Park Golf Course**. 7194 Cty. Rd. 132, Ovid 14521; 607-869-9909

✳ Lodging

Halfway up the west side of the lake, **Driftwood B&B** has six airy rooms, some with lake views. There are also three cottages (one, two, and four bedrooms) available by the week and 260 feet of private beachfront, kayaks, rowboat, and a dock. A full breakfast is served. $$–$$$ 7401 Wyers Point Rd., Ovid 14521; 607-532-4324, 888-532-4324; www .driftwoodny.com

Silver Strand at Sheldrake, a restored lakefront Victorian, has a lovely old porch, six very attractively furnished bedrooms, a three-bedroom guest cottage and Hilltop House with 3 to 4 bedrooms. All rooms in the main house have private baths, air conditioning, and private balconies; some have fireplaces. Guests have use of kayaks, a rowboat, a hot tub, a swimming beach, bikes, and games. $$–$$$ 7398 Wyers Point Rd., Ovid 14521; 607-532-4972, 800-283-5253; www.silverstrand.net

TILLINGHAST MANOR BED AND BREAKFAST, OVID

When you stay at **Tillinghast Manor** you take a step back in time. Much of the lumber used in the mansion's construction was personally sawed and worked by George Jones, the man who built this elegant Victorian house in 1873 with a cupola, lovely long windows, and high ceilings. There are five guest rooms, some with shared baths. Furnishings are a mix of antiques and period furniture. Breakfasts are hearty—eggs, homemade jams, and home fries. Children and pets are welcome. $$ 7246 S. Main St., Ovid 14521; 607-869-3584

Laura Kozlowski

FOOD, FUN, AND HARD CIDERS ARE PART OF THE PICTURE AT THE FINGER LAKES CIDER HOUSE

✳ Dining Out

WINERY AND BREWERY RESTAURANTS The **Copper Oven at Cayuga Ridge Estate Winery** produces a mean pizza using homegrown ingredients and local produce, cheeses, and meats. 6800 NY Rt. 89, Ovid 14521; 607-220-8794

Crystal Lake Café in the Americana Vineyards is another dining gem in a vineyard setting. Cuisine centers on local ingredients, artisan breads, and cured and smoked meats like shrimp po'boy and barbecued pulled pork. Sunday brunch is amazing. On-site is a really nice gift shop with interesting and unusual items like blown glass bottle lanterns. 4367 E. Covert Rd., Interlaken 14847; 607-387-6804; www.americanavineyards.com

Come to the **Finger Lakes Cider House** on an organic farm and enjoy ciders from several regional producers as well as locally made cheeses, breads, and other good foods. Along with dinner you can try cider flights from producers like Slatestone Black Diamond and Cloudsplitter. Get lucky and catch the live music. 4017 Hickok Rd. #1, Interlaken 14847; 607-351-3313; www.fingerlakesciderhouse.com

The **Restaurant at Knapp Vineyards** is a good place to stop for a bite to eat while touring the vineyards. Eat indoors or on the patio. 2770 Emsberger Rd., Romulus 14541; 607-869-9481; www.knappwine.com

LAKE VIEWS Arrive by car or boat at **Kidders Landing** where you can enjoy well-priced, light fare like sandwiches and burgers by the lake. 7930 Cty. Rd. 153, Interlaken 14847; 607-532-3446; www.kidderslanding.com

ICE CREAM **Cayuga Lake Creamery** on Route 89 is famous for its homemade ice cream. Family-owned and -operated, the Creamery uses fresh, local ingredients in making its flavors and is open year-round. Eat inside or on the deck. 8421 NY Rt. 89, Interlaken 14847; 607-532-9492; www.cayugalakecreamery.com

✳ To See

Interlaken Historical Society Museum exhibits eighteenth- and nineteenth-century farm tools. The Nivison Grain Cradle building houses the Farmers' Museum; and the

New Historical Society Museum, located in the Trumansburg Telephone Company building, displays artifacts, period clothing, and historic photos. 8394 Main St., Interlaken 14847; 607-532-8899; www.interlakenhistory.org

✳ To Do

BIKING There are several trails around Cayuga Lake. The 90-mile **Cayuga Lake Loop** with a gently rolling grade reveals views of the lake, fields, and farms. The paved 30.6-mile **Gorge Trail** starts at Ithaca Commons and takes you by Buttermilk Falls State Park, Robert Treman State Park, and Taughannock Falls State Park.

The **Eastern Route**, a 36.2-mile trail on mostly paved roads with several rolling hills and a few steep inclines, starts in Union Springs. Along the way stop at the **Frontenac Museum, MacKenzie-Childs, Wells College, Long Point State Park, King Ferry Winery**, and the **Rural Life Museum**. Head south on US 90 through Aurora and on to King Ferry. Stay right to go into Long Point, and at the stoplight, turn left onto NY Rt. 34B, and go north to Scipioville. At the turn veer left onto Ridge Rd., and follow it straight to NY Rt. 326. Turn left onto NY Rt. 326 W., and follow signs to return to Union Springs.

BOATING Dinner, lunch, champagne brunch, and sightseeing cruises are offered on the lake by **Cayuga Lake Cruises** departing from Ithaca's M/V Columbia Pier. 607-256-0898; www.cayugalakecruises.com. The **Erie Canal Cruise Line** features cruises on the Erie Canal. 800-962-1771; www.canalcruises.com. **Ithaca Boat Tours** offers a variety of one- to two-hour cruises sailing out of the Ithaca Boat Center. 607-697-0166; www.ithacaboattours.com

Water to Wine Tours depart from Interlaken at 11 a.m. and return at 4 p.m., stopping at wineries and a winery bistro for lunch. Cost of $85 (lunch extra) includes tasting fees, complimentary soft drinks, and cruise. The company also offers Happy Hour Cruises and other specialty cruises. 607-229-6368; www.winolimo.com

For fun on Cayuga Lake, rent a kayak, canoe, paddleboard, and the gear at **Puddledockers** in Ithaca. Lessons also available. 607-273-0096; www.puddledockers.com

MARINAS AND LAUNCHES Among the marinas and launch areas (some also offer boat rentals) are **Allan H. Treman State Marine Park**, one of the largest inland marinas in the state 607-272-1460 summer, 607-273-3440 winter; **Barrett's Marine**, Waterloo 315-789-6605; **Finger Lakes Marine Service**, Lansing 607-533-4422; **Beacon Bay Marine**, Cayuga 315-252-2849; **Frontenac Harbor** in Union Springs 315-889-5532; and the **Marina** in Seneca Falls 315-568-0200. Also launch at **Long Point State Park** (off NY Rt. 90, Aurora) and **Deans Cove** (NY Rt. 89, west side of Cayuga Lake).

Oak Orchard Marina and Campground at May's Point, Seneca Falls, is set on a 3,000-foot riverfront site with rental cottages overlooking the Erie Canal. There are tent and trailer sites, a pool, a playground, boat rentals, hiking, hayrides, a boat launch, and hookup facilities. 315-365-3000 summer, 609-965-4647 winter; www.oakorchard.com.

Hibiscus Harbor Marina in Union Springs on the east side of Cayuga Lake has 205 slips, a marine store, Wheel House Restaurant, an outside deck, bathrooms, showers, a pool, tenting area, and boat rentals. Live music on Sundays in-season. 315-889-5008; www.tradeayacht.com/central-new-york-marinas

GOLF There are several public golf courses around Cayuga Lake that are a lot of fun to play and very inexpensive, with really nice views of the lake. Green fees are typically under $30. (If you have pull, beg your way onto the **Cornell University Golf Course** in Ithaca.)

Nine-hole courses with green fees often less than $20 include **Cayuga Links Golf Course** at New York Chiropractic College, Seneca Falls, with several elevated greens, a small clubhouse, driving range, pro shop, and carts, 315-568-6597; **Cedar View Golf Course** in Lansing with some views of the lake, 315-364-7598; **Indian Head Golf Course** between Auburn and Seneca Falls, a rather flat nine-hole with some hills, popular with locals.315-253-6812; **Newman Golf Course** on the lakeshore in Ithaca, 607-273-6262; and **Wells College Golf Course**, a beautiful track in Aurora designed by Robert Trent Jones, 315-364-8024

New to the area (2007), another nine-hole course, **King Ferry Golf Club** overlooking the eastern shore of the lake, evokes a Scottish links–style layout with feathery fescue defining the fairways. With green fees from just $13, it's a real deal, too. 1309 Clearview Rd., King Ferry 13081; 315-364-7343; www.kingferrygolfclub.com

The front nine at the 18-hole **Hillendale Golf Course** in Ithaca is somewhat hilly, while the back nine is considered a bit harder. There is a restaurant, bar and one of the better practice facilities in the area. 218 Applegate Rd. N., Ithaca 14850; 607-273-2363; www.hillendale.com

Trumansburg Golf Course is a well-maintained, very pretty older (1969) course with a pro shop, bar, and restaurant. 23 Halsey St., Trumansburg 14886; 607-387-8844; www.trumansburggolf.com

Silver Creek Golf Club (See Seneca Lake East Side section)

FISHING Considered one of the top 10 bass lakes in the United States, Cayuga Lake is a fisherman's dream come true. In addition to the great bass fishing, anglers pull in lake trout, landlocked salmon, brown trout, and rainbow trout. Fly fishermen have more than 102 miles of trout streams and 28 miles of warm water streams to enjoy.

Cayuga Lake's AA rating means the water is fit for drinking and holds a healthy population of game fish. The fishing season runs from April to November on the lake and September to April on the Salmon River.

Eagle Rock Charters in Cayuga offers half, full, and evening light-tackle fishing charters aboard *Eagle Rock II*, a 27-foot Baha cruiser. Eagle Rock Charters also has a one-hundred-year-old five-bedroom rental house overlooking Cayuga Lake, 3.5 miles from the boat. Bring a valid New York State fishing license, seasonal clothing, soft-soled shoes, a cooler to transport your catch home, snacks, beverages, and rain gear. 315-889-5925; www.eaglerockcharters.com

HIKING Hiking trails range from easy to difficult. Some of the best are highlighted by a view of one of the many waterfalls in the area. Ask for the Waterfalls brochure from Visit Ithaca. 607-272-1313; www.visitithaca.com

Major water drama is provided by **Taughannock Falls** plunging 215 feet, a sight you can see free from the overlook off Rt. 89. Hike the Gorge (.75 miles), South Rim (1.25 miles), or North Rim (1.5 miles) trails. Enjoy a good look at the **Lick Brook Falls** in Sweedler Preserve when you hike the 1.6-mile loop. Short but difficult, this part of the Finger Lakes Trail takes you down a steep hill and then back up the hill. 607-275-9487

Other notable falls include **Ithaca Falls** with a drop of 150 feet and one of the most powerful and awesome falls; **Denison Falls** in the Cayuga Nature Center; **Enfield Falls**, **Lucifer Falls**, and **Fish Kills Falls** in the Robert Treman State Park; **Buttermilk Falls** and **Pulpit Falls** in Buttermilk Falls State Park, and **Potter's Falls** and **Businessman's Lunch Falls** along Six Mile Creek. Swimming is permitted in the lifeguarded area below Enfield Falls and below Buttermilk Falls.

OTHER TRAILS

The **Cayuga Trail** takes off from NY Rt. 366 off the southwestern tip of Cayuga Lake. This 6.5-mile difficult loop goes along an abandoned rail bed, up steep hills, through thickly planted woods, and along a creek. **Esker Brook Nature Trail** in Montezuma National Wildlife Refuge, west of Auburn, a moderately easy 1.5-mile loop along dirt paths, passes through woods, wetlands rich with wildlife and waterfowl, old apple orchards, and around ponds. 315-568-5987

Also check out the **Cornell Lab of Ornithology** (see "Ithaca's Discovery Trail" in Ithaca section), with more than four miles of nature trails winding through wildlife habitats in the Sapsucker Woods Sanctuary. 607-254-BIRD; www.birds.cornell.edu

KAYAKING AND CANOEING Oak Island on Oak Street off US 20 just west of Lock 4 in Waterloo is a lovely town park with a pavilion, launch area, and picnic tables. Slide your kayak or canoe into the canal for a paddle up the canal all the way to Seneca Lake. The pavilion can be rented for a nominal fee, and if you clean it up, you get your money back. What a deal.

PARKS, NATURE PRESERVES, HIKING, AND CAMPING Whether you're looking for a place to pitch your tent, park your RV, or rent a cabin, around Cayuga Lake you have choices.

A short drive from Ithaca, the 751-acre **Buttermilk Falls State Park**, with several creeks and streams, waterfalls, and a gorge trail, is more like a full-service "camp resort," with tons to do. Facilities include 46 campsites, several cabins, swimming, picnic areas, ball fields, and nature programs. NY Rt. 13, Ithaca 14850; 607-273-5761/3440; www.parks.ny.gov/parks

Robert H. Treman State Park has 1,070 acres running through rustic Enfield Glen, four hiking trails, 72 campsites, 14 cabins, swimming, two pavilions, a picnic area, and a camper recreation program. The upper and lower falls are connected by hiking trails; the most dramatic part is the upper half mile, where the scenery was often used as a backdrop for early Western movies. A beautiful stone path and steps lead to 115-foot Lucifer Falls. 105 Enfield Falls Rd., Ithaca 14850; 607-273-3440; www.parks.ny .gov/parks

Sned Acres Family Campground has lovely views of the water, tent and trailer sites, hookups, picnic tables, grills, restrooms, showers, a store, playgrounds, and on-site trailer rentals. Cabin rentals are $42 per night. 6590 S. Cayuga Lake Rd., Ovid 14521; 607-869-9787; www.sned-acres.com

Spruce Row Campsite and RV Resort, 7 miles north of Ithaca, has large open and shaded RV and tent sites on 125 acres, a pool, hayrides, playgrounds, miniature golf, a recreation building, paddleboats, a store, and full hookups. 2271 Kraft Rd., Ithaca 14850; 607-387-9225; www.sprucerow.com

Towering Taughannock Falls, the highest vertical falls east of the Mississippi River, plunging 215 feet straight down through a rock amphitheater, is the focal point of **Taughannock Falls State Park**. Located in Trumansburg, the 783-acre park has several trails, 16 cabins, 76 campsites, picnic areas, toilets, fishing, swimming, and boat rentals. Even in winter the frozen and flowing ice create a visual feast, and you can go whizzing down the sledding slope, skate on the rink, and hike the gorge trail. NY Rt. 89, Trumansburg 14886; 607-387-6739; www.taughannock.com

On a smaller scale, **Cayuga Lake State Park** in Seneca Falls on the lake's western shore is graced by level lawns, lots of trees, campsites, and a playground. 315-568-5163, 800-456-2267; www.parks.ny.gov/parks. For picnicking, fishing, and swimming there is **Frontenac Park** in Union Springs on the eastern shore of the lake 315-889-7341 and **Long Point State Park** 4 miles south of Aurora 315-497-1030; **Stewart Park** in Ithaca has playing fields, a playground, a picnic area, a concession stand, tennis courts—even a restored carousel. 607-273-8364; www.cityofithaca.org/516/stewart-park

FOR THE BIRDS Wildlife is front and center at the **Montezuma National Wildlife Refuge** off NY Rt. 5 and US 20E west of Auburn. Each spring and fall, ducks, geese, herons, and other shorebirds are seen at this major resting and breeding area. The refuge includes a visitor's center, a viewing platform from which you may be able to spot a nesting eagle, an easy-to-follow 1.5-mile walking loop, and a 3.5-mile wildlife drive. 3395 NY Rts. 5 and 20, Seneca Falls 13148; 315-568-5987; www.fws.gov

SKYDIVING Ah, the adrenalin rush of jumping out of a perfectly good airplane. **Finger Lakes Skydivers**, near Ovid, can make it all happen. Your first jumps are tandem—jumping with an experienced skydiver. After a short instructional session, you go up in the plane and then, harnessed to your instructor, you exit through the large door of the plane, spread out your arms, and for 30 seconds free-fall before opening your canopy. Relive the thrills over and over again when you jump with a free-fall photographer. The cost is $199 for the first tandem jump; free-fall training jumps are $60–$135 800-SKY-DIVE; www.skydivefingerlakes.com

SWIMMING The waters of Cayuga Lake are cool and clean. Several points of entry include the Wells College dock, Aurora, off Myers Point; Long Point State Park; and Frontenac Park. Also try the pools at the bottom of the falls at Buttermilk Falls State Park and Robert Treman Park and at the public area in the lake at Taughannock Falls State Park.

FAMILY FUN **Bakers' Acres** in Groton is a wonderland of display gardens, greenhouses, groves of apple trees, a cider press, and three barns for drying flowers—plus a woodland path leading to a pond. Have lunch in the Tea Room, enjoy Bob's great barbecued chicken, and check out the antiques in the Lodge. Classes and workshops in gardening, cooking, and herbs are offered. FYI, Professor Bob Baker was the creator of the famous Cornell recipe for barbecued chicken. 1104 Auburn Rd., Groton 13073; 607-533-4653; www.bakersacres.net

Cayuga Nature Center in Ithaca is a 241-acre fun-filled place with exhibits of live animals, a nature store, a working farm, and a number of special programs including summer camp and teen adventure. Get up close to farm animals and little creatures like snakes and creepy-crawlies, and explore the 5 miles of nature trails. (See "Ithaca's Discovery Trail" in Ithaca section)

See a boa constrictor, water flume, and two-story kinetic ball, and explore the workings of a walk-in camera at Ithaca's

KAYAKS

Sciencenter. It's a great place to spend a day, with more than one hundred exhibits, many hands-on. (See "Ithaca's Discovery Trail" in Ithaca section)

The **Ithaca Farmers' Market** on the waterfront sells local produce, plants, baked goods, meats and cheeses, crafts, clothing, and furniture. There is a pavilion, picnic area, docking facilities, and plenty of parking. Everything is made or grown within a 30-mile radius. There are also a variety of special events throughout the season such as dancing, a strawberry festival, chili contest, a bee-day, a ping-pong tournament, and live performances. Come hungry. Third St. off NY Rt. 13, Ithaca 14850; 607-273-7109; www.ithacamarket.com

Eco tours on Cayuga Lake are offered by **Tiohero Tours**, an independent branch of Cayuga Wooden Boatworks that specializes in boatbuilding and restoration. Tiohero's floating classrooms promote awareness of the lake, its history, legends, and boat skills. Great fun for kids of all ages. 866-846-4376; www.tioherotours.com

Tours and special events at **Lively Run Goat Dairy** are offered by the Messmer family. Learn about dairy goats and cheese making, sample a variety of cheeses, and perhaps milk a goat. Purchase gourmet foods, cheeses, local handcrafts, and gifts, and even enjoy a picnic. 8978 Cty. Rd. 142, Interlaken 14847; 607-532-4647; www .livelyrun.com

The **Seneca Museum of Waterways and Industry** on Fall Street will give you a crash course on how important the waterways of the Finger Lakes were to the area's development. 315-568-1510; www.senecamuseum.com

FOR MORE INFORMATION **Finger Lakes Tourism Alliance**: 800-548-4386, 315-536-7488; 309 Lake St., Penn Yan 14527; www.fingerlakes.org

Finger Lakes Travel: Break the Ice Media: 888-408-1693; www.fingerlakestravel ny.com

Ithaca/Tompkins County Convention & Visitors Bureau: 904 E. Shore Dr., Ithaca 14850; 800-28 ITHACA; www.ithacaevents.com; www.visitithaca.com

Seneca County Tourism: 2020 US 20, Seneca Falls 13148; 800-732-1848; www .fingerlakescentral.com

Trumansburg Area Chamber of Commerce: P.O. Box 478, Trumansburg 14886; 607-387-9254; www.trumansburgchamber.com

B&B and Vacation Rentals of Greater Ithaca: www.bbithaca.com

Cayuga Lake

✱ What's Happening

SPRING **Annual Finger Lakes Carp Derby**, Peoples Park, Seneca Falls. More than $2,000 in prizes to catch the big one. 315-568-5112

Annual Seneca County Fair, Seneca County Fairgrounds, Waterloo. A whole week of fun: tractor pulls, midway attractions, demolition derby, parades, barbecues, rides, animals, and more. www.senecacountyfair.org

Bacon on the Lakein is all about—what else—bacon. Receive a wineglass at your starting point winery and recipe cards as you sample wines and bacon-infused dishes at each of the 17 wineries you visit. 800-684-5217; www.cayugawinetrail.com

Canalfest, Seneca Falls Canal Promenade. Arts and crafts show with artisans, entertainment, food, antique boats, steamboats, and fireworks. 315-568-2906

Wine & Herb Festival, Cayuga Lake wineries. Visit participating wineries, taste new wines, sample foods made with fresh herbs, and take home potted herbs ready for planting. 800-684-5217

Ithaca Festival, Ithaca. Crafts, singing, theater, mimes, fireworks, and food. 607-273-3646

Maple Sugar Festival, Cayuga Nature Center, Ithaca. See how maple syrup is tapped and made into sugar. 607-273-6260

Old Home Days, Interlaken. Parade, auctions, yard sales, and entertainment. 607-532-8731

Vintage Car Show, on the Commons, Ithaca. Antique cars. 607-277-8979

SUMMER **Empire Farm Days**, Rodman Ltd. & Sons Farm, Seneca Falls. A huge farm show with tractor pulls, flower vendors, food stands, animal care demos, and horse activities. 585-526-5356

Grassroots Festival of Music and Dance, Trumansburg Fairgrounds, Trumansburg. Musical concerts on three stages (usually the third weekend in July). 607-387-5098; www.grassrootsfest.org

Route 90 Fifty-Mile Long Garage Sale, last weekend in July. Runs on NY Rt. 90 from Montezuma, along the west side of Cayuga Lake to Homer, with hundreds of sales, antiques, collectibles, and more. Take in the BBQs, bake sales, and breakfasts along the way. 800-499-9615; www.tourcayuga.com

FALL/WINTER **Apple Harvest Festival**, Ithaca. A gala weekend filled with local produce including apples, cider, and pies; a craft fair, entertainment, and storytellers. 607-277-8679

Cayuga Wine Trail Shopping Spree, Cayuga Lake wineries. Taste wine, sample holiday hors d'oeuvres, and take home recipes (December). 800-684-5217

Grape Stomping Festival, Cobblestone Farms, Romulus. Grape picking as well as crushing the purple fruit, music, hay rides, food, and fun. 315-549-2505

"It's a Wonderful Life" Festival, Seneca Falls (December). 315-568-2703; www .therealbedfordfalls.com

King Ferry Winery Harvest Festival, King Ferry. Grape harvesting tours, wine tasting, and winemaking demonstrations.

Thirsty Owl Wine Company Barrel Tasting & Polka Party, Ovid. Skips the stomping and goes straight to the tasting with great food and live music morning to night. 866-869-5805; www.thirstyowl.com

Trumansburg WinterFest, Trumansburg. The Christmas tree is the center of attention as it is lit with a sing-along, music, crafts, horse and carriage rides, and a dessert contest (first weekend in December). 607-387-6501; www.trumansburgchamber.com

SENECA LAKE

The Native American translation for Seneca—"a place of stone"—hardly does the lake justice. More than 50 vineyards cover hundreds of acres on fertile hillsides that gently slope to the water's edge. They are, quite simply, a stunning sight.

From Seneca Lake, 38 miles long and more than 618 feet deep in some places, you can reach the Atlantic via the New York State canal system. Seneca Lake is a coveted water playground for boaters, sailors, anglers, and swimmers, while race enthusiasts flock to Watkins Glen at the southern end of the lake for NASCAR events.

The lake is now ringed by small villages, summer houses, camps, and parks. Geneva commands the northern end; Watkins Glen anchors the southern end. Other towns near or around the lake include Waterloo, just west of Geneva; Dresden; and Dundee.

A few miles south of Watkins Glen, Montour Falls is home to the beautiful SheQuaGa Falls, plunging 165 feet into a rocky pool. At the foot of Main St., the falls are illuminated at night, a spectacular sight.

Geneva and Waterloo

The site of Kanadesaga, once capital of the Seneca Nation, was renamed Geneva in the eighteenth century. The land opened up to settlers at the time of the Phelps-Gorham purchase in 1783, and Geneva was officially laid out in 1794, with Water St. (now Exchange St.) as the heart of the business district. In the early 1800s steamboats transported products and passengers from one end of the lake to another, and railroads followed in the 1900s.

Prominent companies in the early days were the Geneva Waterworks (1776), J. W. Smith Dry Goods (1847), Geneva Optical Company (1873), the Nester Malt House (1890), and the Geneva Carriage Company (1891).

As you drive west into the city along NY Rt. 5 and US 20, the expansive Seneca Lake State Park, dotted with trees, picnic tables, and grills, is a good place to picnic and swim. Then stop at the Lakeside Park and the Chamber of Commerce Center for regional information. A number of piers and mooring slips are located near the Ramada Geneva lakefront, so boaters can tie up and walk into Geneva about two blocks away.

While in town, take time to note the fine old houses that reign along South Main St., characterized by pillars, leaded windows, round towers, and generous lawns and gardens. Tree-lined Pulteney Square, the original center of town, also features exquisite three-story brick Federal townhouses (circa 1820), many with superb views of the water.

Exchange Street—the main drag—and the adjoining streets contain a mixture of shops, restaurants, local stores and an original movie house. Handsome period-style lighting and brick sidewalks along with ongoing renovations of the turn-of-the-century buildings are transforming this area into one of the better small towns in the state. With a resurgence of the restaurant scene in Geneva, you are sure to find an interesting place for a meal and brew.

The red brick buildings of the in-town campus of **Hobart and William Smith Colleges** settle comfortably into the landscape. A liberal arts education is offered at

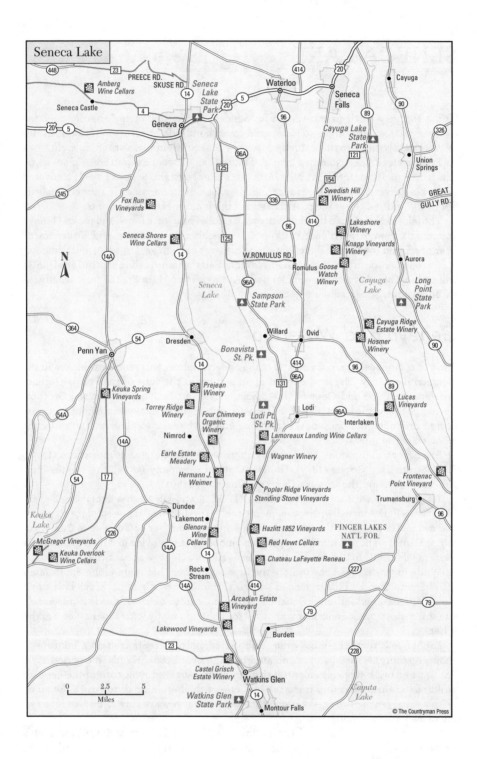

Seneca Lake

PREECE RD.
SKUSE RD.
Amberg Wine Cellars
Seneca Castle
Seneca Lake State Park
Waterloo
Seneca Falls
Cayuga
Geneva
Cayuga Lake State Park
Union Springs
GREAT GULLY RD.
Fox Run Vineyards
Swedish Hill Winery
Seneca Shores Wine Cellars
Lakeshore Winery
W. ROMULUS RD.
Knapp Vineyards Winery
Seneca Lake
Romulus
Goose Watch Winery
Aurora
Sampson State Park
Cayuga Lake
Long Point State Park
Willard
Ovid
Cayuga Ridge Estate Winery
Penn Yan
Dresden
Bonavista St. Pk.
Hosmer Winery
Keuka Spring Vineyards
Prejean Winery
Lodi
Lucas Vineyards
Torrey Ridge Winery
Four Chimneys Organic Winery
Lodi Pt St. Pk.
Interlaken
Nimrod
Lamoreaux Landing Wine Cellars
Earle Estate Meadery
Wagner Winery
Hermann J. Weimer
Poplar Ridge Vineyards
Standing Stone Vineyards
Frontenac Point Vineyard
Trumansburg
Keuka Lake
Dundee
Lakemont
Hazlitt 1852 Vineyards
FINGER LAKES NAT'L FOR.
McGregor Vineyards
Glenora Wine Cellars
Red Newt Cellars
Keuka Overlook Wine Cellars
Chateau LaFayette Reneau
Rock Stream
Arcadian Estate Vineyard
Lakewood Vineyards
Burdett
Cayuta Lake
Castel Grisch Estate Winery
Watkins Glen
0   2.5   5
Miles
Watkins Glen State Park
Montour Falls

© The Countryman Press

Hobart for men, the oldest college in western New York (1822), while next door William Smith (1908) for women, shares many facilities with Hobart.

Just east of Geneva on NY Rts. 5 and 20, two blocks of red brick buildings define the business section of Waterloo. It's the kind of place that typifies hometown America—so it's appropriate that Waterloo is the birthplace of Memorial Day, first observed on May 5, 1866. You can't miss **The National Memorial Day Museum** on Main St.—it's the red brick building with all the flags and patriotic bunting. 315-539-9611; www.waterloony .com

Also see the restored **Peter Whitmer Farm**, where the Church of Jesus Christ of Latter-day Saints was formed in 1830.

A pleasant unexpected discovery of your visit to Waterloo could be a visit to the new **American Civil War Memorial** in Lock Park along the canal. Designed and installed by Pietro Smith, the sculptures and cenotaphs set among the trees and gardens are a powerful tribute to our country's history. Plaques describe the significance of each artfully rendered site.

SMITH OPERA HOUSE IN GENEVA.

While in Waterloo, stop at **Mac's Drive-In**, a Finger Lakes icon and the only '50s-style carhop in the area. This red-and-white-peppermint place, now in its 55th season, sells burgers, sandwiches, and other light food along with ice cream. It's also noted for creamy root beer in a frosty cold mug. 315-539-3064; www.macsdrivein.net

The **Finger Lakes Tea Company** grows and sells various kinds of teas. 678 NY Rt. 318, Waterloo 13165; 315-856-8031

MEMORIAL DAY MUSEUM IN WATERLOO, CONSIDERED THE BIRTHPLACE OF THE HOLIDAY

✳ Lodging

Geneva offers one of the widest ranges of places to stay in the Finger Lakes, from full-service hotels and grand estates to B&Bs. Take your pick.

IN THE GRAND MANOR The 1890s Romanesque **Belhurst Castle** is about the closest thing you'll come to a European castle in this part of the world with rich oak doors and woodwork, stained glass windows, and towers and turrets worthy of King Arthur. Once a private home, today Belhurst operates as an inn, spa (Isabella), and restaurant, with three distinct hotels: the Chambers in the Castle;

historic **White Springs Manor** (two miles west of the castle) with 13 rooms overlooking a vineyard in Seneca Valley; and the Vinifera Inn next door to the castle with in-room Jacuzzis and fireplaces. In the castle, many rooms are appropriately king-like, one with a spiral stairway leading up to a lookout. Dine in Edgar's or Stonecutters lounge, and if you're up for a glass of wine (and you're an in-house guest), simply head to the wine spigot on the second floor and help yourself. Because they believe in doing things the old-fashioned way, reservations are by phone only, answered by a real person. $$–$$$$ 4069 NY Rt. 14S, Geneva 14456; 315-781-0201; www.belhurst.com

Inspired by the Villa Lancellotti in Frascati outside of Rome, **Geneva on the Lake**, an Italianate Renaissance mansion, was built above the lake in 1910. Stay here and you may rub elbows with visiting artists, performers, and sports stars. Beautifully renovated and furnished with rich fabrics, oriental rugs, tapestries, and Stickley furniture, each of the 29 rooms is unique. Lounge by the 70-foot pool at the end of the gardens or have a go on the rope swing. Lunch is served on the terrace overlooking Seneca Lake and, weather permitting, at 4:00 p.m. the resort's pontoon boat is ready to take you on a sunset cruise. Then it's dining in the Colonnade Pavilion or in one of the intimate dining rooms, where tables are set with linens, crystal, and candles. When it comes to romance, Geneva on the Lake gets a high five. $$–$$$ 1001 Lochland Rd. on NY Rt. 14, Geneva 14456; 800-3-GENEVA, 315-789-7190; www.genevaonthelake.com

TRIED AND TRUE In and around Geneva, there are several chain hotels and motels, including the **Hampton Inn Geneva**, popular with business travelers for its convenient location $$–$$$$ (43 Lake St., Geneva 14456; 315-781-2035; www.hamptoninn.hilton .com) and **The Ramada Geneva Lakefront** notable for its lakeside location and Pier House Restaurant with an open-air patio and attractive rooms. $$–$$$$ 41 Lakefront Dr., Geneva 14456; 800-990-0907; www.genevaramada.com

RAMADA GENEVA LAKEFRONT

B&BS The in-town **1907 Bragdon House B&B** on South Main is but a short walk to Hobart and William Smith Colleges. Once the private home of the former mayor of Geneva, this delightfully decorated bed-and-breakfast features beautifully appointed guest rooms with luxury queen- or king-size beds, high-thread-count linens, robes, and five working fireplaces. A home-cooked breakfast prepared by innkeepers Diane Wenz and Jennifer Foe is served either in the dining room or on the porch overlooking the lake. $$–$$$ 527 S. Main St., Geneva 14456; 315-781-6320; www.bragdonhousebb.com

Located on the edge of a large vegetable crop farm, **Gentle Giants Bed & Breakfast**, a restored 1856 Italianate Victorian, has a comfortable parlor with a piano, books, and games. Out back is a large barn, home to registered Belgian horses—the "gentle giants." There are two comfortable rooms, and for breakfast you'll enjoy fresh eggs and produce from the farm. This is a casual, comfy place without pretensions. $$ 1826 Cty. Rd. 4, Geneva 14456; 315-781-2723; www.gentlegiants.pair.com

Through the Grapevine B&B, on NY Rt. 96 through Waterloo, is a charming 1870 brick Italianate home built by Col. Frederick Manning of the Union Army's 148th Regiment. Two guest rooms with private baths are decorated in the Victorian mode with queen beds and pillow-top mattresses covered by Amish-made quilts. Sit back in the white wicker chairs on the wide front porch and watch the world go by. A full breakfast is served. $$ 108 N. Virginia St., Waterloo 13165; 866-272-1270; www .throughthegrapevinebnb.com

✳ Dining Out

While Seneca Lake has many on-the-lake restaurants, there is a lot happening on some of the smaller streets in the city, like Linden where boutique cafés such as the Microclimate Wine Bar are making downtown Geneva a place for the food inspired. An interesting initiative between the Geneva business community and Hobart and William Smith Colleges challenges designers to come up with award-winning plans to transform small, out-of-the-way areas—perhaps a few parking spaces—into a "parklet," providing spots to dine in the open air.

TRADITION, TRADITION Dine like a baron in **Belhurst Castle**, an 1890s Romanesque castle by the lake. Leaded-glass French doors, carved aged wood, mosaic-tiled fireplaces, and beamed cathedral ceilings set the mood. Dine inside in Edgar's or the more casual Stonecutters. (Also see the description of Belhurst in Lodging) $$–$$$ 4069 NY Rt. 14S, Geneva 14456; 315-781-0201; www.belhurst.com

Geneva on the Lake: Tables are beautifully set with linens, crystal, candles, silver, and fine china. Dinner is served each evening in the Lancellotti Room, in intimate smaller rooms, or on the Terrace. No matter where you dine, you overlook the gardens with their neatly trimmed hedges and borders of flowers and the lake beyond. Lunch might be fresh seafood salad served in a phyllo pastry shell, while dinner might be orange and ginger glazed duck breast or pan-seared sea bass, with baked Alaska for the grand finale. (Also see the description of "Geneva on the Lake" in Lodging.) $$–$$$ 1001 Lochland Rd. on NY Rt. 14, Geneva 14456; 800-3-GENEVA; www .genevaonthelake.com

CASUAL FARE Located in a renovated colonial home across from Hobart College, **Dana's Time Out** sports bar is geared to New York sports fans and features an all-sports satellite system with multiple televisions. To accompany the Bills game, chow down on generous portions of steaks, pasta, seafood, and hearty sandwiches. There is also a late-night menu. $–$$ 258 Hamilton St., Geneva 14456; 315-781-2107

Halseys Restaurant is a good place to go before or after a production at the Smith Opera House nearby. Indulge in wood-fired pizzas, filet mignon, seafood, and some interesting vegetarian dishes along with a good selection of wines. $–$$ 106 Seneca St., Geneva 14456; 315-789-4070; www.halseysgeneva.com

Dine inside or outside on the deck near Geneva's waterfront at **Nonna's Cosentino's Trattoria**, known for homemade Italian sauces and dishes like lasagna, manicotti, and braciola as well as steak, veal, and seafood pasta. $–$$ 1 Railroad Pl., Geneva 14456; 315-789-1638; www.nonnastrattoria.com

Next to the Smith Opera House and a hot spot for local businesspeople, **Parker's Grille and Tap House**, with its green-painted walls, woodwork, booths, bar, and high-top tables, evokes an old-time traditional bistro. Menu items include burgers, Philly steak, and homemade soups along with a veggie basket and a large selection of beer and ale. In the warmer weather, grab a table on the sidewalk patio. $–$$ 100 Seneca St., Geneva 14456; 315-789-4656

The popular **Pier House Restaurant**, serving breakfast, lunch, and dinner is definitely into fish and seafood. Lunchtime they serve a salmon burger and other fish and seafood dishes, as well as a charcuterie board or roasted corn and bell pepper soup. For dinner there are tasty traditional items like Atlantic scallops, pork ribeye, and seafood fettuccine along with NY strip steak. And while you're eating, enjoy the views of the lake through large windows or from the patio. $–$$ 43 Lakefront Dr., Geneva 14456; 315-789-0400; www.genevaramada.com

Pinky's Restaurant is not fancy—just a longtime favorite among locals, with a jukebox in the corner. The menu includes everything from soup to nuts, along with great onion rings, homemade pasta sauces, and wine. $ 14 Castle St., Geneva 14456; 315-789-9753

WINERY AND BREWERY RESTAURANTS Bring in your old LPs and ask them to be played on the turntable at **Lake Drum Brewery**, a small-batch brewery, cidery, and coffeehouse in downtown Geneva. Check out the news on the chalk-board, settle into one of the couches, and munch on popcorn. It's all goodwill and hugs wrapped in a small package, plus a very cool vibe. $$ 16 E. Castle St., Geneva 14456; 315-789-1200; www.lakedrumbrewing.com

Lake Street Station Winery occupies a former Texaco gas station, where patrons can still fill up—we're talking glasses and tummies, not cars. Their wines are created from a collaboration with Hazlitt and Three Brothers Wineries, while their food is hearty pub-style. Look for live music weekends. $$ 41 Lake St., Geneva 14456; 315-325-4089; www.lakestreetwine.com

For a robust lineup of wine and beer also check out **Microclimate**, **Naked Dove Brewing Company**, **OPUS Espresso & Wine Bar**, and **Billsboro Winery** on NY Rt. 14, housed in a rustic barn.

LAKE VIEWS On NY Rts. 20 and 5, **Abigail's Restaurant** is a modern, casual restaurant, offering a large menu for lunch and dinner. In the warmer months you can dine on their deck overlooking the Cayuga-Seneca Canal—some patrons arrive by boat via the canal. An all-you-can-eat deli bar buffet is reasonably priced, and dinner choices include several Italian specialties. $–$$ 1978 NY Rts. 5 and 20, Waterloo 13165; 315-539-9300; www.abigailsrestaurant.com

Ports Café is often recommended as a good place to eat by area bed-and-breakfasts. Ports specializes in cooked-to-order food, fresh seafood, grilled meats, and local produce and cheese, as well as Finger Lakes micro beer and wines by the glass. $–$$ 4432 W. Lake Rd., Geneva 14456; 315-789-2020; www.portscafeny.com

The Crow's Nest next to the Seneca Marina serves seafood and fish, along with burgers and other sandwiches. Eat by the water or inside. $–$$ 415 Booty Hill Rd., Geneva 14456; 315-781-0600

Also see: **Belhurst, Geneva on the Lake, Pier House Restaurant**

DIM SUM The Lin family's **Tea Shop and Dim Sum Restaurant** specializes in teas and Chinese food. The Lins also grow tea on-site and offer exotic teas including scented, wild, oolong, red, black, and white tea. Order items like egg rolls, steamed soybeans, Chinese pizza, steamed and fried dumplings, and other specialties. $–$$ 678 NY Rt. 318, Waterloo 13165; 315-856-8031; www.fingerlakestea.com

QUICK BITE **Cams Pizzeria** tosses out creative thin-crusted pizzas, super subs, Buffalo wings, calzones, and sausage rolls. It's a winner. $–$$ 476 Exchange St., Geneva 14456; 315-789-6297

Char Burrito Bar is minimalist in style but expansive in its southwestern fare, with made-to-order burritos. $–$$ 68 Castle St., Geneva 14456; 315-840-0591

Uncle Joe's Pizzeria occupies a classic old train station, and its pizzas, like the double-decker originals, are on track with locals. $–$$ 99 N. Genesee St., Geneva 14456; 315-781-1199; www.unclejoesgeneva.com

✳ To See

ARCHITECTURE For an overview of the many interesting buildings in Geneva, take a **self-guided walking tour** of S. Main St. organized by the **Geneva Historical Society**. It starts at 380 S. Main, an 1832 Greek Revival originally built as a church. Each house of interest is described in the brochure, including the Smith Opera House and Williamson House, an elegant Federal home. The S. Main Historic District has often been compared to Charleston, South Carolina, because of its stately Federal-style row houses. Stop by the Geneva History Museum to get a copy of the tour. 543 S. Main St., Geneva 14456; 315-789-5151; www.genevahistoricalsociety.com

MUSEUMS, EXHIBITS, AND HISTORIC SITES **The Cracker Factory**, a nineteenth-century three-story brick industrial building, has been repurposed to house the Mills & May Furniture Works as well as the dwelling for the building's creative owners. The second floor is home to a letterpress studio, an apartment, and spaces for fun events and weddings. Unique features include exposed brick walls and high ceilings. 35 Lehigh St., Geneva 14456; 315-789-1226

Geneva History Museum, headquarters for the Geneva Historical Society, is in an 1829 Federal-style house with four period rooms and regularly changing exhibitions, as well as collections of furniture, decorative arts, and period clothing. The museum shop sells local history publications and gift items. 543 S. Main St., Geneva 14456; 315-789-5151; www.genevahistoricalsociety.com

Mike Weaver Drain Tile Museum in the restored 1821 John Johnston farmhouse on NY Rt. 96A in Geneva contains more than 500 drain tiles ranging in date from 500 B.C. to plastic tiles of recent times. 3523 E. Lake Rd., Geneva 14456; 315-789-3848

WINE & BEER TASTING TOUR

Start: Geneva

Stay: Ramada Geneva Lakefront (see listing in Geneva)

Travel: South on NY Rt. 14 down west side of lake to Watkins Glen

1st Stop: Situated in a nineteenth-century barn, **Billsboro Winery** invites you to taste dry classical European varietals. If you are lucky you'll be there for a special occasion like Pizza on the Patio night. 315-789-9538; www.billsborowinery.com

Optional: Stop at **Weaver-View Farm Country Store** in an 1850's restored barn. The Weavers, a horse and buggy Mennonite family with seven children, have been working diligently since they bought the farm in 2012 to restore the property. The store features a variety of Amish- and Mennonite-made goods, from quilts and gifts to jams and jellies. (See "Gifts" in the Geneva section)

2nd Stop: Fox Run Vineyards offers tastings and tours showcasing their award-winning wines such as riesling, pinot noir, chardonnay, cabernet sauvignon, cabernet franc, merlot, gewürztraminer, reserve chardonnay, rosé and reserve pinot noir. Try their semidry blush, Arctic Fox, and port. President and co-owner Scott Osborn presides over a lovely barn with a deck overlooking the lake, a large wine-tasting area, a gift shop, a café, and wine tours. 315-536-4616, 800-636-9786; www.foxrunvineyards.com

Note: If you are interested in seeing a LEED (Leadership in Energy and Environmental Design)-certified winery where environmentally sustainable wine-growing practices are followed, stop next at **Red Tail Ridge Winery** just down the road. 315-536-4580; www.redtailridgewinery.com

3rd Stop: Anthony Road Wine Company, Penn Yan, features a Martini-Reinhardt selection, chardonnay, riesling, cabernet franc, pinot gris, and late-harvest vignoles; blends include a Tony's series and Devonian white or red. Wine tasting is in an attractive building with a good view of the lake. 315-536-2182, 800-559-2182, www.anthonyroadwine.com

4th Stop: Climbing Bines Hop Farm & Brewery (See "Sampling the Breweries" in What's Where in the Finger Lakes)

Peter Whitmer Log Home in Waterloo, a reconstructed 1810 log home, was the birthplace of the Church of Jesus Christ of Latter-day Saints in 1830. 1451 Aunskt Rd., Waterloo 13165; 315-539-2552; www.hillcumorah.com

If you happen to be boating on the lake, you'll see the impressive white-pillared The **Rose Hill Mansion** on the eastern shore. Built in 1839, this stately 24-room Greek Revival mansion is furnished in the Empire style and is one of America's most distinguished examples of the period. 3373 NY Rt. 96A, Geneva 14456; 315-789-3848; www.genevahistoricalsociety.com

THEATER The **Smith Opera House**, an ornate structure built in 1894, still operates today as a performing arts venue featuring dance, theater, music, and films. The

5TH STOP: Earle Estates Meadery is a large retail store and wine-tasting facility with its own beehives and honey. Owners John and Esther Earle are known for their honey and fruit-influenced wines such as Pear-Mead, Peach Perfection, Cherry Charisma, Raspberry Reflections, and Strawberry Shadows as well as a light, fruity chardonnay, riesling, Cayuga White, and seyval blanc. The wine bottles alone are worth the price. Ask to try Big Jake Worthog Spiced Hard Cider. It's a kick. The family also owns the **Torrey Ridge Winery** down the road, certainly worth a stop. 607-243-9011; www.meadery.com

6TH STOP: Miles Wine Cellars, accessible by car and boat, arguably has one of the most serene settings on the lake. Savor estate wine and try their new Ghost wine, a blend of chardonnay and Cayuga in honor of the "spirits" that are said to reside in the house—ask about the stories that swirl around these legends. If you are ready to call it a day, check into the **Inn at Miles Wine Cellars** with three beautifully furnished rooms. 607-243-7742; www.mileswinecellars.com

7TH STOP (overnight, wine tour and dinner): Glenora Wine Cellars, Dundee, has a first-rate inn, winery, and restaurant set amid the vineyards. Taste their riesling, chardonnay, barrel-fermented chardonnay, merlot, cabernet sauvignon, cabernet franc, blanc de blancs,

and French-American hybrid wines such as Cayuga White and seyval blanc. Glenora also produces several fruit wines and a fine brut sparkling wine. Both the dining room of **Verai-sons Restaurant** and the guest rooms overlook the lake and vineyards. Some of the guest rooms have whirlpool tubs for two and fireplaces while all rooms have patios. 607-243-5511, 800-243-5513; www .glenora.com (See listing for the inn in the Seneca Lake West Side section)

GLENORA WINE CELLARS, DUNDEE

interior was renovated in 1931 in the Baroque style. Many famous musicians have performed here, including Itzhak Perlman, who praised its magnificent acoustics. 82 Seneca St., Geneva 14456; 315-781-LIVE; www.thesmith.org

EDUCATION **Hobart and William Smith Colleges**, two four-year institutions, provide programs in the liberal arts and sciences, enrolling approximately 1,900 students. The two colleges share a common curriculum and some facilities, but each awards its own degree and has its own dean, admissions office, student government, and athletic programs. Hobart for men was founded in 1822; William Smith for women, in 1908. The focal point for the campus, Coxe Hall, a grand Jacobean-style building, houses the administration and Bartlett Theatre. 300 Pulteney St., Geneva 14456; 315-781-3000; www.hws.edu

✳ Shopping

ANTIQUES **Geneva Antique Co-op** is like one huge garage sale chock-full of every-thing from vintage fur coats and old photos to antique furniture, glassware, and books. 475 Exchange St., Geneva 14456; 315-789-5100; www.geneva-antique-coop.com

16 Rose Hill Antique Consignment Shop, Geneva, sells fine antiques and collect-ibles on the grounds of Rose Hill Mansion. NY Rt. 96A, Geneva 14456; 315-789-5915

FACTORY OUTLET **Waterloo Premium Outlets** is a huge complex of factory outlets selling clothes, cosmetics, entertainment, food, home furnishings, housewares, jew-elry, luggage, shoes, and specialty items. NY Rt. 318 between exits 41 & 42 off the NY State Thruway, Waterloo 13165; 315-539-1100; www.premiumoutlets.com

FARMERS' MARKETS **Geneva Area Farmers' Market** sells local produce including fruits and vegetables, breads, and flowers (Thursdays in season). 666 S. Exchange St., Geneva 14456; 315-789-5005

J Minn's Farms features fruits and vegetables with sweet corn, cabbage, cauli-flower, broccoli, and brussels sprouts. NY Rt. 14A, between Geneva and Hall, Geneva 14456; 585-526-6944

Red Jacket Orchards one mile west of Geneva is a large operation owned by the Nicholson family for three generations. More than 450 acres are in fruit produc-tion with several varieties of apples, strawberries, sweet cherries, prunes, plums, and apricots. Products for sale include cider, fruit butters, relishes, chili sauces, honey, cheeses, jams, and jellies. In the Fruit Cellar you can select your own fruit and often taste the different kinds as well. Pick your own strawberries and cherries in season. 957 NY Rts. 5 and 20, Geneva 14456; 315-781-2749, 800-828-9410; www .redjacketorchards.com

GIFTS **Earthly Possessions** carries lots of unique gifts, such as scented candles, handcrafted jewelry, bath products, and other items. 70 Seneca St., Geneva 14456; 315-781-1078

Mary Ann's Treasures has all kinds of "treasures," from Boyd's Bears, dolls, and handmade quilts to candles, crafts, and seasonal gifts. 209 W. Main St., Waterloo 13165; 315-539-3889

Stomping Grounds has just about everything you could think of, from gifts and antiques to books, prints, and memorabilia. 22 Castle St., Geneva 14456; 315-789-1000; www.stompinggrounds.com

Weaver-View Farms Amish Country Store 8 miles south of Geneva, in a classic 1850s barn on an 85-acre working farm, is a wonderful repository of Amish/Mennonite quilts and handcrafted gifts. Also ask about their historic farmhouse rental. 386 NY Rt. 14, Penn Yan 14527; 315-781-2571; www.weaverviewfarms.com

Watkins Glen

In 1948 the green flag waved the start of world-class motor racing in Watkins Glen at the southern end of Seneca Lake. In those days, the cars raced along village streets and hillsides. Now the thunder of Grand Prix auto racing has moved to its own course, but you can use a self-guided tour map to trace the route the racers used to follow. On the hills overlooking the town, **Watkins Glen International Speedway** is the site of several

THE RACES ARE ON AT WATKINS GLEN INTERNATIONAL SPEEEDWAY

major racing weekends a year, including NASCAR events and the U.S. Vintage Grand Prix. 607-535-2486, 800-461-RACE.

Watkins Glen is a small lakeside village with a narrow main street, a fine lakeside hotel, and an attractive wide-board pier stretching into the harbor. Each summer outdoor concerts are held in the park.

✳ Lodging

When the races are on, demand for places to stay revs up. In addition to basic motel-style lodging like the no-nonsense **Glen Motor Inn** that overlooks the lake (www .glenmotorinn.com), there is the handsome waterfront Watkins Glen Harbor Hotel as well as several B&Bs and small inns.

HARBOR SIDE The Nantucket-style **Watkins Glen Harbor Hotel** hugs the waterfront. The pier and marina are right out the back door. It is the best place to stay in the area if you're looking for an upscale hotel with all modern amenities and facilities. Decorated in soft, muted blues, grays, greens, and neutrals, rooms come with pillow-top mattresses, high-thread-count linens, duvets, and feather

THE WATKINS GLEN HARBOR HOTEL HUGS THE LAKESHORE

pillows. There is a state-of-the-art fitness center, indoor heated pool, HD flat screen TVs, WiFi, and three places to eat and drink including The Blue Pointe Grille, Coldwater Bar, and the patio. 16 N. Franklin St., Watkins Glen 14891; 607-535-6116; www .watkinsglenharborhotel.com

B&BS A beautifully decorated 1830s Greek Revival historic home in Watkins Glen combined with gracious hospitality from hosts David and Brian make for a very pleasant stay for those who choose **The Blackberry Inn Bed & Breakfast**. One bedroom has an en-suite bath, while the other two bedrooms share a hall bathroom. $$$ 209 6th St., Watkins Glen 14891; 607-535-2300; www.theblackberryinnbb.com

Cherry Orchard is set in—no surprise here—an orchard and vineyard just north of Watkins Glen while **Barnstormer Winery** is right next door. Although the house dates back more than a hundred years, extensive modernizing and additions make it more contemporary. Two of the four guest rooms have cathedral ceilings, and there is a very large great room. An attractive stone spa accommodates nine people, and there is an exercise room. A full breakfast is served. $$ 4194 NY Rt. 14, Rock Stream 14878; 607-535-7785; www.cherryorchard.com

In Watkins Glen, **Echoes of the Glen**, an English Tudor-style home is within walking distance of everything in town. There are five rooms with television/DVD, high-speed Internet, and private baths. A complete breakfast is served. $–$$ 300 S. Franklin St., Watkins Glen 14891; 607-535-2896; www.echoesoftheglen.com

THE FOX AND THE GRAPES IS JUST NORTH OF WATKINS GLEN

The Fox and the Grapes sits above Seneca Lake where porches provide plenty of places to relax and enjoy the views. Minutes from Wagner Vineyards and other wineries, the B&B is ideally located. All rooms have private baths, air-conditioning, and ceiling fans, and the great room has a fireplace. A full breakfast is served, and gluten-free items are available with advance notice. $$–$$$ 9496 NY Rt. 414, Lodi 14860; 607-582-7528; www.thefoxandthegrapes.com

The 18-room Victorian mansion **Idlwilde Inn** is a pretty impressive place, with lake views, sunrooms, a grand staircase, a cupola room, and gardens. The 10 guest rooms in the main house and carriage house range from simple and small to grand and spacious with a walk-out deck. Relax on the huge wraparound porch and have breakfast in the sunny dining room. $$–$$$ 1 Lakeview Ave., Watkins Glen 14891; 607-535-3081; www.idlwildeinn.com

Lake House B&B is all about unwinding in the country. This restored hundred-year-plus farmhouse overlooking the lake has four guest rooms, two with private baths, and furnishings include oriental carpets and some Victorian pieces. There's a big old front porch where you can start the day with a cup of coffee and home-baked breads before digging into a sumptuous breakfast. Another guest accommodation is located in a two-story lake cottage that sleeps six in season. A quarter mile away is a beach where you can kayak. $$ 46 Hunt Rd., Rock Stream 14878; 607-243-5637; www.thelakehouseonseneca.com

A special hideaway with lots of charm, the **Manor Bed & Breakfast at Castel Grisch** is tucked into a garden enclave adjacent to **Castel Grisch Winery**. European in style with an octagonal tower and a brick-and-timber exterior, it offers unending views of vineyards and countryside. Castel Grisch has four rooms and suites, an enclosed spa garden room with a hot tub, and a sitting room with a large fireplace, satellite television, and an honor bar. A full breakfast is served. $$–$$$ 3390 Cty. Rd. 28, Watkins Glen 14891; 607-535-9614; www.castelgrisch.com

The Marmalade Cat B&B, with its wraparound porch and English country décor, is furnished with family antiques from across the pond. Located in the heart of Watkins Glen, there are three guest rooms with private baths. And yes, there is a marmalade cat in residence. Breakfast is served, and a full English breakfast is available on request. $$–$$$ 400 E. 4th St., Watkins Glen 14891; 607-398-9020; www.thefoxandthegrapes.com

Hudson Manor B&B, one of the oldest houses in town (1890s), is an immaculate, grand Victorian in a quiet lakeview setting. It has wide pumpkin-pine floors, vintage furniture (many antique pieces), a sitting room with a fireplace, a guest kitchen, and a lighted gazebo. A 65-foot wraparound porch, a large deck, and extensive gardens promise lots of ways to enjoy the outdoors. Five guest rooms have private baths and king rooms have private decks and views of the water. $$–$$$ 104 Seneca St., Watkins Glen 14891; 607-535-5333

Sunset on Seneca Bed & Breakfast is a spacious old lake home directly on a private waterfront in Burdett just east of Watkins Glen. There are three guest rooms with Select Comfort mattresses, private baths, TVs, and free WiFi—even robes. A large, lofty great room, dining room, enclosed porch, and deck all look out to the lake, where there is a substantial dock—a perfect perch for fishing or sunning. $$–$$$ 3221 NY Rt. 414, Burdett 14818; 607-535-6973; www.sunsetonseneca.com

COTTAGE **Arms at the Glen** on Watkins Glen's main street is a modest-size cottage with three bedrooms. It has a great deal of charm with leaded windows, a fireplace, and antiques. $$ 330 S. Franklin St., Watkins Glen 14891; 607-569-3039; www.armsattheglen.com

✷ Dining Out

Seneca Harbor Station, a restored nineteenth-century train station with its 16-foot fanned ceilings, mahogany bar, spiral staircase, and original hardwood floors, is located on the water next to the public fishing pier. The restaurant has a dining deck, large bar, and inside dining rooms with expansive windows looking out to the lake. The ambiance is nautical, and the menu includes items like clam chowder, crab cakes, fisherman's salad, lobster pasta, "boatman's grilled meats," burgers, "sailor sides," and "sweet-water desserts" like Harbor Raspberry Bongo. $–$$ 3 N. Franklin St., Watkins Glen 14891; 607-535-6101; www.senecaharborstation.com

CASUAL FARE For more than 50 years, **Curly's Family Restaurant** has been treating its patrons to some good old down-home cooking. Try their fish dinners, Italian specialties, Texas hot sandwiches, and homemade soups. Located between Watkins Glen and Montour Falls, this is a good place to bring Mom, Dad, and the kids. $–$$ 2780 NY Rt. 14, Watkins Glen 14891; 607-535-4383; www.curlysfamilyrestaurant.com

For locally brewed craft ales and robust pub food along with live entertainment, try the **Crooked Rooster Brew Pub** and **Wildflower Café,** two restaurants side by side with the same menu and kitchen. Love their snack cones, fries, and fried jalapeños, and their Rooster Pie pizza accompanied by Hop Warrior Imperial or Firehouse Blonde Ale. $–$$ 223-301 N. Franklin St., Watkins Glen 14891; 607-535-9797; www.roosterfishbrewing.com

Village Marina Bar & Grill at the Village Marina Seneca Harbor is a good place to enjoy a glass of wine and a sandwich on the deck by the water. $–$$ 2 Seneca Harbor, Watkins Glen 14891; 607-535-7910

Also try the **Heavily Brewing Company** (see "Sampling the Breweries" in What's Where in the Finger Lakes) and **Montour Coffee House & Wine Bar** in Montour Falls south of Watkins Glen, 607-621-7247

QUICK BITE **Classic Chef's** on State Rt. 14 in Montour Falls is one of those good old-fashioned diners serving everything from short orders to complete dinners. 380 N. Catherine St., Montour Falls 14865; 607-535-9975;

Seneca Lodge by the south entrance to the Watkins Glen State Park sells homemade breads, soups, and other freshly made dishes, and has a nice salad bar. 3600 Walnut Rd., Watkins Glen 14891; 607-535-2014

✷ To See

International Motor Raceway Center: 610 S. Decatur St., Watkins Glen 14891; 607-535-9044; www.racingarchives.org

Schuyler County Historical Museum in Montour Falls is housed in an early nineteenth-century building. 108 N. Catherine St., Montour Falls 14865; 607-535-9741

✷ Shopping

ANTIQUES If you walk along N. Franklin St., the main drag in Watkins Glen, you are certain to pass antique shops chock full of intriguing items. Stop at **O'Shaughnessy Antiques, Country Haven Treasures,** the **Putty Jug,** and **Yesterday.**

THE CROOKED ROOSTER BREW PUB

TJ Antiques has been selling high-quality antiques and nostalgic items for three generations. Bikes for two, art, green metal chairs, Victorian sofas, architectural pieces, and many other treasures including handcrafted furniture can be found in TJ's large retail facility. 4031 NY Rt. 14A, Reading Center 14876; 607-535-4588; www.tjantiques.com

THE ARTS **Joyful Adornments** is a glass studio and gift gallery. Find beads, buttons, and jewelry made from handcrafted glass as well as recycled wine bottle jewelry made from your special event wine bottle so you can "wear a memory." 534 Church St., Odessa 14869; 800-517-6440; www.joyfuladornments.com

O'Susannah's Quilts, named one of the top quilt shops in the country by *Better Homes & Gardens* sells a huge range of quilting materials and hosts quilting retreats and classes. There is also The Upstairs Inn for those coming here who want to stay overnight. 111 W. 4th St., Watkins Glen 14891; 607-535-6550; www.osusannahsquiltshop.com

Quintus Gallery, a strikingly beautiful building perched on the shores of Seneca Lake, features work by top contemporary artists. This exceptional venue is available for events. 85 Salt Point Rd., Watkins Glen 14891; 315-527-4263; www.quintusgallery.com

FACTORY OUTLET **Famous Brands** contains three floors of merchandise and close to 20 brands selling discounted items. Famous brands include Merrell, AmeriBag, Carhartt, Duofold, and other brands. 412 Franklin St., Watkins Glen 14891; 607-535-4952; www.famousbrandsoutlet.com

GIFTS **Skyland Farm Craft Gallery** features exceptional craft items from more than 150 regional craftspeople. 4966 NY Rt. 414, Burdett 14818; 607-546-5050

Seneca Lake West Side

✽ Lodging

Heading north from Watkins Glen, whether you're checking out the vineyards or just enjoying the ride, here are some nice places to spend the night.

Enormous barrels announce the entrance to **The Inn at Glenora Wine Cellars**. Set into a hillside overlooking the lake and surrounded by vineyard, this California, redwood-style

ITINERARIES

#1 ENERGY CHARGED

• Start: **Watkins Glen State Park**, NY Rt. 14 Voted one of the top three state parks in the country by *USA Today* readers, Watkins Glen State Park treats you to a breathtaking walk of cliffs and waterfalls winding through a deep chasm. Within two miles, the water descends 400 feet past 200-foot cliffs, generating 19 waterfalls along its course. Cost: $8 per car or park on the street and get in free.

• Mid-morning snack: **Glen Mountain Market** where you can land a delicious iced coffee and deli sandwich to gear up for the rest of your day.

• Board the schooner *True Love* that has sailed the Caribbean waters of St. Thomas since the 1950s and was featured in the 1956 movie *High Society* with Grace Kelly, Bing Crosby, and Frank Sinatra. Today owned by Schooner Excursions, she is available for charter and day sails. www.schoonerexcursons.com

• Adrenaline fans: start your engines at **Watkins Glen International**. Find out what it feels like to drive this storied road course while piloting your personal vehicle [sorry, no motorcycles] around the 3.4-mile Grand Prix circuit behind a paced vehicle. After two laps, your guide will stop at the start/finish line . . . it's picture time! www.theglen.com

• Check into the **Watkins Glen Harbor Hotel** and relax with dinner on the patio or in the Blue Pointe Grille. Afterward sit by the fire pit alongside the water or take a moonlight trail ride at **Painted Bar Stables**. www.paintedbarstables.com

#2 OUTDOOR ENTHUSIASTS

• Morning coffee and treats at **The Village Bakery** in Montour Falls—it's where the locals go.

• See some waterfalls: Take the path to a gushing waterfall in **Havana Glen Park**, then drive to **She-Qua-Ga Falls** in downtown Montour Falls and then to **Aunt Sarah's Falls**, on the northern edge of Montour Falls.

inn with its expansive windows and high ceilings has a tidy, light, open feeling. All rooms have private balconies or patios, and some have a fireplace and whirlpool tub. The winery operation is just up the hill, while the views from the Veraisons Restaurant are spectacular. $–$$ 5435 NY Rt. 14, Dundee 14837; 800-243-5513; www.glenora.com

The Federal-style **1819 Red Brick Inn B&B** in Dundee, located on eight peaceful countryside acres with a pond, has five guest rooms with private baths. An extensive continental breakfast is offered. $$ 2081 NY Rt. 230, Dundee 14837; 607-243-8844; www.1819inn.com

The **Pearl of Seneca Lake B&B**, on the lake in Dundee, is a neat home with four guest rooms with private baths plus WiFi, air conditioning, pillow-top mattresses, and satellite TV. One room is handicapped accessible; another has extra beds. Grounds go right to the lake, where there is a beach, hammock, rowboat, canoe, dock, screen house with picnic table and fire pit. There is also an eight-foot-wide trail through the woods. A full breakfast is included. 4827 Red Cedar Ln., Dundee 14837; 800-50-PEARL; www .thepearlofsenecalake.com

The **South Glenora Tree Farm**, with two converted barns on a 42-acre tree farm, is perfect for those who love nature, the outdoors, and space—the great room is great, great. There are five guest rooms with private baths, some with fireplaces. The main

• Hike in the **Finger Lakes National Forest**.

• Grab a light pub lunch at the waterfront **Village Marina Bar & Grill**. www.village-marina.com

• Experience a 15-mile vista atop the region's only remaining fire tower at **Sugar Hill State Forest**.

• Cool off with a fishing charter or guided paddle on Seneca Lake with **Summit to Stream Adventures**. www.summittostream.com

#3 SEE AND SAVOR

Day 1

• Follow the **Seneca Lake Wine Trail** and visit some of the more than 40 wineries and breweries such as the **Grist Iron Brewing**, **Heavily Brewing Company**, and **Rooster Fish Brewing Company**. Sample lagers, pale ales, stouts, and more on the Finger Lakes Beer Trail.

• Take a lake cruise on Captain Bill's ***Stroller IV*** or cruise and dine aboard Captain Bill's ***Seneca Legacy***.

Day 2

• Visit the **International Motor Racing Research Center** and learn about the history of racing and early ties to Watkins Glen.

• Tour the barns and savor cheeses at **Sunset View Creamery** on Hoffman's Dairy, a century-old farm outside Odessa, 15 miles south of Watkins Glen. The cheese is made from milk from the dairy's own herds. www.sunsetviewcreamery.com

• Stop at the region's first craft distillery, **Finger Lake Distilling**, and taste their flavored vodkas, whiskies, and liqueurs.

• Browse stunning local and regional contemporary art at the **Quintus Gallery**. www.quintusgallery.com

barn has four guest rooms, while the fifth, a two-room suite, is in a former calf barn. Wraparound porches are great for reading or snoozing. $$ 546 S. Glenora Rd., Dundee 14837; 607-243-7414; www.treefarmbb.com

Weaver-View Farms' Farmhouse on NY Rt. 14 was built in 1900 and is now owned by a local Mennonite family. This is a large house with six to eight bedrooms and three baths. Beds are dressed in lovely quilts, porches overlook the lake, rooms are furnished with fine wood pieces, and the house has beautiful oak floors, large windows, and a great kitchen. If you must have a TV, go somewhere else, but if it's peace and tranquility you crave, this is the place. Rent the entire house or a room. Also note weddings can be performed in their barn and the wedding party can stay in the farmhouse. 386 NY Rt. 14, Penn Yan 14527; 315-781-2571

✲ To See

All the Fun of 1901 . . . How Grandpa Had Fun is played out on weekends all summer long at **The Old Havana Courthouse Theatre** located south of Watkins Glen in Montour Falls. 408 W. Main St., Montour Falls 14865; 607-742-0850; www.oldhavanatheatre.com

WINE & BEER TASTING TOUR

Start: Watkins Glen

Travel: North on NY Rt. 414 to Ovid; then pick up Rt. 96A to Geneva

1st Stop: Finger Lakes Distilling in Burdett (See "Distilleries" in What's Where in the Finger Lakes)

2nd Stop: Two Goats Brewing in Burdett (See "Sampling the Breweries" in What's Where in the Finger Lakes)

3rd Stop: Atwater Estate Vineyards, Burdett, occupies a 1930s barn, which is now the tasting room for Atwater's rieslings, cabernet franc, pinot noir, chardonnay, and a sparkling wine as well as dessert wines. Views of Seneca Lake from the tasting room and deck are stunning. There is a small gift shop and picnic tables. 800-331-7323, 607-546-8463; www.atwatervineyards.com

***Optional lunch Stop:* Stone Cat Café** in Hector—perhaps catch the Sunday jazz brunch. 607-546-5000; www.stonecatcafe.com. Or if you are finished for the day, savor a meal at Suzanne Fine Regional Cuisine for an exceptional dining experience or Dano's Heuriger. (See Seneca Lake East Side)

4th Stop: Red Newt Cellar Winery and Bistro, Hector, is another good place for lunch at the Bistro, housed in a chalet-style building where you can eat inside or out on the deck. Taste their riesling, gewürztraminer, pinot gris, and dry rosé as well as cabernet franc, merlot, cabernet sauvignon, and syrah. (See "Casual Fare" in Seneca Lake East Side)

5th Stop: Hazlitt 1852 Vineyards, Hector, is a lively, friendly place run by a fun group of people. The Hazlitt family offers chardonnay, riesling, Schooner White, cabernet, merlot, pinot gris,

WAGNER VINEYARDS OVERLOOK SENECA LAKE

LAMOREAUX LANDING WINE CELLARS, LODI

White Cat, and Red Cat, a blend of catawba and baco noir. The winery is in a wonderful rustic barn filled with antiques and memorabilia. Tasting takes place around two U-shaped bars, and there is a gift shop. 607-546-WINE, 888-750-0494; www.hazlitt1852.com

6TH STOP: Wagner Vineyards & Wagner Valley Brewing Company, Lodi, is one of the largest operations in the Finger Lakes and a huge producer of riesling. Located in a striking octagonal building in the 250-acre vineyard there is also a 20-barrel German-style brewery. Featured wines are chardonnay, gewürztraminer, riesling, cabernet franc, cabernet sauvignon, merlot, and pinot noir as well as sparkling wines and ice wines. Have lunch in the **Ginny Lee** café overlooking the lake and vineyards (see "Casual Fare" in Seneca Lake East Side) and join in the fun summertime on the Brewdeck Friday nights for live music. 607-582-6450, 866-924-6378; www.wagnervineyards.com, www.wagnerbrewing.com

7TH STOP: Lamoreaux Landing Wine Cellars, Lodi, targets the ultra-premium market and produces a full-bodied pinot noir, as well as chardonnay, gewürztraminer, riesling, merlot, cabernet franc, and brut. Blends include Estate White and Estate Red. Lamoreaux's wines have received many awards. The winery and its tasting room, a handsome building with four square columns resembling a modern version of a Greek temple, is set on 130 acres overlooking the lake. Picnic tables are available. 607-582-6011; www.lamoreauxwine.com

8TH STOP: Three Brothers Winery & Estate, Geneva, combines three extraordinary wineries and a microbrewery—Stony Lonesome Wine Cellars, where you find serious vinifera wines; Bagg Dare Wine Company, (a really fun place to linger); Passion Feet Wine Barn (where you can sip a wine slushy); and War Horse Brewing Company. War Horse produces an array of handcrafted microbrew and homemade root beer as well as the world's first riesling ale, a combo of riesling and an American wheat beer. Also try their seasonal beer like raspberry wheat ale and ciders. Each tasting room offers a fun experience. Trust us. 315-585-4432; www.3brotherswinery.com

9TH STOP: Ventosa Vineyards Estate Winery in Geneva is showcased in a Tuscan-style building with a terrace overlooking Seneca Lake. Try their pinot noir, lemberger, cabernet franc, cabernet sauvignon, syrah, merlot, pinot grigio, rieslings, chardonnay, sanglovese, and Tocai Friulano. The large restaurant is open for lunch, and their LaVista é Bella Room can accommodate up to 350 guests. 315-719-0000; www.ventosavineyards.com

DINE: Port's Café or **Halsey's Restaurant** (See Geneva)

OVERNIGHT: Ramada Geneva Lakefront or one of the local B&Bs (See Geneva)

The **Robert Ingersoll Museum** in Dresden is the birthplace of the famous nineteenth-century orator, writer, and a founder of the Stanford & Woodstock Art Communities. See local history exhibits and artifacts. 61 Main St., Dresden 14441; 315-536-1074; www.rgimuseum.org

Drive the Glen tours through mid-July take you on three paced laps of the track where the pros race. 2790 Cty. Rt. 16, Watkins Glen 14891; 866-461-RACE; www.theglen.com

✳ Dining Out

Veraisons in Dundee (Glenora Wine Cellars) invites you to admire the view through large windows that look out to the lake while you enjoy your meal. They call their cuisine "regional fusion," which translates to using the freshest of local produce combined with flavors and textures from around the world, along with wines. Find regional specialties like fresh fish, bison, and local fruits and vegetables. $–$$$ 5435 NY Rt. 14, Dundee 14837; 607-243-9500; www.glenora.com

CASUAL FARE If you love dogs and sausages, you have to stop at the **FLX Wienery** in Dundee, where all the toppings will blow you away and the meat is locally sourced. Here "gourmet wieners" is not an oxymoron—go "Whole Hog" and you'll get it. They have other things, too, like hamburgers and Korean BBQ. $–$$ 5090 NY Rt. 14, Dundee 14837; 607-243-7100; www.flxwienery.com

Seneca Lake East Side

✳ Lodging

The Inn at Chateau Lafayette Reneau, near the southern end of the lake, with 10 rooms, is a Craftsman-style farmhouse set on the grounds of the Chateau Lafayette Reneau Winery. Rooms are simply decorated yet stylish, and each has a view of the lake and/or vineyards. Rates include a full breakfast. $$ 5081 NY Rt. 414, Hector 14841; 607-546-2062; www.clrwine.com

The Inn at Grist Iron accommodates guests in a post-and-beam 1860s farmhouse and a rustic stone-and-cedar lodge with beautifully appointed suites and cottages, most rooms with views of Seneca Lake. On-site is a picnic pavilion, fire pit, stocked fishing pond, and the nearby Grist Iron Brewing Company. $$–$$$ 4880 NY Rt. 414, Burdett 14841; 607-546-4066; www.gristironbrewing.com

Magnolia Place, an 1830s pink farmhouse, is a gracious and beautiful place with eight guest suites. Air-conditioned guest rooms are on the first and second floors, and the second-story rooms open onto a lovely porch with great lake vistas. Three rooms have Jacuzzis, two have fireplaces, and the suite features a double Jacuzzi and a fireplace. $$–$$$ 5240 NY Rt. 414, Hector 14841; 607-546-5338; www.magnoliawelcome.com

The Red House Country Inn, a mid-1800s farmhouse in the Finger Lakes National Forest, has five guest rooms furnished with turn-of-the-century antiques. A full home cooked breakfast is served. $$ 4586 Picnic Area Rd., Burdett 14841; 607-546-8566; www.redhousecountryinn.com

A good deal for a group, the **Skyland Guest House** in Burdett sleeps 18 with six bedrooms, a teen tree loft, 2½ baths, a huge kitchen, outside dining areas, a barbecue, children's play areas, Seneca Lake views from most rooms, and pillow-top mattresses. 4966 NY Rt. 414, Burdett 14818; 607-423-0113; www.skylandguesthouse.com

Yale Manor, a vacation rental property at the northern end of the lake, sleeps 14 guests comfortably. The former manor house of a prosperous 365-acre farm (circa 1908), this stone estate home affords great views of the lake or countryside. There are 5½ baths, four of the seven bedrooms have fireplaces, and the master suite has a jetted tub. Walk down to the boathouse and swim off the private beach. The gourmet kitchen has a five-burner stove where you can prepare meals for family and friends. 563 Yale Farm Rd., Romulus 14541; 888-414-5253; www.yalemanor.com

✷ Dining Out

Come to **Dano's Heuriger** and be transported to another world, where you will be treated to a taste of European cuisine and hospitality. Acclaimed chef and owner Dano Hutnik, who lived and worked in Vienna for several years and has been a featured chef at the James Beard Foundation (among other honors), specializes in Austrian dishes like horseradish beet soup, homemade sausage, pork schnitzel, knodel, and sacher torte, while Karen Gilman Hutnik creates incredible desserts, Viennese-style. Accompany your meal with wines produced around Seneca Lake. Everything is ordered a la carte, so you may try as many items as you wish, and diners are encouraged to share. Located 15 miles north of Watkins Glen on the east side of Seneca Lake, Dano's sunlit dining room, gardens, and deck overlook the water. $$–$$$$ 9564 NY Rt. 414, Lodi 14860; 607-582-7555; www.danosonseneca.com

Suzanne Fine Regional Cuisine: With vegetables, herbs, fruits, and flowers growing in gardens, behind the restaurant, the freshness of the ingredients doesn't get any better. Set on the east side of Seneca Lake in Lodi, Suzanne offers views of the water from the tables on the porch or through expansive windows in the dining rooms. It's a beautiful setting for a perfect meal orchestrated by owners, Robert and Suzanne Stack, who serve dinner Thursday through Saturday. Cuisine is prepared from the freshest ingredients—from local farmers as well as from the Stack's gardens—while the artful presentations entice before you even pick up your fork. The set five-course menu changes with what is being harvested, and the tastes reflect the talent of Chef Suzanne. Best to call ahead for reservations. 9013 NY Rt. 414, Lodi 14860; 607-582-7545; www.suzannefrc.com

CASUAL FARE The **Ginny Lee at Wagner Vineyards** in Lodi serves lunch indoors or outdoors on the deck of Wagner Vineyards. 9322 NY Rt. 414, Lodi 14860; 607-582-6574; www.theginnylee.com

Red Newt Bistro located in Red Newt Cellars serves light lunches including soups and sandwiches. $–$$ 3675 Tichenor Rd., Hector 14841; 607-546-4100; www.rednewt .com

Stonecat Café is tucked between the southeastern shore of Seneca Lake and the Finger Lakes National Forest. The chef sources seasonal organic ingredients for creative cuisine like organic spinach and mushroom risotto and local, pasture-raised chicken grilled under a brick and served with the café's signature rhubarb BBQ sauce. On Sundays Stonecat is the scene for a great live jazz brunch. $–$$ 5315 NY Rt. 414, Hector 14841; 607-546-5000; www.stonecatcafe.com

SUZANNE FINE REGIONAL CUISINE DRAWS FROM ITS OWN GARDENS IN FOOD PREPARATION

✳ To See

The **Air Force Museum at Sampson** was established as a naval training station in 1942. It was here that more than 411,429 young men were taught to be sailors and then sent overseas to participate in World War II. This museum, created by the thousands of members of the Sampson WWII Navy Veterans organization, contains artifacts from the veterans, photos, porthole displays, guns, the ship's bell from FDR's presidential yacht Potomac, and other memorabilia. NY Rt. 96A, Romulus 14541; 585-6203, 800-357-1814; www.sampsonvets.com

✳ To Do

BIKING A bicycle path runs along both shores of the lake. The grade is gently rolling, and views are of the lake, fields, and farms.

Dresden/Dundee/Dresden Route: This 38.7-mile ride takes you along paved roads with some rolling hills. Start on Main St. in Dresden. Highlights are the Robert Ingersoll Museum, the wineries along the Seneca Wine Trail, FLX Wienery (for fabulous hot dogs), Dundee Historical Society, and the Windmill Farm & Craft Market (open Saturday). 800-868-9283

Geneva Skyline Loop: This 35.7-mile route is mostly paved, with some dirt roads. Start in Geneva. Highlights include Seneca Lake State Park, Smith Opera House, South Main Street Historic District, Geneva History Museum (where there are maps), Hobart and William Smith Colleges, and the NYS Agricultural Experiment Station Grounds. 877-FUN-IN-NY

BOATING **Captain Bill's Seneca Lake Cruises** are aboard the luxurious *Seneca Legacy*. Enjoy a full-course lunch or dinner aboard this vessel or a sightseeing cruise on the *Stroller IV*. 607-535-4541; www.senecaharborstation.com. Also glide across the lake with **Seneca Sailing Adventures**. 607-742-5100; www.senecasailingadventures.com

Finger Lakes Water Adventures at Stivers Seneca Marine offers cruises on Seneca Lake on the double-decker *Rose Lummis*, a 1953 Mississippi riverboat. 315-789-5520; www.stiversseneca marina.com

Schooner Excursions offers charter and day sails aboard the schooner *True Love*, which sails out of Seneca Harbor Park Pier in Watkins Glen, May through October. 607-535-5253; www.schoonerexcursions.com

MARINAS There are a number of marinas and launching areas around Seneca Lake. **A&B Marina**, Waterloo, is a full-service marina and campground, offering boat rentals, hoist, and dock installations, skis, kneeboards, and sales. 315-781-1755. **Barrett's Marine** on the Cayuga-Seneca Canal, Waterloo, offers a variety of launches, overnight slips, showers, restrooms, and repair services as well as a hydraulic hoist. 315-789-6605. **Roy's Marina**, 3 miles south of Geneva, is a full-service facility, with rentals, fishing boats, pontoon boats, hoists, launch, dockages, and storage. 315-789-3094. **Stivers Seneca Marine** in Waterloo on the Cayuga-Seneca Canal, off NY Rt. 96A, has a travel lift service, more than 75 boat slips, boat sales and repairs, and marine supplies. Stivers also rents paddle, fishing, and pontoon boats, kayaks, canoes, tubes and skis along with a four-bedroom/two-bath luxury houseboat. And don't miss their **Tiki Bar North** with live music on some nights. 315-789-5520. **Ervay's Marina** and the **Village Marina** are on the south end of the lake.

FISHING Seneca Lake provides excellent fishing grounds. For the latest fishing report, check with one of the local bait shops (such as Barry's Bait and Tackle, NY Rt. 5 and US 20, Waterloo, 315-539-5341).

Summit to Stream Adventures in Watkins Glen offers charter fishing, fly fishing, kayaking, and hiking. 607-535-2701; www.summittostream.com

GOLF Seneca Lake has a handful of golf courses open to the public where green fees are often less than the cart fees.

Big Oak Public Golf Course is a "Jekyll and Hyde" course with two completely different nines—the front wide open and fairly straightforward; the more dramatic newer back cut through trees and wetlands with water on six holes requiring some skillful target shooting. 33 Packwood Rd., Geneva 14456; 315-789-9419; www.bigoakgc.com

Silver Creek Golf Club is a scenic 18-hole public course with watered fairways, tees, and greens that attracts tournaments and outings. Their restaurant can seat up to 300 people. 1790 East River Rd., Waterloo 13165; 315-539-8076; www.silvercreekgc.com

Seneca Lake Country Club is across from the lake. NY Rt. 14 S., Geneva 14456; 315-789-4681

For a good warm-up try these nine-hole tracks: **Fox Run Golf Course** in Rock Stream, 607-535-4413; **Geneva Country Club** with good views of the lake, 315-789-8786; and **Watkins Glen Golf Course,** 607-535-2340

HORSEBACK RIDING **Painted Bar Stables** in Burdett near Watkins Glen offers year-round guided trail rides on beautiful trails ranging from simple to rugged terrain as well as lessons, leasing, boarding, and opportunities to facilitate dream realization and lifelong relationships between people. 4093 Lake St., Burdett 14818; 607-216-8141; www.paintedbarstables.com

PARKS, NATURE PRESERVES, CAMPING, AND HIKING

NORTH SENECA LAKE

Lakeshore Park at the north end of the lake adjacent to the state park in Geneva is a pleasant, grassy park where you can stroll along the water and stop by the Chamber of Commerce to get area information. There are also boat slips and a dock. 607-546-9911

Back Achers in Himrod is a full-service camping facility right on the lake with cottages and campsites. 607-243-7926

THE TOWN PIER GIVES EASY ACCESS TO THE LAKE.

Spray Park in **Seneca Lake State Park**, Geneva, attracts families, with fountains you can run through to cool off, plus bike and walking paths, picnic areas, swimming facilities, boat launch, marina, and beach. 315-789-2331

Lodi Point State Marine Park off NY Rt. 414, east side of Lake Lodi, is a boat launch site with a picnic area and modest accommodations for boaters, picnickers, and anglers. 315-585-6392

Sampson State Park, Romulus, offers tent, trailer, and camping facilities as well as a marina, biking, and hiking. The Sampson World War II Navy Museum is also on the grounds. 315-585-6392

Also check the **Catharine Valley Trail**. www.parks.ny.gov/parks

SOUTH SENECA LAKE

Finger Lakes National Forest, a 16,000-acre woodland, has hiking, cross-country skiing, snowmobiling, horse trails, camping, fishing, hunting, berry picking, and bird-watching as well as primitive camping sites. The 12-mile Interlaken Trail runs along Parmenter Road, crosses the Finger Lakes National Forest from north to south, and passes through varied terrain. Southern portions are steeper and more wooded. On the way, stop at the Foster and Teeter Pond areas. 5218 NY Rt. 414, Hector 14841; 607-546-4470

Havana Glen Park and Campground, south of the lake in Montour Falls, has tent and trailer sites, hiking trails, shower and toilet facilities, playgrounds, and ball fields plus three pavilions for outings. A magnificent gorge is perfect for picnics and soaking up the beauty of the falls and surrounding countryside. 135 Havana Glen Rd., Montour Falls 14865; 607-535-9476

Municipal Campground and Marina in Montour Falls has 90 campsites, 190 boat slips, a public boat launch, picnic pavilions, playground, and ball fields. Boaters can access Seneca Lake through the Old Barge Canal. NY Rt. 14, Montour Falls 14865; 607-210-4124

Smith Park and Campground, off NY Rt 414 in Hector, is a 92-acre site along 2,000 feet of Seneca Lake shoreline with boat launching facilities, swimming, hiking trails, and more than 56 campsites.

Sugar Hill Recreation Area 7 miles west of Watkins Glen off Tower Hill Rd., a venue for big-time archery tournaments, covers about 9,085 acres and is laced with miles of trails for hiking, snowmobiling, biking, and horseback riding. Other facilities include campsites and shelters, picnic grounds, fishing areas, and wildflower fields. Climb the 75-foot fire tower to enjoy a 15-mile vista in all directions. 607-776-2165; www.dec.ny.gov

Warren W. Clute Memorial Park and Campground, Watkins Glen, has campsites, tennis, playground, swimming, a ball field, picnic facilities, a boat launch, and a lakeside pavilion. 421 E. 4th St., Watkins Glen 14891; 607-535-4438

Watkins Glen State Park and Gorge, one of the most beautiful parks in the Finger Lakes, is a deep rock-walled canyon with 19 waterfalls, many cascades, grottoes, and amphitheaters. There are picnic facilities, camping, an Olympic-size swimming pool, and nonstop views. www.nyfalls.com/watkinsglensp.html

FAMILY FUN Younger kids will give you a big high five when you take them to the **Adventure Playland at Amazeing Acres** in Hector. Here they can work their way through a 7,000-square-foot Hedge Maze, try out the paddleboats and kayaks on the pond, quiet their minds in the labyrinth (or at least parents can), and bike into the

CAN YOU HEAR THE LAKE DRUMS?

The Seneca believed they heard the low, distant booms of the drums of their ancestors, thought to be manifestations of evil spirits or divine messages from the god of thunder. Today these booms can sometimes be heard on very still evenings, but no one is sure just what causes them. Some think it's a result of gases building up from the lake bottom that create the noises as they escape.

Finger Lakes National Forest. Open May through October. 9799 Lodi Center Rd., Hector 14841; 607-592-5493; www.fingerlakesmaze.org

Animals are front and center at **Farm Sanctuary**, where tours are given on weekends. The farm, a shelter for animals, has cows, sheep, pigs, and other friendly creatures. Through pictures, videos, and materials, this organization strongly promotes protecting farm animals. 3150 Aikens Rd., Watkins Glen 14891; 607-583-2225; www.farmsanctuary.org

Seneca Grand Prix has a really fun miniature golf course. Hours vary; call ahead. 2374 NY Rt. 414, Watkins Glen 14891; 607-535-7223

Go horseback riding over hill and dale at **Painted Bar Stables** in Burdett. They also offer Adventure Days and camps, riding lessons, trail rides, and horse leases. www.paintedbarstables.com

Enjoy lunch, dinner, and sightseeing cruises as well as miniature golf located right outside Captain Bill's gift shop at **Captain Bill's Seneca Lake Cruises** in Watkins Glen. 607-535-4541; www.senecaharborstation.com

Get the gang together and spend a week in the roomy **Skyland Guest House** in Burdett while you explore the area. It sleeps 18 with six bedrooms and pullouts, has a 20' x 20' kitchen with a counter the size of a bowling alley, outside dining areas with barbecue and place for a bonfire, a children's play loft, Seneca Lake views from most rooms, pillow-top mattresses, and even a horse in the backyard. Skyland Farm has something to delight everyone in the family, from farm animals to a barn crammed with unusual handcrafted items, a fine arts gallery, and food products such as jams, jellies, and candies. 4966 NY Rt. 414, Burdett 14891; 607-546-5050; www.skylandfarm.net

Explore **Watkins Glen State Park and Gorge**, a deep rock-walled canyon with 19 waterfalls, many cascades, grottoes, and amphitheaters. There is an Olympic-size swimming pool, picnic facilities, camping, and nonstop views. 607-535-4511

Destination Farms provide great experiences for the entire family where you can do things like meet baby goats, forage for mushrooms, and learn how farm animals can be rescued and how cheese is made. Visit **Sunset View Creamery** in Odessa; **Lively Run Dairy** in Interlaken; **Shtayburne Farm** in Rock Stream (cheese); **Fulkerson Winery** in Dundee; and **Hawk Meadow Farm** in Dundee (mushrooms). www.watkinsglenchamber.com/farmtours

FOR MORE INFORMATION Geneva Area Chamber of Commerce: 315-789-1776; www.genevachamber.com

Ontario County/Finger Lakes Visitors Connection: 877-386-4669; www.visitfingerlakes.com

Seneca County Chamber of Commerce: 800-732-1848; www.fingerlakescentral.com

Watkins Glen Area Chamber of Commerce: 800-607-4552, 607-535-6243; www.watkinsglenchamber.com

Yates County Chamber of Commerce: 315-536-3111; www.yatesny.com

WINE & BEER TASTING TOUR

Driving south from Glenora or Miles:

1st Stop: Heron Hill Tasting Room in Himrod is one of three locations for this important winery. The winery itself and **Blue Heron Café** are in Hammondsport overlooking Keuka Lake, while another tasting facility is in Bristol on Canandaigua Lake. Taste rieslings, chardonnays, vinifera reds, and Heron Hill's popular Eclipse series as well as their late-harvest and ice wines. 5323 Seneca Point Rd., Canandaigua 14424; 800-441-4241; www.heronhill.com

2nd Stop: If you're up for something different, stop at the **FLX Wienery** in Dundee. It's the kingdom of the brat and the dressed-up hot dog. (See "Casual Fare" in Seneca Lake West Side)

3rd Stop: Fulkerson Winery in Dundee produces more than 20 handcrafted wines including dornfelder, traminette, Matinee, cabernet franc, ice wine, and three elegant rieslings. Climb aboard a horse-drawn vehicle for a vineyard tour. Get supplies and grape juice here to make your own wine. Fulkerson sells juice from more than 30 grape varieties. Also ask about their farmhouse rental that sleeps 10. 607-243-7883; www.fulkersonwinery.com

4th Stop (across street): For Irish-style whiskey made from locally grown grains by an Irish farming family with roots in Kilfountain, Country Kerry, Ireland, visit **O'Begley Distillery** in Dundee. The family has built the distillery from the ground up over a three-year period and is dedicated to bringing you fine whiskies branded as Poitin and Old Kilfountan. 5430 NY Rt. 14, Dundee 14837; 585-750-8560; www.obegley.com

If time permits: Visit **Rock Stream Vineyards** (www.rockstreamvineyards.com); **Barnstormer Winery** (www.barnstormerwinery.com); and see if you can catch some tasty sustenance at **Ahhh La Cart Food Truck Rodeo** often parked at Lakewood Vineyards. www.ahhhlacart.com

5th Stop: Lakewood Vineyards in Watkins Glen is run by four generations of the Stamp family. Lakewood's sparkling wine Candeo is a winner. Also try white catawba, Long Stem White and Long Stem Pink, chardonnay, riesling, and ice wines. This is a kid-friendly place with tours, picnic facilities, and a small playground. 607-535-9252; www.lakewoodvineyards.com

Final Stop: Watkins Glen for dinner and overnight. Dine at **Seneca Harbor Station** or the **Wildflower Café and Crooked Rooster Brew Pub** and try their craft beer. Check into the **Watkins Glen Harbor Hotel** or one of the local B&Bs such as the **The Blackberry Inn**, a beautifully appointed Greek Revival home. (See Watkins Glen section)

Seneca Lake

✳ What's Happening

SPRING **Grand Prix Festival**, Watkins Glen. A full weekend of special events from vintage car parades to races along the original circuit. 607-535-3003; www.grandprixfestival.com

    Memorial Day Celebrations, Waterloo. Parades, picnics, music, and fairs in the birthplace of Memorial Day. 315-568-2906

National Lake Trout Derby, Seneca Lake, Geneva. Fish for prizes on Memorial Day weekend. 315-789-8634

Pasta and Wine, Seneca Lake Wine Trail. Visit 21 wineries along Seneca Lake, and enjoy pasta dishes paired with wine. 315-536-9996

Seneca Lake Wine & Food Festival, Clute Park the last weekend in May. Visit wine, food, and craft vendors. www.watkinsglen.com

FIRST WOMAN DOCTOR

In 1849, when Hobart was Geneva College, Elizabeth Blackwell graduated from Geneva Medical College, becoming the first female physician in this hemisphere.

Spring Wine and Cheese Weekend, Seneca Lake wineries. Follow a route around the lake, sipping wine and nibbling cheese and crackers as you go. 315-536-9996

The Waterfront Festival, Seneca Harbor Park. Concourse de Cardboard (cardboard boat regatta), kayak rides, bands, chicken, and barbecue (June). 607-535-3003; www.thewaterfrontfestival.com

SUMMER **American Legion Fireworks and July 4th Festival**, Geneva. Festival of fun, games, and food. 315-789-5165

Concerts in the Park, Watkins Glen. Every Tuesday evening through mid-August.

Cruisin' Night & Block Party, late July, Geneva.

Dundee Day Downtown Dundee, twenty-four miles of yard sales, arts and crafts, food, and fun. First Saturday after July 4th.

Finger Lakes Wine Festival, Watkins Glen International Race Track. More than 80 wineries participate in this three-day event with wine tasting, wine sales, a Taster's Banquet, Champagne Breakfast, live music and seminars, plus arts and crafts vendors. 866-461-7223; www.flwinefest.com

Geneva Lakefront Park Concert Series, Geneva. Free concerts at 7 p.m. 315-789-5005

Musselman Triathlon, July in Geneva. www.musselmantri.com

NASCAR Sprint Cup Series, Watkins Glen International. 866-461-RACE; www.the glen.com

Ontario County Fair, Ontario County Fairgrounds. Five activity-filled days with animals, games, music, food, pig races, and much more. www.ontariocountyfair.org

Geneva Classic Car Show, Lakeshore Park, Geneva. More than five hundred vintage cars on display, plus arts and crafts vendors, a flea market, food, entertainment, a vintage boat regatta, and fireworks. www.genevachamber.org

Pickin' in the Pasture, Lodi. August celebration of bluegrass and old-time music overlooking Seneca Lake. 607-582-6363

St. Mary's Annual Festival, Waterloo. Entertainment, fire engine rides, games, and food under tents. 315-539-2944

Schuyler County Italian American Festival, Clute Park, Watkins Glen. Enjoy amusements, games, family-friendly activities, food, crafts, entertainment, and more, plus an amazing fireworks display on Saturday night.

Seneca Lake Whale Watch, northern end of lake, Geneva. No whales in this freshwater lake, but a weekend promising a whale of fun. Crafts, games, food, water-ski show, boating excursions, musical performances, displays, fireworks, and wine tasting (August). 315-781-0820; www.senecalakewhalewatch.com

FALL/WINTER **IKEPOD Watkins Glen Grand Prix Festival and Zippo U.S. Vintage Grand Prix**, Watkins Glen. Sports car events, live music, Concours d'Elegance (vintage and classic car show), race reenactment of vintage cars from the 1948–1952 circuit, wine tasting, family fun, kid racer school and derby, road rally, food vendors, and more. 607-535-3003; www.grandprixfest.com

Deck the Halls: Visit each of the wineries along the Seneca Lake Wine Trail, and collect ornaments, recipes, and a wreath as you go. Each place offers wine tasting and something to eat. Early reservations a must. 315-536-9996

Chocolate and Wine, Seneca Lake wineries. Visit wineries, and taste gourmet chocolate delights paired with select wines (February). 607-535-8080

KEUKA LAKE

To the Senecas, Keuka meant "canoe landing." The largest town, Penn Yan, lies at the tip of the northeastern branch; Branchport is nestled around the northwestern branch, and Hammondsport lies at the southern end. With 70 miles of shoreline, Keuka Lake; harbors the most water-hugging restaurants. It is also one of the warmest of the lakes.

During the 1800s, this 22-mile Y-shaped lake, which forks about midway to the north, had been the epicenter of a thriving steamship industry where fanciful steamboats like *Lulu* and the *Yates* cruised the lake. It was a time of dances in lakeside pavilions and grand stays at the Grove Springs Hotel; stops at the Urbana Winery and Gibson's Landing.

The opening of the Erie Canal in 1825 resulted in traffic being diverted to northern ports. For about 40 years (1830–1870) the Crooked Lake Canal linked Penn Yan to Dresden on Seneca Lake; however, the coming of the railroad made the canal obsolete. All that remains today are traces of some of the 28 locks, mill foundations, and towpath. The canal's path is now defined by the Keuka Outlet Trail, popular with hikers and bikers.

By the late 1800s the emphasis on transporting grains had shifted to grapes, bringing new prosperity to the region. Extensive publicity spread the word about the leisure assets of Keuka Lake, attracting affluent visitors who built lovely summer homes along the shores.

Considered the center of the champagne industry in New York State, the hills around Hammondsport and along the lake are carpeted with vineyards.

Penn Yan

Penn Yan, now a pretty serene place, was once nicknamed "Pandemonium" because of its rowdy reputation. About 1808, the leaders settled on "Penn Yan" satisfying two factions who were having trouble agreeing: immigrants from Pennsylvania and Yankees from New England—Penn Yan's version of the Hatfields and the McCoys.

One of the first founders of the town, David Wagener, built a gristmill on the site where the Birkett Mills now stands along the Keuka Lake Outlet. Wagener's son, Abraham, considered to be the father of the town, built the first frame house and first inn, the Mansion House, and constructed the grand manor house above Bluff Point.

Shops and taverns were gradually built both at the north end of Main St. and around the mills. Since then the heart of the business district has drifted more toward where Crooked Canal was built. Keuka College, a four-year coed liberal arts school founded in 1890, has a beautiful 1,300-foot site on the west side of the lake, four miles southwest of Penn Yan.

✳ Lodging

TRIED AND TRUE There are a handful of chain hotels like the **Best Western Vineyard Inn & Suites** (142 Lake St., Penn Yan 14527; 315-536-8473, 800-823-0612; www.vineyardinnandsuites.com); the **Microtel Inn & Suites** (124 Elm St., Penn Yan 14527;

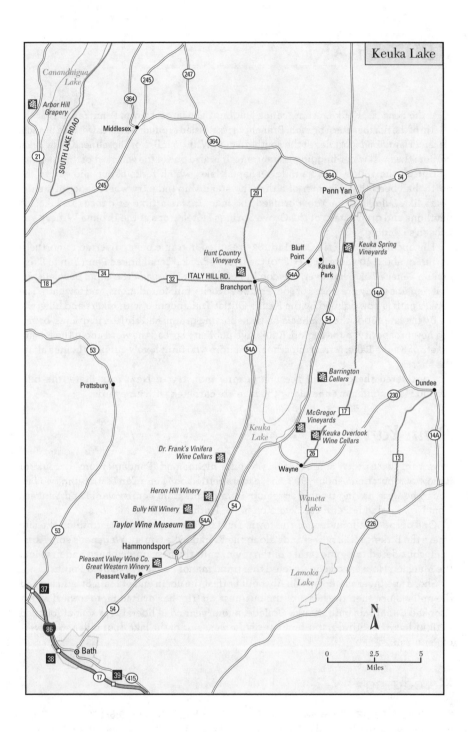

Keuka Lake

Canandaigua Lake

Arbor Hill Grapery

SOUTH LAKE ROAD

Middlesex

Penn Yan

Hunt Country Vineyards

Bluff Point

Keuka Spring Vineyards

ITALY HILL RD.

Keuka Park

Branchport

Dundee

Barrington Cellars

Prattsburg

McGregor Vineyards

Keuka Overlook Wine Cellars

Keuka Lake

Dr. Frank's Vinifera Wine Cellars

Wayne

Heron Hill Winery

Waneta Lake

Bully Hill Winery

Taylor Wine Museum

Hammondsport

Pleasant Valley Wine Co. Great Western Winery

Pleasant Valley

Lamoka Lake

Bath

N

0   2.5   5
Miles

KEUKA LAKE IS THE ONLY FINGER LAKE THAT BRANCHES IN THE SHAPE OF A "Y"

800-337-0050; www.microtelinn.com); and a new **Hampton Inn** downtown (expected to be completed in summer 2016). There are also many bed-and-breakfasts, small inns, and older motels like the nicely renovated **Colonial Motel**, across the lake and close to Keuka College—not the Ritz but good value for money. 17 W. Lake Rd., Penn Yan 14527; 315-536-3056; www.colonialmotelkeuka.com

ELEGANT AND LAKE VIEWS The view from **Esperanza's Mansion** in Branchport high above Keuka Lake doesn't get much better. Once a stop on the Underground Railroad, this stately yellow Greek Revival house with pillars and verandas (circa 1838) and nine suites is the site of many weddings. Additions include a 21-room inn adjacent to the main house. Mansion house suites are each different, some with canopy beds and period decorative fireplaces. Quilts from Belgium resemble large petit point works of art. There is a restaurant, a library, and a tavern. $$$–$$$$ 3456 NY Rt. 54A, Bluff Point 14478; 315-536-4400; www.esperanzamansion.com

B&BS There are more than 35 B&Bs in the area. Here are some to check out.

Adda Trimmer House B&B, a restored 1891 Queen Anne–style home owned by Gary Smith, a professor of hospitality management at Keuka College, is furnished with period wall coverings and fabrics, hand-oiled woodwork, marble and oak floors, painted ceilings, and chandeliers. All rooms have air-conditioning and

VIEWS OF THE LAKE FROM ESPERANZA'S MANSION ARE SPECTACULAR

television/VCR. There are two parlors, a library with fireplace, a formal dining room and music room as well as an outdoor hot tub. Guests enjoy a full breakfast plus complimentary snacks and beverages. Trimmer House is within walking distance of Penn Yan's restaurants and shops. $$ 145 E. Main St., Penn Yan 14527; 315-536-8304, 800-968-8735; www.trimmerhouse.com

Aubergine, a wonderfully restored late-1800s Victorian with a lovely Second Empire slate mansard roof, has three tastefully furnished guest bedrooms with cable TV, WiFi, air conditioning, ceiling fans, hair dryers, and robes. Although the inn is furnished with period pieces, the overall feeling is light, not dark, with a French flair. A continental breakfast is served in the dining room. Sorry—no children or pets. $$ 311 Clinton St., Penn Yan 14527; 315-694-7218; www.aubergineinn.com

The yellow brick **Fox Inn B&B** on Main St. is surrounded by wide lawns with huge trees and rose gardens. Built in 1820, this gracious pillared Greek Revival house should appeal to those who love traditional elegance, antiques, and artwork. Some of the six rooms have fireplaces and whirlpool baths; all have a TV/VCR. There is a large billiard room, a living room with a marble fireplace, a sunporch with flowers and plants, and a formal dining room where gourmet breakfasts are served. $$–$$$ 158 Main St., Penn Yan 14527; 315-536-3101, 800-901-7997; www.foxinnbandb.com

You'll become a B&B believer when you stay at **La Belle Vie B&B**, an 1860s Italianate Victorian home in Penn Yan's Historic District. Exquisite details in the home and furnishings include hand-printed wallpaper, oak floors, queen sleigh bed, walk-in closet, private balcony, and lovely etched glass windows. Find pillow-top mattresses, walk-in showers, individual Takagi water heaters so you will never run out of hot water, designer soaps, privacy room shades, WiFi, and HDTVs. And yes, breakfasts are home cooked. $$$ 208 Main St., Penn Yan 14527; 315-694-7273; www.labelleviebb.com

KEUKA LAKE OFFERS ALL SORTS OF WATER FUN

Chris Brooks

GUESTS STAYING AT LOS GATOS B&B CAN CHOOSE A ROOM IN THE MAIN HOUSE OR IN ONE OF THE TIDY CABINS

Los Gatos Bed & Breakfast is a tidy, well-run place on the hillside with gardens all around. In addition to three rooms with private baths in the main house, there are two wonderful log cabins. Rooms have very comfortable queen beds covered with quilts made by local Mennonites. Innkeepers Susan and Burney Baron make their own jams, grape juice, and bread, and breakfasts from scratch, including eggs from their own chickens. There is a lovely outdoor pool and gazebo, the site of many a wedding. Views of trees, hills, and lake are stunning. On clear, starry nights, tour the skies through their large telescope. $$ (ask about their packages) 1491 NY Rt. 14A, Penn Yan 14527; 315-536-0686, 866-289-7381; www.losgatosbandb.com

Once a stop on the Underground Railroad, **Merritt Hill Manor B&B** in Penn Yan, is one of the grander bed-and-breakfasts in the area. This 1822 Federal-style country home on the crest of a hill offers spectacular views of Keuka and Seneca Lakes and the hills. On 12 acres, the house is surrounded by open pastureland and gardens; a stream runs through the property. The five guest rooms are exceptionally large and come with private baths. A breakfast is served. $$ 2756 Coates Rd., Penn Yan 14527; 315-536-7682; www.merritthillmanor.com

New Vines B&B was designed to celebrate the Finger Lakes wine-growing culture—there is even a small vineyard planted on the property. Unlike many historic B&Bs, this was built specifically to host guests, so the efficient use of space and energy and the modern décor will appeal to those who love clean and new. There are four guest rooms plus a shared living room with a fireplace and a spacious porch rolling out great lake views. $$–$$$ 1138 Travis Rd., Penn Yan 14527; 315-536-4087; www.newvinesbb.com

THE PUBLICK UNIVERSAL FRIEND

Jemima Wilkinson (1752–1819), an imposing figure in flowing robes with long raven hair, grew up in a Quaker family in Rhode Island. After a nearly fatal fever in 1776, she believed that she had died and returned to earth to preach to a "lost and guilty, gossiping, dying World." Calling herself the Publick Universal Friend or simply "the Friend," she began attracting followers to her "Society of Universal Friends," eventually creating a communal settlement near Dresden.

In 1790, the Society established a gristmill and harvested the first wheat sown east of Seneca Lake, and soon it became the largest community in the region. The society opposed war and slavery, fostered peaceful relationships with Native Americans and African Americans, and honored celibacy. Eventually the community was disturbed by conflicts over ownership of the land and tales of dictatorial rule and strange practices. After Jemima's death in 1819, the group gradually disintegrated. The Universal Friend's three-story mansion where members of the Society lived still stands and is now privately owned.

English inside and out, **Tudor Hall B&B** is right on the lake at the site of a former steamboat landing. All three suites have private baths, views of the lake, and sitting areas. There are terraced gardens, a private beach, and several boats: a rowboat, canoe, paddleboat, and powerboat that innkeepers Priscilla and Don Erickson use to take their guests on lake cruises. A 20-foot pontoon boat is available for rental. Gourmet breakfasts are served by candlelight using crystal and china—the whole works. $$ 762 E. Bluff Dr., Penn Yan 14527; 315-536-9962; www.p-port.com/tudorhallbb

Catch the lake views from your balcony when you stay at **Steamboat Castle**, set on a former steamboat landing on the water with a lovely tiered yard. This B&B has five bedrooms, all with private baths. On the waterfront you can relax or go swimming, canoeing, or kayaking. Guests rave about the breakfasts. There is also a lakeside cottage with a big open living room, fireplace, and a wall of windows overlooking the water. It has three bedrooms, two baths, and it sleeps six. $$$–$$$$ 2893 W. Lake Rd., Penn Yan 14527; 315-536-6759; www.steamboatcastle.com

Universal Friend B&B circa 1845, a well-furnished country home near the wineries, is a very good value with three bedrooms and a mantra of "Be kind, be unselfish, and promote full equality for all." $$ 3269 Italy Friend Rd., Branchport 14418; 315-536-4541; www.universalfriendbandb.com

The grounds of the **Wagener Estate**, a gracious, circa-1794 Colonial farmhouse, still have many of the fruit trees from the old orchard. A large porch overlooks the lawns with a peek of the lake, and a hammock invites a late-afternoon snooze. Recently the property was acquired by the great-great-great-grandchildren of the original Wageners who built the house. The new owners, George and Maryann Reigelsperger, have renovated the home and are dedicated to bringing back the "WOW" of this five-bedroom B&B. In the morning find a breakfast ranging from country, to a three-course gourmet spread. $$–$$$ 351 Elm St., Penn Yan 14527; 315-536-4591; www.wagenerestate.com

The Willows B&B is a classic lakeside contemporary; rustic outside, but decorated in soft, serene colors inside where four queen-size-bedded rooms, with private baths, offer all desired amenities. There is a great deck complex on the lake framed by grand feathery willows, and waterfront activities include kayaks, swim floats, and fishing. $$$ 6893 E. Bluff Dr., Penn Yan 14527; 315-536-5653; www.thewillowsonkeukalake.com

VACATION RENTALS **Wright's Cottages on Waneta Lake,** located between Seneca and Keuka Lakes, include six furnished board-and-batten cottages with fireplaces and 250 feet of lakefront. Sleeping four to six people, cottages come with fully equipped kitchens, television/VCR (only two have cable), and campfire pits. There is a long dock, raft and plenty of water craft, while a scenic trail runs along the lake. This is a quiet place—if you crave nightlife, go somewhere else. Bring your own towels and bedding. $$–$$$ 309 Lake St., Penn Yan 14527; 607-292-6786; www.wrightscottages.com

✱ Dining Out

Keuka is the star when it comes to restaurants right on the lake. Several provide docks and tie-up facilities so that you can arrive by boat. Many of the wineries have restaurants; some restaurants offer Amish and Mennonite food.

ELEGANT AND ROMANTIC **Esperanza Mansion** is one of the more romantic places to dine with views of the lake. Eat by candlelight in the dining room, the tavern, or on the terrace. $$–$$$; $ 3456 NY Rt. 54A, Bluff Point 14478; 315-536-4400; www.esperanza mansion.com

CASUAL FARE The **Antique Inn** is a casual, rustic, family-style place with reasonably priced good food. Try the spaghetti sauce—they make it themselves. The fried fish, fried oysters, and liver and onions are local favorites. Eat in the dining room or bar. $–$$ 2940 NY Rt. 54A, Penn Yan 14527; 315-536-6576

Let yourself go with the mouthwatering homemade soups, sandwiches, and bakery items at the **Flour Shop.** $–$$ 223 Main St., Penn Yan 14527; 315-536-6491

FLX Wienery is one of those fun and crazy places serving things like gourmet hot dogs, sausage, and hamburgers, foiedog with bacon caramel, and roasted farm fresh veggies, plus Finger Lakes wines. Or hey, what about a rhubarb milkshake? 5090 NY Rt. 14, Dundee 14837; 607-243-7100; www.flxwienery.com

Locals know the food is always good, prices are reasonable, and you get good service at **Timmy G's** (formerly Holly's Red Rooster). With new owners, the interior has been updated a bit, but you still find early 1900s pictures from Penn Yan. $–$$ 12 Maiden Ln., Penn Yan 14527; 315-536-9800

La Cocina is a cute little place serving wonderful Mexican food. A tin ceiling, wide plank floors and colorful décor set the mood for dishes like enchiladas suiza—corn tortillas stuffed with chicken or beef. 16 Maiden Ln., Penn Yan 14527; 315-536-6512; www.lacocinapy.com

The **Keuka Restaurant** is one of those places you'll return to again and again. In addition to an extensive dinner menu with items like sushi-grade tuna, pastas, and awesome steaks, there is an impressive pub menu. Sit in high-back booths, tables, or at the long bar. $–$$ 12 Main St., Penn Yan 14527; 315-536-5852; www.keuka -restaurant.com

Lloyds Limited "A Pub" is pure Finger Lakes vintage: tin ceiling, historic photos of area on walls, beer and wine memorabilia, old copies of *Reader's Digest*, blow-up beer bottles, 1910 skates, old keg taps—you name it. Starting life as a bar, Lloyds has added booths and casual pub dinners—pizza, chicken wings, potato skins, and other finger foods as well as Finger Lakes wines. $ 3 Main St., Penn Yan 14527; 315-536-9029

Silverbird Woodfired features an eclectic menu: coleslaw cut fresh with every order, turkey burgers, and wood-fired artisan pizzas along with some super espressos, lattes and cappuccinos. While there check out the antique gaming machines. 133 E. Elm St., Penn Yan 14527; 315-536-5892

A hot spot for locals and anyone else who hears about it, **Water Street Wine Bar** in Birkett Landing rolls out three tiers of wines at reasonable prices: California, Finger Lakes, and a Discovery Series from all over, plus a lineup of local craft beer on tap. A light tapas menu features flatbread pizzas, cheeses, charcuterie boards, and other items. Décor is stylish and hip, utilizing reclaimed wood from wine barrels. Eat indoors or out. $$–$$$ 130 Water St., Penn Yan 14527; 607-569-2528

QUICK BITE For a bit of nostalgia and great homemade pie, stop at the little **Penn Yan Diner.** The menu includes all the usual suspects. $ 131 Elm St., Penn Yan 14527; 315-536-9259

ICE CREAM **Seneca Farms** in Penn Yan makes their own ice cream. Simply the best. Also try their fried chicken and burgers. 2485 NY Rt. 54A, Penn Yan 14527; 315-536-4006

✳ To See

Arts Center of Yates County offers classes and workshops and showcases the work of painters, sculptors, photographers, clay artists and potters, jewelry makers, wood- and metalworkers, and multimedia artists at the Flick Gallery. 127 Main St., Penn Yan 14527; 315-536-8226; www.ycac.org

The Birkett Mills, an imposing yellow brick building on Main St.—check out the giant griddle display—still grinds flour, including its highly prized buckwheat flour, and sells a variety of food products. 1 Main St., Penn Yan 14527; 315-536-3311

Garrett Memorial Chapel, between Branchport and Penn Yan, is a lovely Gothic stone Episcopal chapel built in memory of Charles William Garrett, the son of a wealthy wine merchant. Poems the young man had loved are represented on the stained glass windows of the crypt. 5251 Skyline Dr., Keuka Park 14478; www .garrettchapel.org

Catch the light streaming through the magnificent stained glass windows designed by Gabriel Loire of Chartres Cathedral fame at **Norton Chapel** on the Keuka College campus. 141 Central Ave., Keuka Park 14478; 315-279-5000

The Yates History Center comprises the **Oliver House Museum** and the **L. Caroline Underwood Museum**. The Oliver House, the nineteenth-century brick home of the Oliver family, is filled with local history and genealogical information including pieces from the Victorian period, a large array of china, and a collection of historical materials from Yates County, often used for research by students and genealogists. The L. Caroline Underwood Museum contains collections from Caroline's family in addition to exhibit rooms, a gift shop, and the Spencer Research Center. 107 Chapel St., Penn Yan 14527; 315-536-7318; www.yatespast.com

✳ To Do

WALKING TOUR This National Register Historic District is highlighted in a comprehensive Historic Main Street Walking Tour. Pass by the Holowell House, a late-nineteenth-century Queen Anne home; the Victorian King-Post House; the Bordwell House, a brick Italianate residence; and others. The tour guide is available at the Visitors Center on Rt. 14A south of the village.

ON THE WATER To help people understand, preserve, and utilize Keuka Lake and its wetlands, the **Finger Lakes Museum and Aquarium** in Penn Yan has several projects well underway. Linked to the Townsend-Grady Wildlife Preserve by Sugar Creek, a navigable tributary of Keuka Lake, the museum is building a system of boardwalks to provide visitors with an up-close view of the ecologically rich area while offering several exhibits and programs. In the works, the largest freshwater aquarium in the Northeast will geologically replicate a cross-section of a glacially carved Finger Lake, and Creekside Center, a kayak and canoe livery on Sugar Creek, leading to Keuka Lake's west branch, will give visitors ready access to the water. 315-595-2200; www.fingerlakemuseum.org

✳ Shopping

In and around Penn Yan, handcrafted and food items play a starring role.

ARTS AND CRAFTS **The Quilt Room** sells Mennonite handmade quilts, wall hangings, and craft items. 1870 Hoyt Rd., Penn Yan 14527; 315-536-5964

The Windmill Farm and Craft Market on Rt. 14A features more than 200 vendors selling crafts, farm produce, plants, antiques, quilts, cheeses, baked goods, and furniture. Twice a year there are two Custom and Classic Car Shows and swap meets. Open Saturdays in season and some holidays. 3900 NY Rt. 14A, Penn Yan 14527; 315-536-3032; www.thewindmill.com

BOOKS AND GIFTS **Long's Cards & Books** sells much more than books. They have games, stationery, office supplies, gifts, souvenirs, and arts & crafts supplies. 115 Main St., Penn Yan 14527; 315-536-3131; www.longscardsandbooks.com

SPECIALITY FOODS **The Keuka Candy Emporium** will send older folks back to a world of nostalgia with their vintage candy selections, while their homemade truffles and fudge can send everyone into a sugar high. SkyBars, Mallo Cups, Necco Wafers—all those and many more fill old barrels for you to pick from. They serve a number of funny flavors of cotton candy daily along with ice cream with all the toppings. This is for kids of all ages for sure. 17 Main St., Penn Yan 14527; 315-531-4700; www.keukacandyemporium.com

Oak Hill Bulk Foods in Penn Yan between Keuka and Seneca Lakes sells a variety of foods in sizable quantities displayed in more than 20,000 square feet. Find grocery items, Amish cheeses, snacks, unusual foods like raspberry nut snack mix, corn chips with flax, and other good things. Linger in the café with coffee and one of their impossible-to-resist bakery temptations. 3173 NY Rt. 14A, Penn Yan 14527; 315-536-0836; www.oakhillbulkfoods.com

Hammondsport and Bath

Voted "America's Coolest Small Town" by readers of *Budget Travel* magazine, Hammondsport is located at the head of Keuka Lake. Hammondsport's shops and restaurants are arranged around a park of trees, gardens, and a gazebo. Walk a couple of blocks to the lakeshore, where there is a public park and the old Hammondsport Depot. Summertime take in band concerts in the square on Thursday evenings. Considered the wine capital of the state, Hammondsport has several vineyards within its

WINE & BEER TASTING TOUR

START: Penn Yan to Hammondsport

END: Branchport

STAY: Los Gatos B&B

TRAVEL: South NY Rt. 54, north on NY Rt. 54A

1ST STOP: Keuka Spring Vineyards welcomes visitors to sample their premium wines in a hillside tasting room overlooking the lake. For more than two decades, the Wiltbergers have been producing a variety of fine wines including chardonnay, riesling, Cayuga Whites, seyval blanc, vignoles, cabernet franc, cabernet sauvignon, merlot, pinot noir, and Crooked Lake Red. On this historic property is a gambrel-roofed barn, an 1840s homestead, and a picnic area. 243 NY Rt. 54, E. Lake Rd., Penn Yan 14527; 315-536-3147; www.keukaspringwinery.com

2ND STOP: Rooster Hill Vineyards' wines include riesling, gewürztraminer, pinot noir, lemberger, cabernet franc, and others. Located in Penn Yan, the Tuscan-style wine tasting room and wraparound porch reveal stunning lake vistas. 489 NY Rt. 54, Penn Yan 14527; 315-536-4773; www.roosterhill.com

3RD STOP: Barrington Cellars, Penn Yan, a family-owned winery, features wines made from *Vitis labrusca* grapes (a native variety) and French hybrids. Owners Ken and Eileen Farnan offer rieslings, Pink Cat, Isabella rosé, and dessert wines. Be sure to take in the great views of the lake from the balcony. 2794 Gray Rd., Penn Yan 14527; 315-536-9686; www.barringtoncellars.com

4TH STOP: McGregor Vineyard and Winery, Dundee, a pioneer of dry red wines, produces the highly prized Black Russian Red as well as chardonnay, rkatsiteli, cabernet franc, merlot, pinot noir aged in French oak, rieslings, gewürztraminer, and sparkling wines. Set on a hill overlooking Bluff Point—one of the most scenic views in the state—the winery is located in an attractive rustic-style building. Close to 100 percent of the grapes are estate grown and hand picked. Picnic on the terrace and purchase homemade gourmet foods, cheeses, and other items. 800-272-0192, 607-292-3999; www.mcgregorwinery.com

5TH STOP: Ravines Wine Cellars on Keuka Lake, Hammondsport, specializes in elegant European-style fine dry wines including riesling, a crisp Cayuga White, chardonnay, pinot noir, pinot rose, cabernet franc, and meritage. Also find local specialty foods: freshly baked wine crackers, cheeses, and artisan chocolates. 14630 NY Rt. 54, Hammondsport 14840; 607-292-7007; www.ravineswine.com

Heron Hill Winery

HERON HILL WINERY, HAMMONDSPORT

6TH STOP: Domaine Leseurre Winery in Hammondsport is relatively new to the Finger Lakes winery scene. The small facility sits above Keuka Lake offering great views while you sample Céline and Sébastien Leseurre's fine French wines. 13920 NY Rt. 54, Hammondsport 14840; 607-292-3920; www.domaineleseurre.com

7TH STOP: Hammondsport is a good place to spend some time. Walk around the village then tour the **Pleasant Valley Wine Company/Great Western** contained in eight historic stone buildings. In 1873

COLOBEL GRAPES FROM THE BULLY HILL VINEYARDS

Great Western became the first American champagne to win a gold medal in Europe at the Vienna exposition. Storage areas house enormous wine vats and barrels, caves are carved into the valley's hillside, and a working model of the Bath–Hammondsport Railroad is on the grounds. Visit the Great Western Winery visitor's center, with a theater, memorabilia, and wine equipment spanning 140 years (see "To See" in Hammondsport and Bath).

If breweries hold your interest, stop at the **Brewery of Broken Dreams**. (See "Sampling the Breweries" in What's Where in the Finger Lakes)

8TH STOP & LUNCH: Bully Hill Vineyards (formerly the Taylor Wine Company) has produced many award-winning wines from French-American hybrids. The winery's lovely weathered barns, hillside gardens, and the W. S. Taylor Art Museum—containing an extensive collection of Taylor's artwork—enhance the visit. Have lunch on the deck or inside (see "Winery Restaurants" in Hammondsport and Bath). Views of the lake are spectacular. 8843 Greyton H. Taylor Memorial Dr., Hammondsport 14840; 607-868-3610, 607-868-3210; www.bullyhill.com

Note: If you decide to continue touring the next day, the **Keuka Lakeside Inn**, **Black Sheep Inn**, or the **McCorn Winery Lodging** are good lodging choices, while for dinner **The Village Tavern** has a huge selection of craft beer (see Hammondsport and Bath).

9TH STOP: Turning north along the west side of Keuka Lake, visit **Heron Hill Winery** in Hammondsport located in a handsome building showcasing a breathtaking view of the lake. Taste chardonnay, johannisberg riesling, pinot noir, Eclipse, Gamebird Red and White, and blends from hybrid and *Vitis vinifera* grapes. 9301 Cty. Rd. 76, Hammondsport 14840; 607-868-4241, 800-441-4241; www.heronhill.com

10TH STOP: Founded in 1962 by one of the Finger Lakes's most important winemakers, **Dr. Frank's Vinifera Wine Cellars**, Hammondsport, is a must stop. Dr. Konstantin Frank showed how the prized European grape varieties could be grown in the region and how world-class table wines could be produced. Arguably the most critically acclaimed winery in the region, Dr. Frank's produces barrel-fermented chardonnay, gewürztraminer, riesling, pinot noir, rkatsiteli, and cabernet sauvignon, while Chateau Frank is a premium sparkling wine made in the méthode champenoise style. Their pinot noir vines are the oldest in the Finger Lakes, producing a complex, full-bodied wine. 9749 Middle Rd., Hammondsport 14840; 607-868-4884, 800-320-0735; www.drfrankwines.com

11TH STOP: Hunt Country Vineyards, Branchport, is an operating family farm, with a renovated 1820s barn, wine tasting room, deck, and gift shop. Owners Art and Joyce Hunt focus on specialty wines and feature riesling, barrel reserve chardonnay, Foxy Lady (blush), Classic White, seyval, Cayuga, vignoles, and Vidal ice wine. Scenic trails are open to hikers and cyclists, who are invited to bring their lunch for picnicking. 4021 Italy Hill Rd., Branchport 14418; 800-946-3289, 315-595-2812; www.huntwines.com

FINAL STOP: Vineyard View Winery in Keuka Park just south of Penn Yan sits on a hill above the lake. They carry rieslings, cabernet franc, Nikki's Red, and dessert wines. 2971 Williams Hill Rd., Keuka Park 14478; 315-694-7262; www.vineyardviewwinery.com

PULTENEY SQUARE, BATH

Steuben County Convention and Visitors Bureau

boundaries, including the Great Western and Pleasant Valley Wineries. The Glenn H. Curtiss Museum tells the story of this man's amazing accomplishments at the dawn of the air age.

The buildings along Pulteney Square and Liberty St., as well as the Erie Freight House, are especially interesting. Several private homes are on the National Register of Historic Places. Walking tours include Greek Revival, Queen Anne, Italianate, and Tuscan buildings. For a dose of the 1950s, take in a movie at one of the few drive-in theaters still left in the country.

South of Hammondsport, Bath—site of the longest-running county fair—was named after Lady Bath of England, by founder Colonel Charles Williamson, whose dream was to create the state's first planned community. Believing that Bath's location at the junction of the Susquehanna, Conhocton, and Chemung Rivers would be a surefire combination to creating a highway to the West, the "Baron of the Backwoods" promoted the site as the next great metropolitan area.

In 1793 when 15 families moved into the village, Williamson did not foresee that the Erie Canal and the coming of the railroad would negate the importance of the rivers. But his dynamic personality and boundless energy prevailed to some extent and eventually Bath was developed with a gristmill, sawmill, several residences, theater, and a racecourse.

The comparatively tiny lakes of Lamoka and Waneta, just east of the southern end of Keuka Lake, are hardly on some of the area maps. Less than 4 miles long and 1,000 feet above sea level, Lamoka is the site of a prehistoric Indian settlement, one of the oldest such sites in the state, while Waneta encompasses but 778 acres. Both offer superb fishing. Peaceful places.

Today there is a lot of excitement in the Keuka Lake region as new breweries and cideries open, many with tasting rooms.

✳ Lodging

EASY AND INEXPENSIVE MOTELS If you're a no-frills kind of person and care mostly about being on the shore at an economical price, the efficiently run **Keuka Lakeside Inn** might be your winning find. It sits on a little piece of land jutting into the water and is simply furnished in a '60s-type style. Rooms have been redecorated in fresh, upbeat color, and half of them have views of the lake, along with WiFi, HDTVs, coffeemakers, and fridges. There is a pretty gazebo, boat launch, and public beach. $–$$ 24 Water St., Hammondsport 14840; 607-569-2600; www.keukalakesideinn.com

Vinehurst Inn & Suites in Bath has whirlpool suites as well as standard rooms and family accommodations. There is an exercise room and family activity area with volleyball, croquet, and other games. Rates include a continental breakfast. $–$$ NY Rt. 54, Hammondsport 14840; 607-569-2300; www.vinehurstinn.com

B&BS **Amber Waves Farm Bed & Breakfast** was built specifically as a B&B on more than 300 acres of a working cattle farm. Therefore, guests enjoy the latest in amenities, including two-story wraparound porches, yet can experience the peace and tranquility of the countryside with the pastures and woodlands and fishing ponds. Themed rooms are cleverly decorated, like the Americana Room showcasing U.S. memorabilia. $$–$$$ 8266 Cty. Rd. 74, Pulteney 14874; 602-522-7733; www.amberwavesfarmbb.com

With four spacious bedrooms—including two with Jacuzzi tubs—WiFi, TVs in each room, outdoor patio seating, a grill, fire pit, and full sit-down breakfasts, **Amity Rose B&B** is a sanctuary where you can get away from your daily routine while enjoying the relaxed pace and comfortable atmosphere of small-town living. $$ 8264 Main St. Extension, Hammondsport 14840; 607-569-3402; www.amityrose.net

Doug Kerr

VILLAGE TAVERN, HAMMONDSPORT

Black Sheep Inn and Spa is one of those rare historic octagonal treasures in the region. Rooms are artfully decorated in a mix of period furnishings and colors. The Taylor suite with a king-size bed occupies its own wing and is very private. Take part in Art Evenings in the studio and savor the owner/chef's delicious breakfasts where ingredients have been sourced from local farmers. Also ask about massages. $$–$$$$ 8329 Pleasant Valley Rd., Hammondsport 14840; 607-567-3767; www .stayblacksheepinn.com

Blushing Rose B&B in an 1843 Italianate home contains period-furnished rooms on the lacy, flowery side with quilts, wainscoting, stenciling, dried flower arrangements, and lots of small knickknacks. Relax on the large porch and walk to the public beach. Four rooms have private baths on the second floor. $$ 11 William St., Hammondsport 14840; 607-569-2687, 866-569-2687; www.blushingroseinn.com

Located northwest of Hammondsport in the countryside, **Feather Tick 'n Thyme**, in an 1890s Victorian country home, sits in the middle of 220-plus acres surrounded by open fields and trees. The four guest rooms (with smallish private baths) are furnished with a mix of antiques, quilts, and period reproductions. This is a very quiet, peaceful place with walking paths. This B&B can host weddings in their on-site barn. $$ 7661 Tuttle Rd., Prattsburgh 14873; 607-522-4113; www.bbnyfingerlakes.com

The bright turquoise **J. S. Hubbs Bed and Breakfast**, circa 1840, has an amazing kitchen, lovely gardens, and a perfect location in the heart of Hammondsport. Three rooms are decorated in subdued colonial-style furnishings. $$ 17 Shethar St., Hammondsport 14840; 607-569-2440; www.jshubbs.com

Owned by artists, Joannie and Bruce, **MoonShadow Bed and Breakfast** overlooking Keuka Lake is contemporary in design, rendered in a palette of cheerful colors and filled with artwork on the walls and in the gallery—browse their website and you'll be entranced. Breakfasts are homemade, the surroundings are magical. $$ 10249 Gibson Rd., Hammondsport 14840; 607-794-2398; www.moonshadowbedandbreakfast.com

THE BLACK SHEEP INN AND SPA, HAMMONDSPORT

MCCORN WINERY LODGING IS HOUSED IN A FORMER WINE-MAKING FACILITY

Enjoy the lovely views of the lake from the porch of the 1887 pillared stone Victorian **Gone with the Wind** on Keuka Lake. Located near Hammondsport, each of the rooms is different: one has a Southwestern theme, another a rustic feeling, while the Rhett and Scarlet Hideaway has a private veranda and a king-size bed. There is a fireplace, a private cove with a gazebo, dock, and a rowboat. It's a peaceful setting, with several hiking trails and no televisions or phones to distract. Still, there is WiFi and air conditioning along with full breakfasts to keep your comfort level high. $–$$ (cash or check) 14905 W. Lake Rd., Branchport 14418; 607-868-4603; www .gonewiththewindonkeukalake.com

McCorn Winery Lodging hugs the side of a steep hill looking out to the lake. With three guest rooms and a wonderful sunporch with views to the waterfront (along with a set of binoculars), this former winery has been reborn as a B&B. It has its quirks, like a stream running underneath the floor and some furniture made out of wine barrels. There are several steps leading down to the entrance, but the owners will help with your bags should you need assistance. 30 Pulteney St., Hammondsport 14840; 607-377-2194; www.mccornwinerylodging.com

The chef-owned **Pleasant Valley Inn & Restaurant** is a grand pink 1848 Victorian two miles out of town. Air-conditioned rooms are furnished in a Victorian style. A restaurant in-house serves candlelight dinners Thursday through Sunday. Owners Marianne and Tom Simmons supply their kitchens with herbs grown from their garden and like to use local fruits and vegetables. A continental breakfast is served. $$ 7979 NY Rt. 54, Hammondsport 14840; 607-569-2282; www.pleasantvalleyinn.com

CABINS **Corning Landing**, about 7 miles north of Hammondsport on the east side of Keuka Lake, has two new log buildings on 170 feet of beachfront with grand tall windows, porches, patios, boat launch, and a swimming raft. The lofty Main Building has four bedrooms, two baths, while the North Cabin has three bedrooms and one bath along with a rec room with a wet bar. 11586 E. Lake Rd., Hammondsport 14840; 607-868-3244; www.corninglandingonkeuka.com

Farmer Phil's Cabins west of Hammondsport are spacious, well designed, and immaculate. Think lofty ceilings, antler chandeliers, lots of wood, front porches. Rustic yes, roughing it no. Perfect for outdoor-types and hunters. 7678 Cty. Rd. 55, Howard 14843; 607-368-5741

✱ Dining Out

WINERY RESTAURANT Besides good food and good portions, **Bully Hill Restaurant** offers a wonderful hilltop view of the vineyards, gardens, and the lake. There are two dining rooms as well as a large deck with umbrella tables. Try the Maryland blue crab cakes with hot pepper or cream of squash soup. Vegetarian dishes include a garden-medley vegetable burger topped with a portobello mushroom. Cuisine is prepared from fresh ingredients and local produce. Before or after dining, be sure to stop at the **Greyton H. Taylor Wine Museum**. $–$$ 8834 Grey H. Taylor Memorial Dr., Hammondsport 14840; 607-868-3490; www.bullyhill.com

LAKE VIEWS Come by car or boat to the **Lakeside Restaurant** overlooking the west side of the lake from this restored Victorian home and dine outdoors or inside. Lunch might include a warm steak salad and mâche greens or a killer burger. At dinner try prime rib served with garlic-mashed potatoes or eggplant and portobello stacks. There are 17 boat slips and a dining room for private parties. $$ 13780A W. Lake Rd., Hammondsport 14840; 607-868-3636; www.lakesidekeuka.com

Come by boat or car to the lively **Waterfront Restaurant** about 7 miles from Hammondsport on the west side of the lake. Eleven boat slips are often full, especially on Sundays in the summer, when the popular clambake is held along with a live music concert, Jimmy Buffet–style. Sit on one of the multiple open-air decks or in the air conditioned dining room. Grilled meats, fish, and pasta are popular fare as well as fish and chips; crab legs and clams a specialty. $–$$ 648 W. Lake Rd., Hammondsport 14840; 607-868-3455

CASUAL FARE Since it opened **Timber Stone Grill** has received high praise for its very fresh and creative cuisine and service. Its bouillabaisse, flatbreads, coriander-encrusted ahi tuna, and other dishes call on locally sourced ingredients. Find a wide selection of regional wine and beer served in a cool, rustic setting. 70 Shethar St., Hammondsport 14840; 607-224-0006; www.timberstonegrill.com

On a corner of the village square in Hammondsport, **The Village Tavern** pulls in the crowds—especially for their Friday fish fries. Eat outside or in. The menu offers fish and seafood along with pasta, vegetarian, and meat dishes. The tavern is known for its extensive list of Finger Lakes wines and more than 130 different brews. The inn also has four guest rooms. $$ 30 Mechanic St., Hammondsport 14840; 607-569-2528; www.villagetaverninn.com

Union Block Italian Bistro's menu features authentic Italian dishes made from fresh, local ingredients accompanied by whole grains and interesting olive oils and vinegar combos. $$ 31 Shethar St., Hammondsport 14840; 607-246-4065; www.union blockitalian.com

QUICK BITE **Chat-a-Whyle** has been family owned and operated for years. Got to try their sticky buns. 28 Liberty St., Bath 14810; 607-776-8040

Crooked Lake Ice Cream Parlor on the Hammondsport Square evokes an old-fashioned ice-cream parlor with its original tin ceiling and soda fountain dating from 1948. Counter and booths look like the originals, too. The hot fudge sundaes, topped with mounds of whipped cream and a cherry, are amazing. 35 Shethar St., Hammondsport 14840; 607-569-2751

Keuka Artisan Bakery & Deli has all those decadent pleasures you crave, like sticky cinnamon buns, molasses cookies, carrot cupcakes, and more, plus super deli sandwiches served on the best sprouted grain bread (other choices, too). Great breakfast sandwiches as well. It's a cute place with white iron tables and whimsical touches. 49 Shethar St., Hammondsport 14840; 607-224-4001; www.locu.com

Maloney's Pub is the closest thing you'll find to an Irish pub in town, with a great variety of beer and local wines and great live entertainment. 57 Pulteney St., Hammondsport 14840; 607-569-2264; www.maloneyspub.com

✳ To See

At the turn of the twentieth century, Hammondsport was buzzing with activity around the work of aviation pioneer Glenn H. Curtiss. Recognized as the father of naval aviation, Curtiss cocreated the first powered aircraft, built the first transatlantic aircraft, and attained a number of world speed records. His daring adventures with early motorcycles, dirigibles, and airplanes thrilled the country—his *June Bug* was the first aircraft to fly more than 1 kilometer; and he organized a Flying Circus, bringing colorful barnstormers to Hammondsport.

The **Finger Lakes Boating Museum** showcases more than 100 very interesting recreational and commercial wooden boats built in the Finger Lakes including Lightnings, Penn Yan motorboats, Lymans, rowboats, runabouts, canoes, and others. Housed in the

THE FINGER LAKES BOATING MUSEUM

AVIATION EXHIBIT

former Taylor Wine Company buildings, see the restoration of *Pat II*, a 39-foot launch and former mailboat on Skaneateles Lake, and take lessons and workshops in boating and restoration offered throughout the year. 8231 Pleasant Valley Rd., Hammondsport 14840; 607-569-2222; www.flbm.org

The **Glenn H. Curtiss Museum** is filled with actual planes and memorabilia including *June Bug II*; a Curtiss "Jenny"; a tractor biplane; 1913 flying boat; vintage autos, motorcycles, and bicycles; antique toys; and several other aircraft. In the workshop, see how airplanes are constructed and restored and explore the Children's Innovation Arcade. 8419 NY Rt. 54, Hammondsport 14840; 607-569-2160; www.glennhcurtissmuseum.org

In 1860 the **Pleasant Valley Wine Company**, producer of Great Western Champagne, was founded south of Hammondsport. It's not just that this is the winery that started it all, but the fabulous stone buildings and Great Western Winery Visitor Center make this a must-see. The Visitor Center provides a comprehensive history of wine with exhibits, displays, and wine tasting. Don't miss the Wine Cask Theater. 8260 Pleasant Valley Rd., Hammondsport 14840; 607-569-6111; www.pleasantvalley wine.com

The first wine museum in America, the **Greyton H. Taylor Wine Museum** at Bully Hill Vineyards, has an impressive collection of antique winemaking equipment, a replica cooper shop in a rustic barnlike building, and memorabilia relating to the early New York wine industry. See also a collection of presidential wineglasses, including one from Lincoln's table the night he and Mary went off to Ford's Theatre. 8843 Greyton H. Taylor Memorial Drive, Hammondsport 14840; 607-868-3610; www.bullyhill.com

Bath Veterans Administration Medical Center Historical Museum and National Cemetery was established in 1878 as a museum containing artifacts dating from the

Civil War to the present. The cemetery holds the graves of five Medal of Honor recipients and 29 unknown soldiers from the War of 1812, along with thousands of other veterans. 4772 Veterans Ave., Bath 14810; 607-664-4772.

Magee House contains early-American artifacts, such as an original mail carrier's bike. 1 Cohocton St., Bath 14810; 607-776-9930; www.steubenhistoricalsociety.org

PHOTO OPS **Bluff Point**, off NY Rt. 54A to Skyline Dr., between Branchport and Penn Yan at one end of an 11-mile bluff separating the two branches of Keuka Lake. The Wagener Mansion is at the top of the bluff; the Garrett Memorial Chapel is barely visible in the trees on the east side of the hill. From here you can scan the east side of the lake to Marlena Point.

Old Railroad Station on the waterfront (on Water St.) next to the public beach in Hammondsport now houses the village offices.

✳ To Do

BIKING The bike trip around the outer perimeter of Keuka Lake is 46 miles. Grades are moderate, so it's a pretty easy ride; the Outlet Trail is 7.5 miles.

From the center of Hammondsport, it's about a 3-mile round-trip to the Great Western Winery and Pleasant Valley Visitor Center. In another direction from town, going up Middle Rd. to Bully Hill Winery, it's a 4.5-mile round-trip.

Green oval signs mark Bike Route 17, part of a 435-mile route that goes from the Hudson River to Lake Erie. Travel through small villages along rural roads with paved shoulders.

Bluff Point Skyline Drive, a 7.5-mile road that runs along the crest of the gently mounded peninsula between the two branches of Keuka Lake, is one way to reach the area at the fork known as Bluff Point and Garrett Memorial Chapel. Take West Bluff and East Bluff Drives to make a loop around the shorelines. A good place to push off on this 14.3-mile trip is Keuka College in Keuka Lake State Park. The trip can take all day if you visit vineyards along the way.

MARINAS AND LAUNCHES Branchport: **Basin Park Marina** (315-595-8808); **Harbor Club Boat Storage** (315-595-6669); **North End Landings and Marina** (315-595-2853).

Penn Yan: **East Bluff Harbor Marina** (315-536-8236); **Morgan Marine** (315-536-8166); and **Penn Yan Boat Launch** (315-536-3015). Boats can be launched from the **Village Boat Launch** located off Keuka St. and from **Keuka Lake State Park** 7 miles south of Penn Yan.

Hammondsport: **Keuka Lakeside Inn** (607-569-2600; keukalakesideinn.com); **H. L. Watersports** in Harbor Lights Marina (607-868-4848); **Keuka Bay Marine Park** (607-569-2777; www.keukaonline.com); and **Village Shores Marina** (607-569-2770).

FISHING Seth Green, a world-class fisherman, proclaimed that Keuka Lake has the finest fishing grounds in the world. Although other Finger Lakes might make the same claim, there is no doubt that these waters are mighty good for catching rainbow trout, yellow perch, black bass, pickerel, and other lake fish.

See lake, brown, and rainbow trout in various stages of growth from eggs to full size at the **NY State Fish Hatchery**. 7169 Fish Hatchery Rd., Bath 14810

If you want an up-to-the-minute report on where the fish are biting, log on to www.fishfingerlakes.com

KEUKA LAKE HAS SOME OF THE FINEST FISHING IN THE WORLD

GOLF **Bath Country Club** is hilly and scenic with water coming into play on six holes. 330 May St., Bath 14810; 607-776-5043

Lakeside Country Club, Penn Yan, runs right through a vineyard. Older push-up-style greens tend to fall toward the lake; greens rebuilt in 1995 are more level, some two-tiered. Fairways climb up and down the slopes, revealing wonderful views of the lake and Keuka College. 154 E. Lake Rd., Rt 54, Penn Yan 14527; 315-536-6251

HIKING The **Keuka Lake Outlet**, a 6-mile ribbon of water connecting Keuka Lake with Seneca Lake, is banked by a linear park, a good place to hike and bike. The 7.5-mile trail running from Penn Yan to Dresden takes you past mill ruins, through Lock 17 and the remains of other locks.

The trails in **Urbana State Forest** between Prattsburg and Hammondsport, west of the southern end of the lake, give you two ways to go: the long route (7.1 miles) and the shorter loop (4.8 miles). Both take you along dirt trails, up a hill to a plateau (where it's easier), through woods, and by Huckleberry Bog. The well-marked trails go over streams and follow country lanes. From NY Rt. 17, go north on NY Rt. 53, then east on Bean Station Rd. Look for FLT signs (Finger Lakes Trail) after you pass Colegrove Rd. 607-776-2165

The **Finger Lakes Trail** runs approximately 562 miles and is the longest continuous foot trail in New York State. Five branch trails and fifteen loop trails extend from the main trail. It is maintained by volunteers and private landowners and is free to the public, but some portions may be closed during hunting seasons.

PARKS, NATURE PRESERVES, CAMPING, GUIDE SERVICES, AND OUTFITTERS Fish from a floating fishing platform or follow self-guided auto trails to see the animals and birds at **Birdseye Hollow State Forest** in Bradford. 607-776-2165

A summer day camp for children with serious illnesses, **Camp Good Days and Special Times Recreational Facility**, is located in Branchport. 315-595-2779; www.campgooddays.org

RED JACKET

On NY Rt. 54A just south of Branchport, a granite monument marks the site of the longhouse (1752) and burial spot for the mother of the Seneca chief Red Jacket. This famous Native American orator of the Seneca tribe—whose Seneca name was Sagoyewatha—is believed to have been given his English name because of a British army jacket he was given and wore constantly.

Flint Creek Campground, midway between Canandaigua and Penn Yan, has 120 sites with fire rings, picnic tables, a playground, a pool, mini golf, showers, laundry, electric hookups, and a pavilion. 800-914-3550, 716-554-3567; www.flintcreekcampground.com

Hickory Hill Family Camping Resort in Bath, has camping sites, two pools, a playground, hiking trails, full hookups, miniature golf, a recreation room, hayrides, a basketball court, plus cottage and cabin rentals. 607-776-4345, 800-760-0947; www.hickoryhillcampresort.com

Indian Pines Park, on the west side of Keuka Lake near Penn Yan, offers swimming, a pavilion, a picnic area with grills, a playground, and volleyball. 315-536-3015

Keuka Lake State Park at Bluff Point is a 621-acre park with a pavilion, boat launch, hiking trails, bathhouses, fishing, and 150 campsites for tents and trailers. 315-536-3666

Outlet Trail Park in Penn Yan has a pavilion, a picnic area with grills, and a playground. 315-536-3111

Red Jacket Park located on the east shore of Keuka Lake's eastern branch has a pavilion, swimming, a picnic area with grills, and a playground. 315-536-3015

Wagon Wheel Campground is close to vineyards and Keuka Lake, with 95 sites, a pool, fishing ponds, a recreation hall, entertainment, showers, laundry, and LP gas. 10378 Presler Rd., Prattsburgh 14873; 607-522-3270; www.wagonwheelcamp.com

GUIDE SERVICES Go hunting with **Eagle Eye Outfitters**, a Penn Yan–based company offering guides for deer hunts with shotgun and bow and arrow, as well as turkey hunts, duck hunts, and fishing trips. Lodging, transportation, stands, ground blinds, and dressing a deer are included. All hunts include home-cooked meals, and meat processing is available. 315-536-9768; www.eagleeyeoutfitter.com

FAMILY FUN See early airplanes, motorcycles, and other vintage aviation memorabilia at the **Glenn H. Curtiss Museum**. Learn how airplanes are constructed and restored in the workshop and explore the Children's Innovation Arcade (see "To See" in Hammondsport and Bath).

Keuka Karts Go-Kart Track in Penn Yan is good fun for kids of all ages. Take a spin in a single or double go-cart. 2451 NY Rt. 54A, Penn Yan 14527; 315-536-4833

Shopping

Hammondsport's stores are arranged around the village square and down a couple of side streets. For airplane models and other transportation-related items, try the gift shop at the **Glenn H. Curtiss Museum**. Many of the wineries have nice shops selling everything from corkscrews to books on wines.

ANTIQUES **Opera House Antiques** (607-569-3525), **Over the Bridge Antiques** (607-569-2708), and **Wild Goose Chase Antiques II** (607-868-3946) are all located in Hammondsport.

LIME BERRY GALLERY & WINERY SELLS WINES AND UNIQUE GIFTS

Lime Berry Gallery & Winery

GIFTS **Browsers** is a small department store selling clothing, gifts, wind chimes, flags, wooden bowls, glassware, and much more. 33 Shethar St., Hammondsport 14840; 607-569-2497

The Cinnamon Stick has two levels selling dolls, candles, teddy bears, glassware, and much more, plus a whole room filled with Christmas items. 26 Mechanic St., Hammondsport 14840; 607-569-2277; www.cinnamonstick.com

Keuka Oil Company offers infused oil in a tempting range of flavors along with gourmet foods and spices. 27 Shethar St., Hammondsport 14840; 607-738-2695; www.keukaoilcompany.com

Lake Country Patchwork has a good selection of everything a quilter needs 67 Shethar St., Hammondsport 14840; 607-569-3530

Lime Berry Gallery & Winery in Melissa and Joe Carroll's 1800s "Wine Tasting Schoolhouse" not only has wines like Bunny Bunny Blush and classic rieslings but an intriguing collection of art in their gallery. Bring a picnic lunch, pair your food with one of Lime Berry's wines, and enjoy lingering in their garden overlooking the lake. 10014 Day Rd., Hammondsport 14840; 607-569-3300; www.corningfingerlakes.com

FOR MORE INFORMATION **Finger Lakes (Yates County) Chamber of Commerce**: 315-536-3111; www.fingerlakeschamber.com

Central Steuben Chamber of Commerce: 607-776-7122; www.centralsteubenchamber.com

Finger Lakes Tourism Alliance: 800-548-4386, 315-536-7488; www.fingerlakes.org

Hammondsport Chamber of Commerce: 607-569-2989; www.hammondsport.org

Keuka Lake Wine Trail: www.keukawinetrail.com

Steuben County Conference and Visitors Bureau: 607-974-2066, 800-284-3352, 866-WINE-FUN (866-946-3386), or 607-936-6544; www.corningfingerlakes.com
Yates County Tourism: 800-868-9283; www.yatesny.com

Keuka Lake

✳ What's Happening

SPRING **Easter Egg Hunt**, Village Square, Hammondsport. Children hunt for hidden eggs and prizes. 607-569-2989

Keuka Arts Festival, Penn Yan Boat Launch. More than 75 vendors showcase their art, wines, food, and music in this fine art and skilled crafshow (June). 315-531-9232; www.keukaartsfestival.com

SUMMER **Keuka Lake Art Association Show**, downtown Hammondsport. Local and regional artists show and sell their work. 607-569-2989

Finger Lakes Chamber Festival, with chamber music featuring Manhattan Chamber Orchestra in unique venues around Keuka Lake.

Steuben County Fair, Fairgrounds, Bath. The oldest continuously held agricultural country fair in the country (August). 607-776-4801

Yates County Fair, Penn Yan: The fun takes place the second week in July. Go hog wild and catch the action of Rosaire's Racing Pigs; see demolition derbies, racing, tractor pulling, horses, and fireworks. And of course there are games and oodles of food. 315-536-3830; www.yatescountyfair.org

Annual Antique Show & Sale, Yates County Fairgrounds, Penn Yan. More than 1,000 dealers and free coin appraisals (August). 315-536-5039

FALL/WINTER **Annual Seaplane Homecoming**, Glenn H. Curtiss Museum, Hammondsport. 607-569-2160; www.seaplanehomecoming.org

Wine Country Dog Show Circuit, Sampson State Park, Romulus. More than 2800 dogs compete, with all AKC breeds represented (September). 607-582-6317

The Genundowa Labor Day Bonfire with Native American flute music from Chief Joe Firecrow. www.genundowa.com

Annual Hunt Country Harvest Festival, Hunt Country Vineyards, Branchport. Features horse-drawn wagon tours of the vineyards along with grape stomping, music, and crafts (October). 800-946-3289

Fall Foliage Festival, Cohocton. Family fun, fireworks, parade, games, and food (October). www.fallfoliagefestival.com

Harvest Celebration of Food & Wine, Keuka Lake wineries. Enjoy German music and food; taste world-class German-style wines at participating wineries. 800-440-4898; www.keukawinetrail.com

Keuka Holidays. Keuka Lake wineries. Visit wineries along the Keuka Lake Wine Trail, enjoy hearty winter foods and wine. 800-440-489

Starshine in the Village, Penn Yan. A celebration of the holidays (December). 800-387-6501

CANANDAIGUA LAKE

Canadice, Conesus, Hemlock, & Honeoye Lakes

The western frontier of the Finger Lakes is anchored by 16-mile Canandaigua Lake, along with the Canadice, Honeoye, Hemlock, and Conesus, which range from 3 miles to 8 miles in length and are often called "The Little Lakes." Rich in natural beauty, there are many undeveloped areas of woodlands and meadows. The largest town, Canandaigua, sits at the northern end of Canandaigua Lake; Naples is at the southern end.

HISTORY "People of the Great Hill," the Senecas, populated the western Finger Lakes long before Columbus found his way to the New World. One of the Senecas' largest communities was on a breezy hilltop in Victor. Known as Ganondagan, it had more than 150 bark longhouses, four corn storehouses, and an estimated population of 4,500.

In the seventeenth century the people of this "Town of Peace" were at the center of a thriving beaver fur trade. The fur was sent to Holland and France to use in making beaver hats, a hot fashion item of the times. To eliminate the Senecas' competition in the fur trade, in the 1660s the Marquis de Denonville and his French troops invaded Ganondagan and destroyed it.

At one time, this region belonged to Massachusetts, then New York State. Congressmen Oliver Phelps and Nathaniel Gorham put together a syndicate and negotiated to purchase the land, which they then marketed and sold to settlers. Phelps and Gorham could thus be called some of our country's earliest land developers. Settlers arrived, towns were established, and communities like Canandaigua and Clifton Springs sprung up. Today the Seneca Art & Culture Center at Ganondagan is a New York State Historical Site.

Canandaigua

Canandaigua, "the chosen spot," maintains a small-town environment for its 10,000 residents. The main part of town is just north of the lake. The wide Main St., divided by a landscaped grassy strip, is lined by retailers and banks along with art galleries and specialty shops.

The revitalized waterfront park, the weathered boathouses, the handsome New York Wine and Culinary Center (see "Dining Out"), and the postage-stamp-size Squaw Island—the smallest New York State Park—are major assets, while the Granger Homestead and Carriage Museum, Sonnenberg Gardens, and the Mansion State Historic Park are important historical attractions.

Canandaigua's notable citizens include benefactor Mary Clark Thompson, while famous visitors have included the Marquis de Lafayette (1824), Susan B. Anthony (1872), Helen Keller, Stephen Douglas, and Humphrey Bogart.

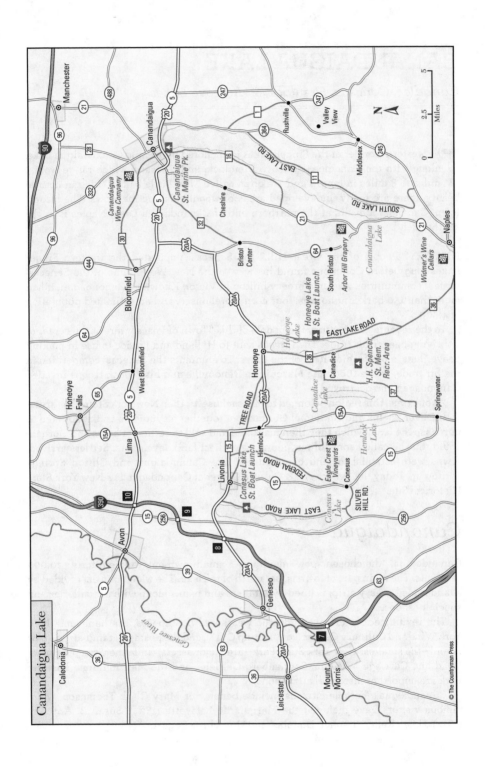

Canandaigua Lake

© The Countryman Press

SONNENBERG GARDENS & MANSION

✳ Lodging

The crowning jewel of the **Bristol Harbour Resort** is its lovely rolling Robert Trent Jones golf course set on 454 acres along the lake. An Adirondack-style inn has 31 rooms with views of the lake, fireplaces, and heated tile bathroom floors. The resort also rents mid-rise condominiums, townhouses, and patio homes that hug the water's edge and range along the fairways. There is a marina, private beach, pool, spa, restaurant, tennis courts, and boat slips. Cross-country skiing is on-site and downhill skiing is just 7 miles away. Golf and stay packages are available. $$–$$$$ 5410 Seneca Point Rd., Canandaigua 14424; 585-396-2200, 800-288-8248; www.bristolharbour.com

The Inn on the Lake is a modern resort and conference center on the shores of Canandaigua Lake. The lobby showcases marble floors, artwork, and plush furniture. Arrive by boat and come in for the night or a meal. Many rooms as well as the large dining room overlook the water. Luxury linens, cable television, and high-speed Internet access are standard in all rooms. Facilities include Jacuzzis, indoor and outdoor pools with spa, fitness center, The Shore restaurant, The Lounge and Deck, and the Sandbar Patio Bar and Grill. $$–$$$$ 770 S. Main St., Canandaigua 14424; 585-394-7800, 800-228-2801; www.theinnonthelake.com

Fun upbeat décor, South Beach–style art deco accents like the motel's original neon light, turquoise pool chairs, and slick furniture shapes in luscious colors have been integrated into the newly renovated **Miami Motel**. It's retro, kitschy, reasonable with extras like luxury linens, beds, and WiFi. We're talking personality. $–$$ 4126 NY Rt. 5, Canandaigua 14424; 585-394-6700; www.motelmiami.com

For those who like to stick to the tried-and-true, Canandaigua also has chain hotels including the **Holiday Inn Express**, 300 Eastern Blvd., Canandaigua 14424; 585-396-3669

THE INN ON THE LAKE, CANANDAIGUA

B&BS This delightful stone-fronted bungalow-style **1837 Cobblestone Cottage** is comfortable and upbeat with a lot of extras. Exceptional homemade breakfasts; cookies; creative goodies like strawberry, tomato, and ricotta bruschetta and creamsicle pies; your own fireplace; king-size beds; fabulous sheets; and a fire pit to enjoy at night all contributes to Cobblestone Cottage's desirability. There are three bedrooms, all with private baths. $$$–$$$$ 3402 W. Lake Rd., Canandaigua 14424; 585-721-6765; www.1837cobblestonecottage.com

You've got to think romance when you visit the **1795 Acorn Inn B&B**. Walled gardens, private brick patios, an outdoor Jacuzzi, and a hammock tucked into a hidden corner provide an intimate setting. Built in 1795 for the stagecoach trade, the inn is furnished with a mix of antiques and period reproductions—interesting collections without clutter—plus oriental rugs, original art, shelves of books, a fireplace, and floor-to-ceiling windows. Five guest rooms have private baths, queen-size beds, luxury bedding, sitting area, air-conditioning, bathrobes, and TV/DVD. The Hotchkiss Room, has a fireplace, canopy bed, French doors leading to a private garden terrace, and whirlpool tub. A bounteous candlelit country breakfast is served on antique English china. Although the entire inn has been soundproofed, this is not a place for young children. $$–$$$ 4508 NY Rt. 64S, Canandaigua 14424; 585-229-2834, 866-665-3747; www.acorninnbb.com

Across from the Granger Homestead, the historic **Bed & Breakfast at Oliver Phelps** is perfect if you want to be in the heart of town. Four guest rooms with private baths are decorated in fresh colors and fabrics enhancing the traditional décor. Its large common room is often booked for parties. Breakfasts are sumptuous. $$–$$$ 252 N. Main St., Canandaigua 14424; 585-396-1650; www.oliverphelps.com

Bella Rose Bed and Breakfast, a Victorian rose-hued home in Canandaigua's historic district, has a lot to love, from a fully stocked fridge, wraparound porch, and original stained glass windows to a cozy fireplace in the parlor. And wait until you see the three guest rooms. Cool things include jetted tubs, a fireplace, pillow-top mattresses, Italian linens, windows that open, and a private balcony—even towel warmers, robes, and slippers. $$–$$$$ 290 N. Main St., Canandaigua 14424; 800-508-2134, 585-393-9937; www.bellarosebb.com

The former Alfred Morris Gifford House, circa 1820, the **Inn on the Main** is located in the historic district. Features include carved fireplaces, polished hardwood floors, oriental rugs, large windows, and five guest rooms with private baths. Queen-size four-poster beds, Jacuzzi tubs, antique claw-foot tub/shower, and a two-bedroom suite with a private entrance and kitchen afford plenty of options. Amenities include TV/VCR/DVD, WiFi, and free local calls. A full country breakfast is served. $$–$$$ 176 N. Main St., Canandaigua 14424; 585-394-0139, 877-659-1643; www.innonthemain.com

With walk-in showers, soaking tubs, balconies, fireplaces, rustic chic décor, and spacious suites, the three bedrooms and public areas of **Chalet of Canandaigua** are designed for those who cherish privacy, class, and peaceful surroundings. There are walking trails, a pond, and lovely grounds, and you are in the heart of wine country. $$$–$$$$ 3770 NY Rt. 21, Canandaigua 14424; 585-394-9080; www.chaletbandb.com

Two miles out of town, tree-lined drives lead up to the stone mansion **Morgan Samuels Inn** (circa 1810). Find exquisite gardens, museum-quality antiques, carpets, and oil paintings. There are 11 fireplaces and several common rooms including a parlor and a glassed-in Victorian porch. Comfortable and elegant, the six well-appointed guest rooms all have fireplaces and private baths. The suite contains French inlaid wood pieces from the 1800s; another room has hand-painted furniture. Some rooms have Jacuzzis, and three have balconies. There is also a tennis court and a full breakfast is served. Crave a five-course gourmet dinner? They can set it up. $$–$$$ 2920 Smith Rd., Canandaigua 14424; 585-394-9232; www.morgansamuelsinn.com

Two decks and gardens overlooking the west side of the lake or the woods, establish a mood of serenity at the **Onanda by the Lake B&B**. The two-story colonial (circa 1844) has three guest rooms with private baths. The Premier suite has a fireplace, whirlpool tub, and deck. Have breakfast where you wish, perhaps the sunporch, dining room, or your deck. Walk to Onanda Park where you can swim, kayak, and hike. 4926 W. Lake Rd., Canandaigua 14424; 585-396-9487; www.onandabythelake.com

COTTAGES A cross between a B&B and a vacation rental, **The Quiet Place** portfolio includes about 25 cabins and cottages in the Canandaigua area promising delicious pleasures like complete privacy, fireplaces, views of hills and lakes, hot tubs, and all sorts of enticements for those who want to get away and unwind. There is Bloomfield Cabin with a queen bed, Jacuzzi, indoor and outdoor fireplace, and a huge panoramic window; there is Whispering Woods with two bedrooms, a great room, and a jetted hot tub on the deck; and the lofty Sunset Lodge with a wraparound deck and two bedrooms. Linens, towels, TV/VCR/DVD, coffee, and other essentials are provided. Just bring your groceries. $$–$$$ 585-657-4643; www.thequietplace.com

✳ Dining Out

There's hardly a better place to appreciate the beauty of the lake than from a perch on **Bristol Harbour Resort**'s terrace high above the water, with the rolling golf course and vineyards all around. This is, by far, one of the nicest places to wine and dine in the area. Inside the lofty dining room and bar, both made of heavy timbers, the views through the large windows are almost as good as those from the terrace. Chairs are made of bent twigs and branches. $–$$ 5410 Seneca Point Rd., Canandaigua 14424; 800-288-8248; www.bristolharbour.com

BEST IN CANANDAIGUA

ROMANTIC ESCAPE: 1795 Acorn Inn
ELEGANT LODGING: Morgan Samuels Inn
RUSTIC CHIC: Chalet of Canandaigua
FUN & REASONABLE: Miami Motel

LAKESIDE DINING: The Inn on the Lake
WINE LUNCH & DINNERS: New York Wine
and Culinary Center
PRIVACY: The Quiet Place

Even if you're not hungry, come for the views at **The Inn on the Lake's Shore Restaurant**. Dishes include classics like shrimp cocktail, Caesar salad, and filet mignon. For brunch, designer omelets allow you to create your own. Entertainment is provided weekends. There is also the **Lakeside Lounge** and **Sandbar Patio Bar**. $–$$$ 770 S. Main St., Canandaigua 14424; 585-394-7800, 800-228-2801; www.theinnonthelake.com

New York Wine and Culinary Center overlooking the city pier serves really delicious, creative fare prepared from local ingredients, like warm lentil salad with house-cured pork belly and Concord grape gastrique, perhaps served with reserve chardonnay or Brooklyn pilsner. Suggested New York wines and beer are included on the menu along with distilled spirits. Dine inside or under the awning on the terrace overlooking the harbor. 800 S. Main St., Canandaigua 14424; 585-394-7070; www.nywcc.com

CASUAL FARE The chef and co-owner of **Café Sol**, located in a remodeled country store, is considered one of the best cooks in the Finger Lakes, so you are in for a treat as she uses fresh, local ingredients in items like her tapas and fish. Enjoy live entertainment some nights. Serving breakfast, lunch, and dinner, but check days open as they vary. $–$$ 4503 NY Rt. 64, Canandaigua 14424; 585-229-2233; www.cafesolroute64.com

MACGREGOR'S GRILL AND TAP ROOM IS ACROSS THE STREET FROM THE NEW YORK WINE & CULINARY CENTER

IN ADDITION TO WINERIES, SEVERAL BREWERIES AND DISTILLERIES HAVE BEEN ESTABLISHED IN THE FINGER LAKES

Casa de Pasta has just a few tables, a bar, and little fuss in décor. Favorite dishes include veal parmigiana, spaghetti, and other Italian specialties. If you like Northern Italian food, you'll like the menu, which features white sauces along with the usual tomato-based fare. Produce is obtained from local farmers whenever possible. $$ 125 Bemis St., Canandaigua 14424; 585-394-3710; www.casa-de-pasta.com

Eddie O'Brien's Grille & Bar serves specialty sandwiches and wraps as well as full-course dinners. If you're up for a steak, come here. $–$$ 182 S. Main St., Canandaigua 14424; 585-394-8810; www.eddieobriens.net

Beer lovers should check out **MacGregor's Grill and Tap Room**, which has a huge selection of brews on tap and in bottles. Facing the waterfront and looking very colonial in its white-frame building and red, white, and blue bunting, MacGregor's offers sports, pub food, wine, and beer. Popular with the younger set, this is a good place to get a brew and simple meal like finger foods, burgers, and sandwiches. $–$$ 759 S. Main St., Canandaigua 14424; 585-394-8080; www.macgregorsgtr.com

Nick's Chophouse and Bar is known for its hand-rubbed steaks and chops along with an impressive menu of martinis and wines. $–$$$ 5 Beeman St., Canandaigua 14424; 585-393-0303; www.nickschophouseandbar.com

Rio Tomatlan serves reasonably priced, really tasty Mexican-style cuisine like tacos, tortillas, quesadillas, enchiladas and homemade salsas and guacamole. Their margarita made with 100% agave reposedo tequila is outstanding. $–$$ 106 Bemis St., Canandaigua 14424; 585-394-9380; www.riotomatlan.com

Family owned and run, **Schooner's Restaurant** is a good down-home restaurant, offering generous portions of pasta, steak, soups, salads, and seafood in a yacht-like setting. Wednesday is chicken 'n' biscuit night; Friday is fish and chips—a favorite. $–$$ 407 Lakeshore Dr., Canandaigua 14424; 585-396-3360; www.canandaiguarestaurants.com

Simply Crepes wraps up all those delicious tastes in their homemade crepes from breakfast to dessert. They have other things, too, like manicotti and great

THE NEW YORK WINE AND CULINARY CENTER IS A GOOD PLACE TO START YOUR TOUR OF THE REGION'S WINES, BREWERIES, AND DISTILLERIES

drinks. Many of the ingredients are locally sourced so are indeed fresh. My favorite: goat cheese and arugula crepes. $$ 101 S. Main St., Canandaigua 14424; 583-394-9090; www .simplycrepes.com

WINE AND BEER To get an overview of wine and beer in the state, start at the **New York Wine and Culinary Center** in Canandaigua. A cork's throw from the harbor, it showcases the various wines and beer from New York State producers. There is a wine and beer tasting room, retail shop, Taste of New York Lounge, demonstration kitchen, meeting rooms, private dining room for small groups, restaurant, deck, and exhibit hall. Experience hands-on programs in the gleaming stainless-steel kitchen including cooking classes presented by well-known guest chefs. An outdoor garden along with a thriving beehive help you learn about this prospering viticultural area. 800 S. Main St., Canandaigua 14424; 585-394-7070; www.nywcc.com

✳ To See

ARCHITECTURE In Canandaigua, notable houses and buildings in the area include those along North Main Street, Gibson Street, and Howell Street.

The **Ontario County Courthouse**, built in 1857 with pillars and a dome, was the venue for a number of hotly contested trials over the years, including many that challenged the 1850 Fugitive Slave Act and the Susan B. Anthony trial (1872). The courthouse was enlarged in 1909, and in 1988, two new wings were added. 27 N. Main St., Canandaigua 14424; 585-396-4239; www.co.ontario.ny.us

THE GRANGER HOMESTEAD AND CARRIAGE MUSEUM

THE GREENHOUSE AT SONNENBERG GARDENS

MUSEUMS AND HISTORIC SITES At the **Seneca Art & Culture Center at Ganondagan** a new permanent year-round interpretive facility has opened telling the 2,000-year-old story of the Seneca and Haudenosaunee contributions to culture and society. Among the exhibits is a re-created bark longhouse depicting how the Senecas lived—their tools, clothing, cooking utensils, weapons, ornaments, and accessories. Each summer the Music and Dance Festival brings skilled artists to perform and demonstrate crafts such as bow making; cornhusk doll making; wood, bone, and antler carving; and other arts. G. Peter Jemison, a descendant of Mary Jemison, a white woman captured and adopted by Native Americans, has been a strong leader in the center. 7000 Cty. Rd. 41, Victor 14564; 585-924-5848; www.ganondagan.org

The **Granger Homestead and Carriage Museum** represents a fine example of Federal architecture, built in 1816 by Gideon Granger, who was postmaster general for Jefferson and Madison. Inside is a collection of period furnishings, some original to the house, along with lovely hand-carved woodwork. The extensive Carriage Museum includes restored leisure, sporting, and commercial conveyances such as the *Eagle*, Canandaigua's first fire engine (1816); a private road coach used by the Vanderbilts; a tinker's wagon; several sleighs; and a rare Coachee (1790s), one of only five known in the country. 295 N. Main St., Canandaigua 14424; 585-394-1472; www.grangerhomestead.org

See hundreds of original deeds for area lands and maps at the **Ontario County Historical Society Museum** including the Native American copy of the 1794 Pickering Treaty between the six nations of the Haudenosaunee (Iroquois) Confederacy and the U.S. government. There is also a valuable collection of Native American signatures along with artifacts, early farm and home implements, and a huge library of family histories, photographs, and other materials. 55 N. Main St., Canandaigua 14424; 585-394-4975; www.ochs.org

Built in 1887 as the summer home of bank magnate Frederick Ferris Thompson and his wife Mary Clark, one of Canandaigua's most generous benefactors, the Victorian mansion at **Sonnenberg Gardens & Mansion State Historic Park** features turrets,

SUMMER EVENTS ARE HELD AT CMAC

towers, stone, and heavily carved wood details. On the 50-acre grounds are several formal theme gardens created between 1902 and 1919, along with unique specimen trees and a large greenhouse complex. The 40-room mansion contains several period pieces. In the summer meals are served on the veranda. 151 Charlotte St., Canandaigua 14424; 585-394-4922; www.sonnenberg.org

PERFORMING ARTS Every Friday evening during July and August, free concerts are held in the **Atwater Park Gazebo**. Main St., Canandaigua 14424; 585-396-0300

Performances take place inside an amphitheater at the base of a grassy hill at the **Constellation Brands-Marvin Sands Performing Arts Center** (CMAC) Sit inside or bring lawn chairs and blankets and picnic on the lawn while listening to great music—classical, pop, rock, jazz, and blues. Occasionally non-music events are held, such as the recent performance by A Prairie Home Companion's Garrison Keillor. 3355 Marvin Sands Dr., Canandaigua 14424; 585-394-4400; www.cmacevents.com

✳ To Do

FAMILY FUN At the summit of Bristol Mountain, thrill to seven challenge courses, 10 zip-lines, and a huge number of platforms with **Bristol Mountain Aerial Adventures**. 5662 Rt. 64, Canandaigua 14424; 585-374-1180; www.bristolmountain adventures.com

Long Acre Farms' amazing Maize Maze in the fall is great fun. It's a working family farm focusing on outdoor entertainment and weekend festivals. There is a goat pen and petting area, a five-acre play area—filled with a wooden pirate ship and playground equipment, a tire climb and pumpkin land in the fall—as well as a farm market store, an ice cream shop, and a bakery. They even offer helicopter rides. It's just north of the Thruway but worth the trip. 1342 Eddy Rd., Macedon 14502; 315-986-9821; www .longacrefarms.com

Cool off on a summer's day at **Roseland Waterpark**, a 58-acre playground with water slides, a giant wave pool, Adventure River, two body flumes, Splash Factory, three tube rides, a 30-acre private lake, river rafts, and a playground. 250 Eastern Blvd., Canandaigua 14424; 585-396-2000; www.roselandwaterpark.com

See how the Native Americans lived at the **Seneca Art & Culture Center at Ganondagan** in Victor, and get an up-close look at historic carriages at the **Granger Museum** (See "To See" in Canandaigua).

Soar above Letchworth Park and the beautiful lake-dotted countryside in a hot air balloon. **Liberty Balloon Company** in Groveland offers flights from Conesus Lake, Canandaigua Lake, Letchworth State Park, Geneseo, and other sites. 585-243-3178; www.libertyballoon.com

See the world's largest herd of white deer at the former **Seneca Army Depot** near Romulus. www.senecawhitedeer.org

DRIVING AROUND THE LAKE It's a beautiful drive all the way around the lake, especially on W. Lake Rd. (Cty. Rd. 16) and E. Lake Rd., which generally follow the shoreline. A local favorite, NY Rt. 21 to Cty. Rd. 12 called the "High Road to Naples," is a quicker way to get from one end to another and runs along the top of the hills on the west side, revealing some lovely scenic vistas. The farther south you go, the better the views. Watch for the signs of wineries on the Canandaigua Wine Trail. www .canandaiguawinetrail.com

Naples

When you notice the purple fire hydrants, you're reminded that in Naples, grapes are big. Most of the year it's business as usual for this quiet place south of the lake, but come September some 75,000 people pour into town for the annual Grape Festival. The main street is lined with booths of more than 250 artists and food vendors; jazz, country, blues, and other musical groups entertain; and, of course, everyone enjoys the World's Greatest Grape Pie Contest. After all, this is the "Grape Pie Capital of the World," a moniker justly deserved when you consider that during the grape harvest, the more than seventy thousand pies sold are baked in the kitchens of about two dozen women.

Naples stands on the site of the original Seneca village of Nundawao and is the burial place of Conesque, the chief of the Senecas, who died in 1794. A plaque notes that it is here that George Washington first took command of the American army on July 3, 1775.

Original landmarks include the Morgan Fire House Hook and Ladder Co. firehouse, a three-story frame structure (1891 to 1916); the Ephraim Cleveland House (1794); and Memorial Town Hall. There is also the Cumming Nature Center, Bristol Valley Theatre, and several area vineyards, including Hazlitt Wine Cellars and Inspire Moore.

WINE & BEER TASTING TOUR

START: Canandaigua

TRAVEL: NY Rt. 21 south down the west side of lake to Naples; north on NY Rt. 245 to NY Rt. 364

1ST STOP: New York Wine & Culinary Center in Canandaigua is the perfect place to start any exploration of Finger Lakes wineries. Here you get an overview and tastings of wines, beer and ales all in one place. Great restaurant, too, celebrating regional foods (see "Dining Out" in Canandaigua).

2ND STOP: Heron Hill Winery Tasting Room at Bristol in a century-old barn. 5323 Seneca Point Rd., Canandaigua 14424; 585-394-0173

3RD STOP: Arbor Hill Grapery, Naples, sells everything remotely connected to grapes including chardonnay, riesling, pinot noir, Cayuga White, maréchal foch, traminette, vidal blanc, catawba, niagara, and Celebration sparkling wine. Try their homemade grape pies and other gourmet foods. 585-374-2406, 800-554-2406; www.thegrapery.com (see listing under "Specialty Foods" in Naples).

4TH STOP: Widmer's Wine Cellars, Naples, on the hills overlooking the Naples valley, offers sherries, sparkling wines, Lake Niagara, Crackling Lake Niagara, and port as well as Manischewitz. There are wine tastings, tours of underground cellars and the bottling facility, and the gift and wine shop. The **Widmer Antique Museum** displays a collection of old winemaking equipment. 585-374-3200, 800-836-5253; www.widmerwine.com

5TH STOP: Naples, venue for the annual Grape Festival. Have lunch at the **Brown Hound Bistro** or **Brew & Brats at Arbor Hill** in a historic carriage barn serving local Bristol Springs Brand craft beer like American Pale Ale and Porter paired with Hartmann's Old World Sausage (see "Casual Fare" in Naples).

6TH STOP: Imagine Moore Winery, Naples, uses sustainable farming practices to grow their grapes and works with local farmers to create their riesling, grüner, veltliner, chardonnay, cabernet franc, pinot noir, and blaufränkisch. 585-374-5970; www.imaginemoorewinery.com

7TH STOP: Hazlitt's Red Cat Cellars, Naples, is the winery's second location and is housed in the old Widmer Wine Complex. Taste wine, take a hike on their one-mile loop, have a picnic and spend the night in the **1852 House**. 1 Lake Niagra Ln., Naples 14512; 585-531-9000

LAST STOP: Take NY Rt. 245 north up the west side of the lake finishing at **Wilhelmus Estate Winery** in Canandaigua. One of the newer wineries in the area (2007), Wilhelmus produces vinifera and hybrid varietals. Take a look at their oak barrel and wine motif furniture, some with a nautical theme. 585-374-3200; www.wilhelmusestate.com

ALSO CHECK OUT: Casa Larga Vineyards north of Canandaigua in Fairport. Its premium category includes limited-release, hand-selected, barrel-fermented and aged and unfiltered oak reserve pinot noir, French oak reserve chardonnay, and American oak reserve chardonnay. 585-223-4210; www.casalarga.com. Also check out **CB Craft Brewers**, Honeoye Falls, with 23 kinds of craft beer on tap brewed on the premises. Food available weekends. 585-624-4386; www.cbcraftbrewers.com

✳ Lodging

B&BS **Monier Manor**, an 1850 Italianate Victorian home located on two lovely acres, has four guest rooms with private baths, queen-size, four-poster beds, and a deck with a hot tub. Bring an appetite for breakfast. $$ 154 N. Main St., Naples 14512; 585-374-6719; www.moniermanor.com

Those looking for quiet seclusion will like **Vagabond Inn**, a 7,000-foot rustic inn on a mountain with an enormous 1,800-square-foot great room and fireplace constructed of native stone and black walnut. There are seven luxury suites like the Lodge Suite with a massive river-stone fireplace and a king-size bed, dining area, hot tub, and bar, while the Bristol Suite has two decks and a private porch as well as a king-size canopy bed, fireplace, and two-person Jacuzzi. A full breakfast is served, a kitchen is available for guests to use as well as an Internet terminal, and there is DirecTV in each room. $$–$$$$ 3300 Sliter Hill Rd., Naples 14512; 585-554-6271; www.thevagabondinn.com

HORSES, HORSES, HORSES **Mountain Horse Farm B&B**, a beautifully constructed log lodge, is set on 33 acres of a Morgan horse farm with pastures, rolling meadows, and trails. The Nokota and Morgan guest rooms, named after horses, are furnished in a contemporary style with colorful Southwest spreads and blankets. Special amenities include robes, a wine chiller, chocolates, flat-screen TVs, and WiFi. A hearty home-cooked breakfast is served. $$ 7520 W. Hollow Rd., Naples 14512; 585-374-5056; www.mountainhorsefarm.com

✳ Dining Out

The Historic Naples Hotel & Restaurant is a small inn with a porch and taproom complete with a stuffed deer head. The dining room has a more formal feel, with white tablecloths and period chairs while the food is centered on old favorites like chicken alfredo and veal cutlet. $$–$$$ 111 S. Main St., Naples 14512; 585-374-5630; www.napleshotelny.com

Kismet New American Bistro serves beautiful, seasonally inspired dinners in an upscale, intimate dining setting. Look for interesting dishes like rabbit with fresh figs, il pollastro, and pecan-crusted tofu. $$–$$$ 114 N. Main St., Naples 14512; 585-374-9171; www.kismetnewamericanbistro.com

Roots Café epitomizes the farm-to-table trend with items such as sweet potato veggie burger; the menu includes vegan and gluten-free dishes. Brought to you by the Inspire Moore wines people next door, Roots is located in a Victorian house painted in whimsical turquoise and purple. Eat on the porch in warm weather or inside where the décor is retro eclectic. 197 N. Main St., Naples 14512; 585-374-9800

CASUAL FARE Down-home cooking at **Bob's 'n Ruth's Vineyard** includes soups, desserts, baked goods, and all the usual suspects. Dine at a counter or booth or in the Vineyard Room where tables are set with linens and crystal. There is also the deck just off the Vineyard—especially pretty in the fall when the hill is ablaze with color. In a hurry? Go to the outside pickup window for simple sandwiches and ice cream and take them to one of the picnic tables in the grove of trees adjacent to the restaurant. $–$$ 204 N. Main St., Naples 14512; 585-374-5122

Brew & Brats at Arbor Hill serves local Bristol Springs Brand craft beer like Frog Hollow Pale Ale and Turtle Crawl Porter. B&B partners with Hartmann's Old World

Sausage from Canandaigua to bring high-quality sausages to enjoy with your beer. The barn's walls are hung with farm implements. Very cool. $–$$ 6461 NY Rt. 64, Naples 14512; 585-374-2870; www.brewandbrats.com

Freshly baked desserts and a diverse selection of Finger Lakes wines are featured in the funky and fun **Brown Hound Bistro** set in a charming one-hundred-year-old house. Eat and drink in the bar/dining room or on the awning-protected deck. You've got to love items like "Wild Bill's Hangover" for breakfast or lunch, and the Bistro burger, house-ground beef and pork. And for dinner there is "Doggone Delmonico." On most weekends, tune into the live music. $–$$ 6459 NY Rt. 64, Naples 14512; 585-374-9711; www.brownhoundbistro.com

✳ To See

PERFORMING ARTS **Bristol Valley Theater** offers musicals, comedy, and mystery thrillers as well as children's theater, held in a former church. Past performances have included *Godspell*, *Rent*, and *Family Matters*. 151 S. Main St., Naples 14512; 585-374-6318; www.bvtnaples.org

The Gell Center draws writers and poets who come to reflect, write, and learn. The Gleason Lodge is used for meetings and special programs, and the Gell House accommodates overnight guests. 6581 W. Hollow Rd., Naples 14512; 585-473-2590; www.wab.org

Honeoye, Canadice, Hemlock, and Conesus Lakes

West of Canandaigua Lake, the four smaller lakes—Honeoye, Canadice, Hemlock, and Conesus—attract those with attitude: that is "I'm on vacation; leave me alone."

The town of Honeoye has more than 150 historic homes and buildings. Folks here go about their business in a friendly yet unobtrusive manner. A museum on Main St., once a one-room schoolhouse, contains exhibits about the area's agricultural history.

On Honeoye Lake, the size of boat motors is restricted, and this Finger Lake is small enough—5 miles long—so you can hike or bike around it in a day.

New York State purchased Hemlock and Canadice lakes from the City of Rochester to protect and preserve the last two undeveloped Finger Lakes, which have supplied water to Rochester for more than 130 years. Home to the Hemlock-Canadice Lake State Forest, these are the only Finger Lakes with no shoreline development, and only non-motorized craft are allowed.

Quiet and pretty Conesus Lake, the most western of the Finger Lakes, is ringed by private homes and many camps along with a few bed-and-breakfasts. NY Rt. 256 along the western side of the lake runs less than 20 feet from the water's edge in some places.

✳ Lodging

CHECKING IN **Greenwoods Bed & Breakfast Inn**, a roomy two-story log inn evoking an Adirondack great camp, has all the comforts of a fine country house. It's a peaceful place with trails to explore and three ponds. Five guest rooms are large and well-appointed. The Timberlake Suite has a canopy bed, fireplace, and outside entrance leading onto a wide deck overlooking gardens and a fishpond; on the top floor great views are a highlight of the Comstock Room. All rooms come with queen-size feath-erbeds, and public rooms include a well-stocked library, game room, and media room with a 40-inch television. There is an outdoor spa, deck, and trails cut into the hills behind the house. A full breakfast is served. $$ 8136 Quayle Rd., Honeoye 14471; 585-229-2111, 800-914-3559; www.greenwoodsinn.com

✷ Dining Out

CASUAL FARE **The Rabbit Room at the Lower Mill** is open for lunch on the first floor of this historic mill, while on the second and third floors you can catch the art on display. Dinner, is served Thursdays, often accompanied by live music. Lunch items include homemade falafel and quinoa salad. The beamed ceilings and wood floors lend a rustic, warm feeling. $–$$ 61 N. Main St., Honeoye Falls 14471; 585-582-1830; www.the lowermill.com

Beachcomber Inn on Conesus Lake appears to have been around for a long time, with its weathered gray siding and deck. You'll know you're there when you see the post with hand-painted signs pointing to faraway places like Cancun and Nice. The deck is popular with locals who come for a quick bite and a beer. 5909 West Lake Rd., Conesus 14435; 585-243-3640; www.beachcomberny.com

✷ To See

The three floors of this historic repurposed building now called the **Lower Mill Restaurant and Galleries** feature fine arts, handcrafts, small businesses, and the Rabbit Room Restaurant. The restored brick walls create an excellent ambiance for special events. 61 N. Main St., Honeoye Falls 14471; 585-582-1830; www.thelowermill.com

Clifton Springs

Clifton Springs, north of Canandaigua, developed as wealthy people came here to take in the natural sulfur springs that were believed to have curative powers. Today this village is a showcase for some lovely Victorian homes as well as the impressive spa building. The **Springs Integrative Medicine & Spa** opened in 2000 to attract people interested in holistic healing techniques. It offers a variety of services including acu-puncture, massages therapy, chiropractic, hydrotherapy, facials, and other programs for well-being. (www.thespringsofclifton.com). The **Pierce Pavilion** houses a sulfur spring and is surrounded by ball fields and picnic areas; a sulfur spring runs through the 15-acre Village Park. The history of the Sulfur Cure and the town is told in the Foster Cottage Museum on Main St.

Notable buildings include the Foster Cottage (circa 1854), with its triple dormers and fancy fretwork, now a museum, and **St. John's Episcopal Church** (circa 1879), made of Medina sandstone in the Gothic style and featuring windows by Tiffany.

✷ Dining Out

Holloway House has been welcoming guests since circa 1808 when it was a stop on the stagecoach line. The original fireplace where cooking took place has been reconstructed, and the original wide oak peg floors still exist under the rugs. The restaurant serves dinner and Sunday champagne brunch, and house favorites include New York State maple-mustard pork tenderloin served with New York apples in a light maple sauce and chicken cranberry. Their breads are so good, they're offered for sale. 29 State St., Bloomfield 14469; 585-657-7120; www.thehollowayhouse.com

Located in a historic three-story brick building, **Warfield's Restaurant, Lounge & Bakery** combines the ambiance of the 1800s with an authentic English pub bar, colonial paneling, fireplace, and tapestries, and offer an extensive menu featuring dishes from all parts of the world. There is a main restaurant, lounge, piano bar, bakery, and banquet rooms, as well as the pub. $–$$ 7 W. Main St., Clifton Springs 14432; 315-462-7184; www.warfields.com

CASUAL FARE It's hard to spend a bundle of money at **Minnehan's Restaurant and Fun Center**. Order at the long counter and eat at tables or booths or do takeout. The menu includes burgers, battered fries, onion rings, sandwiches, frozen custard, and yogurt along with milkshakes, sundaes, and floats. A mini-golf course, batting cages, and laser tag are fun for kids. 5601 Big Tree Rd., Lakeville 14480; 585-346-6167; www .minnehansgokart.com

✻ To See

THE ARTS **Main Street Arts**, a two-story gallery, features contemporary art and fine crafts exhibitions, some juried, as well as rotating exhibits. There is a shop on-site, and Main Street offers workshops and demonstrations. 20 W., Main St., Clifton Springs 14432; 315-462-0210; www.mainstreetartsgallery.com

✻ To Do

BIKING With steep inclines and winding roads, the 35-mile **Canandaigua Loop** is for the experienced, fit cyclist. Start at the City Pier on Lakeshore Dr. in Canandaigua on NY Rt. 5 and US Rt. 20. Heading west, turn left on Parrish St. Go up the hill to NY Rt. 21S and south toward Bristol Springs. Here, at almost the halfway point, you can take a break and check out the **Arbor Hill Grapery and Winery**. Turn right onto NY Rt. 64N, and continue to the intersection of NY Rt. 5 and US Rt. 20. On the way up NY Rt. 64, you'll pass the **Wizard of Clay Pottery**. Then go east to Canandaigua, right onto Pearl St., left at the intersection of Main St., right onto Main to the starting point.

Bike rentals and sales are available at the **Geneva Bicycle Center** in Geneva. 315-789-5922

CRUISES **Canandaigua Lady** departs Canandaigua for meal and sightseeing cruises aboard a two-deck 150-passenger paddle-wheel steamboat. Special events include New Orleans Night, Italian Fest, Fall Foliage, and a Hawaiian luau. 585-396-7350. www .cdgaboatcruises.com

MARINAS AND LAUNCHES **Canandaigua Lake State Marine Park** is located at the northern end of the lake near NY Rt. 5 and US 20 (585-394-9420). **Honeoye Lake State Park**, four miles south of Honeoye, has a boat launch and undeveloped trails (585-335-8111); on Conesus Lake and in Naples, **Smith Boys** has slips, gas, winter storage, boat rentals, sales, and service. (585-346-2060; www.smithboys.com). **Seager's Marina** on the city pier is a full-service marina with sales, service, bait, gas, and convenience store. (585-394-1327; www.seagermarine.com). **Sutter's Canandaigua Marina** at the City Pier offers recreational boat rentals, slip rentals, storage, a store, and a picnic area (no public launching; 585-394-0918; www.suttersmarina.com); and there is the **Woodville Boat Launch** on the south end of Canandaigua Lake.

FISHING Canandaigua Lake is well stocked with lake, brown, and rainbow trout, while Naples Creek has six fishing access points. Three additional fishing sites are maintained on the lake, as well as two for ice fishing at Woodville and Onanda Park. You can fish in the lake or from the City Pier, but you must have a license. Fishing licenses can be purchased at City Hall, 2 N. Main St. or at Walmart on NY Rt. 5 and US 20 East.

Canadice, Conesus, Hemlock, and Honeoye Lakes provide excellent fishing. Honeoye has an abundance of smallmouth bass, and its shallow waters make it ideal for ice fishing. Hemlock is stocked with many kinds of fish; Canadice is best for smallmouth bass. Note limitations on boat and motor size that exist for Canadice and Hemlock.

GOLF Golf in the Canandaigua area is typically a good deal, with green fees usually less than $50 including a cart. Many courses have views of the water.

When Robert Trent Jones came to the site for the **Bristol Harbour Golf Course** more than 25 years ago, he said, "In all the world and of all the properties I've seen, this one has just been waiting for a golf course." The front nine plays like a links course,

THE BRISTOL HARBOUR GOLF COURSE OVERLOOKS CANANDAIGUA LAKE

with large bunkers, nasty rough, and fickle winds. The hilly back nine winds through woods. Many holes reveal splendid views of the lake. There is a driving range, inn, and restaurant on-site. 5410 Seneca Point Rd., Canandaigua 14424; 800-288-8248, 585-396-2460; www.bristolharbour.com

CenterPointe Country Club is a semiprivate course with a blend of open fairways and tighter tree-lined fairways. 2231 Brickyard Rd., Canandaigua 14424; 585-394-0346; www.centerpointegolfclub.com

Ravenwood Golf Club, home of the 2003 New York State Amateur Tournament, combines traditional and links with water carries, bunkers, and angled greens. 929 Lynaugh Rd., Victor 14564; 585-374-8010; www.ravenwoodgolf.com

Reservoir Creek Golf Club in Naples is a hilly course characterized by berms and moguls that separate the fairways. There is a pro shop and restaurant along with a vineyard. 8613 Cohocton St. Rt. 21 S., Naples 14512; 585-374-6828; www.rcgolf.com

Victor Hills Golf Club in Victor is a nice 45-hole layout with a restaurant and pro shop. 1450 Brace Rd., Victor 14564; 585-924-3480 (north and south courses), 585-924-0700 (east course); www.victorhills.com

Winged Pheasant Golf Links in Shortsville offers 18 holes of rolling fairways along with a pro shop, carts, lessons, and golf outings. 1475 Sandhill Rd., Shortsville 14548; 585-289-8846; www.thepheasant.com

HIKING **Bare Hill Unique Area,** a moderately difficult 3.1-mile loop, goes along cut grass and stone trails, through woods, by a pond, and up to the top of Bare Hill. Go south from Canandaigua on NY 364, turn right (west) on Town Line Rd., left (south) on Bare Hill Rd., and right (west) on Van Epps Rd. It is here the Senecas used to light a huge fire in celebration of a successful harvest. The view of the lake and valley is worth the trip. 607-776-2165; www.nyhiking.com

Big Oak Trail and Sidewinder Trail in Harriet Hollister Spencer Memorial State Recreation Area, Honeoye, is marked by cross-country ski trail signs and leads north from the parking lot. Big Oak Trail, a 1-mile loop through woods, over a stream, to the top of a hill, is moderately difficult on wide dirt trails with some steep climbs. Sidewinder Trail snakes 3.3 miles through the trees with some ups and downs. 585-335-8111

Conesus Inlet Path Park on the south side of Silker Hill Rd. near the intersection of NY Rt. 256, Conesus, is an easy 1-mile walk along a mowed grass path just south of the lake. The trail starts from the parking area and is marked with round plastic discs. Walk through woods along the wetlands; stop to see wildlife from viewing platforms. You can picnic along the way. 585-226-2466

Hiking around Conesus Lake: Heading south on West Lake Rd., you pass the Savoy Sandy Bottom Nature Trail; nearing the south end of the lake, the terrain gets dramatically hillier. As you round the southern part of the lake, a dirt road to the left will take you to the paved road that runs along the east side of the lake. This is a good stretch of road, but there's not much going on except an occasional house here and there and a marina—which makes it a fantastic place to bike.

Cumming Nature Center in Naples includes 6 miles of walking trails laced throughout the 900-acre park. 585-374-6160; www.rmsc.org

Hi Tor Wildlife Management Area in Naples, winds through this 6,100-acre area of steep hills, craggy outcroppings, ponds, and old logging roads. Trails can be steep and strenuous. Hike the Conklin Gully Trail, a 1.6-mile loop; the main trail, a 4.5-mile loop; or tie into several other trails along the way and backpack for several days. In the Hi Tor area of hills, forests, and wetlands, you'll be rewarded for your more strenuous climbs by some great views of gullies, lake, and cliffs. Park near the Department of Environmental Conservation building. 585-226-2466

ITINERARIES

HIKING GRIMES GLEN PARK

Park: Along or near Vine Street, Naples
Trail: Follow Grimes Creek (bring waterproof shoes—it can be wet)
Side Trip Tasting: Hike up the trail to **Hazlitt 1852 Vineyards** and sample some Red or White Cat wine. (follow the purple markers in the village).
Walk back into town and browse the shops.
Hungry? Stop at **Roots Café** for dinner, where it is all about farm-to-table food and celebrating local art.
Time left? Take in a show at **Bristol Valley Theater**.

Onanda Park's Upland Hiking Trail is a moderately difficult 1.2-mile loop from the park on W. Lake Rd. 7 miles south of Canandaigua. Dirt paths go through woods to observation platforms overlooking gorges and waterfalls. On-site are cabins, a pavilion, a picnic area, a beach, a tennis court, and playgrounds. 585-396-2752

Ontario County Park at Gannett Hill in Naples offers self-guided tours, as well as playgrounds, a fishing pond, a picnic site, and shelters. The Jump Off trail area is the highest point in Ontario County. 585-374-6250

Rush Oaks Openings in Honeoye Falls is a 1.5-mile loop, moderately challenging along mowed and sometimes scruffy trails through fields of grasses surrounded by oak forests. The trail is unmarked, so get a map from the Department of Environmental Conservation. 518-402-9428

Seneca Trail starts in Victor at the Ganondagan State Historic Site or at the northern end of the trail at Fishers Firehall. The 5.8-mile (one way) trail winding through wooded hills, meadows, wetlands, and along abandoned rail beds is moderately difficult. Pick up a map at the center. 585-234-8226.

Letchworth State Park southwest of Rochester in Castile, is one of the most spectacular parks in the eastern United States. Called the "Grand Canyon of the East," it features three gushing waterfalls—some more than 600 feet high—along with plunging gorges and cliffs. Find playing fields, more than 66 miles of hiking and nature trails, snowmobile trails, white-water rafting, picnic facilities, campsites, biking paths, a swimming pool, and nonstop views. Spend part of the day hiking, have a picnic, and then go antique shopping in Mount Morris. www.nysparks.com

HIKING RESOURCES **Finger Lakes Trail Conference** 585-658-9320; **Ontario Pathways** (23-mile rails-to-trails multiuse recreational trail) 585-234-7922; www .ontariopathways.com; **Victor Hiking Trails** (18 miles of foot trails in Victor) 585-234-8226; www.victorhikingtrails.org; **Ontario County Tourism Office/Finger Lakes Visitors Connection** www.visitfingerlakes.com; and **"Let's Go Hike & Bike"** guide (a wonderful clip-on set of cards describing more than 66 regional trails with maps) 800-530-7488; www.letsgohikeandbike.com

HORSEBACK RIDING **Copper Creek Farm** in Shortsville offers horseback riding, lessons, and sleigh and wagon rides. 5041 Shortsville Rd., Shortsville 14548; 585-289-4441

RING OF FIRE

In the days of the Senecas, the start of the annual harvest was signaled by a huge council fire on top of Bare Hill on Canandaigua Lake. Smaller fires blazed along the shores. To commemorate this tradition, on the Saturday of Labor Day weekend, residents around the lake light flares at dusk.

PARKS, NATURE PRESERVES, AND CAMPING **Bristol Woodlands Campgrounds** set on 100 acres in Bristol is often a camping ground for artists during the summer. 4835 S. Hill Rd., Canandaigua 14424; 585-229-2290; www.bristol woodlands.com

Cumming Nature Center in Naples, an extension of the Rochester Museum and Science Center, is a vast natural environment of 900 acres with hiking and cross-country ski trails, tall red pines, and meadowland. The center is a year-round recreation destination with interpretive programs, a visitors center, and a gift shop. 6472 Gulick Rd., Naples 14512; 585-374-6160; www.rmsc.org

Kershaw Park, Canandaigua, on eight acres, has a walkway along the beach, bathhouses, picnic shelters, a gazebo, a sailboard, and canoe launch. 155 Lakeshore Dr., Canandaigua 14424; 585-396-5060

Letchworth State Park—the "Grand Canyon of the East"—runs through a narrow 17-mile bedrock canyon punctuated by three falls. The William Pryor Letchworth Museum contains Native American and pioneer items as well as archeological and natural history displays. A statue of Mary Jemison stands on the Council Grounds. Overnight accommodations are available in cabins and campsites, Pinewood Lodge, and the Glen Iris Inn. Facilities include swimming pools, fishing areas, hiking trails, hot air ballooning, whitewater rafting, and canoeing. 1 Letchworth State Park, Castile 14427; 585-493-3600; www.letchworthpark.com

Ontario County Park at Gannett Hill, off NY Rt. 64, Naples 14512; 585-374-6250. The highest point in Canandaigua, this rolling grassy park with groves of very tall pines offers hiking trails, tent sites, a playground, a pavilion, and great views, especially from Jump Off point, which looks over the Bristol hills. This is one of the best places to view the "Ring of Fire" on Labor Day weekend.

Onanda Park (see "Hiking").

SKIING **Bristol Mountain Winter Resort**, Canandaigua, is not long as ski hills go, but the 1,200-foot vertical rise is impressive. There are 34 slopes and trails, snow-making, night skiing, ski school, rentals, babysitting, and a restaurant. It's the tallest ski area between the Adirondack/Catskill region and the Rockies and has the only Olympic-style pipe in Western New York. 5662 NY Rt. 64, Canandaigua 14424; 585-374-6000; www.bristolmountain.com

FAMILY FUN **Balloons Over Letchworth** in Castile floats you over the vast natural wonderland of Letchworth State Park. The launch site is at the Middle/Upper Falls picnic area. 585-493-3340; www.balloonsoverletchworth.com,

Canandaigua Motor Sports Park rolls out DIRT motor sport stock racing on Saturdays in season. 2820 Cty. Rd. 10, Canandaigua 13036; 585-394-0961; www.canan daiguamotorsportspark.com

The Finger Lakes Gaming & Racetrack runs thoroughbred racing in season. 5857 NY Rt. 96, Farmington 14426; 585-924-3232; www.fingerlakesracetrack.com

Mees Observatory operated by the Rochester Museum and Science Center offers planet gazing and special programs, using a 24-inch telescope. 6604 E. Gannett Hill Rd., Naples 14512; 585-230-9548; www.rochesterastronomy.org

BUILD A CANOE

Wooden boat builder Patrick Smith, of **West Hollow Boat Company** in Naples, shows you how to build a classic cedar canvas canoe using techniques from the 1800s. Smith is a wonderful and patient teacher with a whole repertoire of clever sayings delivered at the perfect moment—for example "It's OK to make a mistake as long as you don't make the same mistake twice." 585-374-5014; www.westhollowboatsco.com

MASTER CANOE BUILDER PAT SMITH DEONSTRATES HOW TO BUILD A CANOE AND WANNIGAN

Roseland Family Fun Center, Canandaigua, is a 58-acre playground for family fun with water slides, a giant wave pool, Adventure River, two body flumes, Splash Factory, tube rides, a private lake, river rafts, and a playground. 585-396-2000; www .roselandwaterpark.com

PHOTO OPS **Canandaigua City Pier's boathouses** form a Rockport-like line of buildings perched on piers in the water.

Bristol Harbour View from the restaurant's clubhouse patio looking over the lake.

Harriet Hollister Spencer Memorial State Recreation Area—stop just past the guardrails after you enter for a stunning view of Honeoye Lake. From NY Rt. 15A, go south on Canadice Hill Road, and turn left into the park.

Kershaw Park Gazebo, Lakeshore Dr., Canandaigua, one of the best views in the area.

Overlook on NY Rt. 21, Carola Barb Park, South Bristol. Look to the left and see Bare Hill (the second mound), the rise where fires announced the start of the American Indian harvest.

✳ Shopping

This area is known for its grape-related products such as wines, jellies, pies, and salad dressings. Local crafts include pottery, hand-blown glass, paintings, wooden duck decoys, fishing lures, kites, and teddy bears, as well as crafts by the Mennonites and Amish.

ANTIQUES In and around Canandaigua are more than 50 antique shops. One of the biggest concentrations of shops is located in Bloomfield southwest of Canandaigua.

Bloomfield Antique Country Mile in Cheshire is a mecca for antique buffs, with more than 175 dealers in close to 10 shops. Find furniture, memorabilia, primitive tools, toys, vintage books, stoneware, glassware, dolls, collectibles, period firearms, and much more. www.bloomfieldantiquemile.com

The unusual **Vintage Tracks Museum** features more than one hundred Crawler tractors and memorabilia from the early 1900s. 3170 Wheeler Station Rd., Bloomfield 14469; 585-657-6608

The Cheshire Union Gift Shop and Antique Center is filled with an assortment of antiques and gift items. Once a schoolroom (1915), it still has the old blackboard on the wall, and the embossed tin ceiling is still in place. Tucked into nooks and crannies are collections of bears, baskets, candles, hand-knit sweaters, and other items. 4244 NY Rt. 21 S., Cheshire 14424; 585-394-5530; www.cugifts.com

Ontario Mall Antiques contains a fascinating and extensive collection of antiques and memorabilia. 1740 Rochester Rd. #332, Farmington 14425; 585-398-3030; www.ontariomallantique.com

Pierce's Antiques and Gifts is housed in a lovely nineteenth-century building where you'll find a large selection of antiques along with Christmas gifts. 2 W. Main St., Clifton Springs 14432; 315-548-4438

CLOTHING **The Country Ewe** sells a variety of clothing and accessory items like Nomadic Traders, Spring Step shoes, Dansko, and Vintage Concepts. 79 S. Main St., Canandaigua 14424; 585-396-9580, 800-708-0820; www.countryewe.com

ARTS AND CRAFTS **Artizann's** features art produced by local artists including paintings, sculpture, fiber arts, stained glass, music, books, jewelry, and culinary artwork. 118 N. Main St., Naples 14512; 585-374-6740; www.artizanns.com

Finger Lakes Gallery and Frame sells a variety of original artwork, prints, and frames. 175 S. Main St., Canandaigua 14424; 585-396-7210; www.galleryandframe.com

Nadal Glass Art Studios offers hand-blown glass in brilliant colors. 20 Phoenix St., Canandaigua 14424; 585-394-7850; www.nadalglass.com

Rochester Folk Art Guild is actually a small village on East Hill Farm where artists have studios and workshops and sell their pottery, hand-blown glass, handicrafts, furniture, weaving, custom clothing, and other items. 1445 Upper Hill Rd., Middlesex 14507; 585-554-3539; www.folkartguild.org

The Wizard of Clay Pottery, Bloomfield, housed in geodesic domes, is an interesting complex with workshops and shelves filled with reasonably priced dinnerware, casseroles, oil-burning lamps, pie plates, pitchers, planters, bells, mugs, bowls, and more. There is also a good selection of earthy red, white, and blue pottery. 20 State St., Bloomfield 14469; 585-229-2980; www.wizardofclay.com

FARMERS' MARKETS **Barron Pratt Farm and Vineyard**, 4990 NY Rt. 21 S., Canandaigua, produces grapes primarily for people to buy by the bushel and use for pies, jellies, and other things. 585-394-9344

Jerome's U-Pick, Naples, invites you to pick your own strawberries, peas, raspberries, grapes, pumpkins, and other fruits and vegetables in-season. 800-UPICKIT; www.jeromesupick.com

Joseph's Wayside Market, Naples, sells every (regional) imaginable fruit in season, along with grape pies, grape juice, flowers, maple syrup, honey, cheddar cheese, baked goods, jams, jellies, and locally made crafts and gifts. 201 S. Main St., Naples 14512; 585-374-2380; www.josephswaysidemarket.com

Also check out: **Canandaigua Farmers' Market, Canandaigua VA Farmers' Market, Cheshire Union Farmers' Market, Honeoye Old Village Market,** and **Victor Farmers' Market.**

SPECIALTY FOODS **Arbor Hill Grapery** sells jelly, grape pies, taffy, cookbooks, salad dressings, wines, corkscrews, pottery—you name it. John Brahm III, the founder and owner of the company, now has more than 50 products that he makes, packages, and sells, like black raspberry celery seed dressing and fortified flavored teas. 6461 NY Rt. 64, Naples 14512; 585-374-2870, 800-554-7553; www.thegrapery.com

Cindy's Pies has an impressive line of customers who love her grape and other fruit pies as well as chicken pot pie. Just ring her doorbell and she'll pass them out over her Dutch door. 5 Academy St., Naples 14512; 585-374-6122

Finger Lakes Wine Center at Sonnenberg Gardens is your one-stop shopping center for wines and gourmet foods from more than 40 Finger Lakes wineries. 151 Charlotte St., Canandaigua 14424; 585-394-9016; www.sonnenberg.org

F. Oliver's features olive oils, vinegars, and infused-flavor oils. 129 S. Main St., Canandaigua 14424; 585-396-2585; www.folivers.com

Monica's Pies sells homemade grape pies as well as other fruit pies, jellies, jams, conserves, and relish (no preservatives). 7599 NY Rt. 21, Naples 14512; 585-374-2139; www.monicaspies.com

Shark's Ice Cream sells yummy ice cream and sweets. 50 State St., Bloomfield 14469; 585-657-4429

Sweet Expressions has sinfully hard-to-resist handmade candies and other sweets. 169 S. Main St., Canandaigua 14424; 585-394-5250; www.sweetexpressionsonline.com

GIFTS **1812 Country Store** is filled with country gifts, quilts, Christmas things, baskets, jams, jellies, cookie cutters, lamps, cards, and antiques. 4270 E. Main St., Hemlock 14487; 585-367-2802; www.1812countrystore.com

Renaissance—The Goodie II Shoppe, in a fanciful landmark building, is well worth a visit for a very special gift. 56 S. Main St., Canandaigua 14424; 585-394-6528

MORE INFORMATION **Canandaigua Chamber of Commerce Tourist Center Information:** 585-394-4400; www.canandaiguachamber.com

Geneva Area Chamber of Commerce: 315-789-1776; www.genevany.com

Finger Lakes Tourism Alliance: 800-530-7488; www.fingerlakes.org

Finger Lake Visitors Connection/Ontario County Tourism Office: 585-394-3915, 877-386-4669; www.visitfingerlakes.com

Honeoye Chamber of Commerce: www.honeoye.com

Ontario County Tourism Office (see Finger Lakes Visitors Connection)

Seneca County Chamber of Commerce: 800-732-1848; www.fingerlakescentral.com

Yates County: 800-868-9283; www.yatesny.com

Canandaigua and Canadice, Conesus, Hemlock, and Honeoye Lakes

❋ What's Happening

SPRING **Antique Market**, Granger Homestead, Canandaigua. Antiques, treasure table, and bake sale (June). 585-394-1472

Canandaigua Lake Trout Derby, weigh-in stations at Inn on the Lake, Canandaigua. Prizes for best catches. 585-394-4400

Maple Sugaring, Cumming Nature Center, Naples. Demonstrations in the process of maple sugaring (March). 585-374-6160

SUMMER **Canandaigua Lake Festival of the Arts**, Kershaw Park, Canandaigua. More than two hundred art and craft exhibits, demonstrations, cloggers, puppet shows, concerts, and face painting (July). 585-967-2009; www.clfestivalofthearts.com

Civil War Reenactment, Bristol Woodlands Campground. Living encampment and scenarios, infantry, artillery, cavalry, battles, and food through July. 585-396-1417

Concerts in the Park, Atwater Park, Canandaigua. Free concerts Fridays at 6:30 p.m. 585-396-0300

Downtown Canandaigua Art Festival, Canandaigua. Juried show with more than three hundred art and craft exhibits and food vendors. 585-396-0300

Finger Lakes Plein Air Competition and Festival, Canandaigua, a juried exhibition open to all artists 18 years and older.

Horse-Drawn Carriage Rides, Granger Homestead, Canandaigua. Narrative rides through the city's historic neighborhoods on Friday afternoons. 585-394-1472

Hill Cumorah Pageant, Manchester, near Palmyra. An outdoor dramatization of the origins of the Church of Jesus Christ of Latter-day Saints (also known as the Mormons), with a cast of six hundred and recorded music from the Mormon Tabernacle Choir. 315-597-5951; www.hillcumorah.org

July 4th Celebration, Kershaw Park, Canandaigua. Family entertainment, activities, food, and fireworks. 585-396-5000

Native American Dance and Music Festival, Ganondagan Historic Site, Victor. Native American foods, wonderful crafts and demonstrations, dance, and exhibits (July). 585-924-5848; www.ganondagan.org

Pageant of Steam, 5 miles east of Canandaigua. A weekend-long festival in August celebrates antique steam-powered vehicles. The hundred acre site is the venue for sawmill demonstrations, parades, live music, a pedal tractor pull, grain threshing, shingle making, an antique car show, a garden tractor pull, and a giant craft and flea market. 585-394-8102; www.pageantofsteam.org

Ring of Fire around Honeoye Lake: Labor Day weekend

Steuben County Fair, Bath. Six days of fun, carnival, rides, livestock, exhibits, shows, truck pull, music, and demolition derby (August). 607-776-4801; www.steubencountyfair.org

FALL/WINTER **Christkindl Market**, Granger Homestead, Canandaigua. Arts, crafts, food, and more for holiday gift giving (November). 585-394-1472, www.grangerhomestead.org

Fall Festival, Macedon. See giant straw-bale maze and pumpkin land, and ride hay wagons into the fields. 315-986-9821; www.epodunk.com

Festival of Trees, Granger Homestead and Carriage Museum, Canandaigua. Theme-decorated Christmas trees, wreaths, mantel decorations, and other festive items (Dec.). 585-394-1472, www.grangerhomestead.org

Naples Grape Festival, Memorial Town Hall Park, Main St., Naples. More than 250 exhibitors, live entertainment, juried arts and crafts, food, and a grape pie contest. 585-374-2240; www.naplesgrapefest.org

Naples Open Studio Trail, Naples. Visit the studios of more than 20 artists in the area (October). 585-374-6563; www.naplesopenstudiotrail.com

Pumpkin Walk, Canandaigua. Hundreds of carved jack-o'-lanterns twinkle in the dark along Ontario Pathways (October). 585-394-6822; www.ontariopathways.org

HOST CITIES: SYRACUSE, CORTLAND, ELMIRA, CORNING, AND ROCHESTER

Five major cities anchor the Finger Lakes region. Syracuse in the northeast corner, a city with roots in the salt and manufacturing industries, is now on the move to rebuild and recharge the vitality of its downtown while becoming a leader in the sustainability and environmental movements. Inner-city historic buildings are being reborn as chic apartments, with exposed brick and beam details, coveted by young professionals and empty nesters. Farther south on the eastern border of the region and just off I-81, Cortland reigns as the hub of downhill skiing for the eastern Finger Lakes.

Elmira, once the home of Samuel Clemens (Mark Twain), sits on the southern fringe of the Finger Lakes just off NY Rt. 17/I-86. Corning, home of the extraordinary Corning Museum of Glass, is just west of Elmira. At the northwestern corner is Rochester, a vibrant city of high-tech business, museums, and upscale suburbs.

Syracuse

Syracuse is perhaps best known as the home of Syracuse University and the site of the New York State Fair, which brings close to a million visitors to the fairgrounds each year. Increasingly, however, the city has much more to offer. In addition to the fair and SU sports, there are a variety of annual festivals and events each season. For example, the Jamesville Balloon Festival at Jamesville Beach Park is always popular with families each June. Taste of Syracuse brings enormous (and hungry) crowds to Clinton Square; Oktoberfest celebrates beer, food, wine, and German music; while the Syracuse Jazz Fest, held on the Onondaga Community College campus, is the largest free event of its kind in the northeast.

At the crossroads of two interstate highway systems, the east–west New York State Thruway (I-90) and the north–south I-81, the Syracuse area is home to important businesses, such as Welch Allyn, Sensis Corporation, National Grid (Niagara Mohawk), and Lockheed Martin; a daily newspaper; an international airport; and excellent hospitals, including SUNY Upstate Medical Center, Crouse Hospital, St. Joseph's, and the Golisano Children's Hospital. Forty-five private and state colleges are in the Greater Syracuse region; in Onondaga County alone there are eight schools, including Syracuse University with more than 18,000 students, and Le Moyne College with 3,400.

On the cultural scene, Syracuse has its own symphony orchestra, Symphoria; opera company; professional theater; and several museums and art galleries, including the Everson Museum of Art. There is Syracuse University's Carrier Dome (a venue for athletic and other events), the gigantic Empire Expo Center (New York State Fairgrounds), the three-building Oncenter Complex (a multipurpose facility), and a new amphitheater near the fairgrounds for big-time entertainment. The many parks and golf courses are further assets.

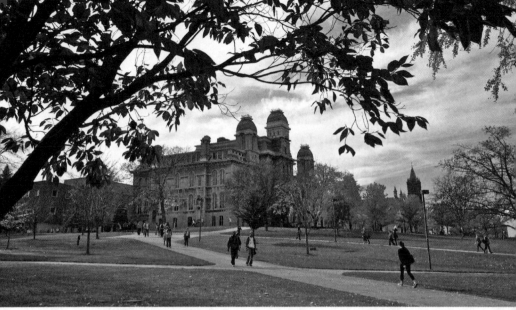

SYRACUSE UNIVERSITY CAMPUS

Chuck Wainright

Just north of downtown is the Inner Harbor at the southern tip of Onondaga Lake. Boaters can dock at the pier and enjoy concerts in the harbor's amphitheater.

Onondaga Lake, once highly polluted, has undergone a massive, multiyear cleanup process and is now reported safe for swimming, fishing, and water sports. Indeed, a new seven-lane, 2,000-meter rowing course has been installed off the eastern shore of the lake. It is used by the Syracuse Chargers Rowing Club and other rowing teams and is the venue for major competitions carrying on a tradition started in the 1870s when the Boating Association of Syracuse University was founded.

Onondaga Lake Park has seven miles of multiuse recreational trails along the western shore of the lake. And there is Wegman's Good Dog Park, a Visitor's Center, Skateboard Park, and Wegman's Boundless Playground. Summer's "Parkway Sundays" reserves Onondaga Lake Parkway just for pedestrians and cyclists.

MANY SHARP CARS ARE ON DISPLAY AT THE SYRACUSE NATIONALS CLASSIC SHOW

Fifty years ago Salina St. in downtown Syracuse was the place to come for fashionable shopping, but when the malls opened in the suburbs, shoppers left. Now Syracuse's inner city is making a comeback. Armory Square, an area of warehouse buildings in the center of town, has been reclaimed and houses chic shops and restaurants. Several in-town hotels and buildings are being renovated, including the former Hotel Syracuse; trendy loft apartments have opened in Franklin Square; and the striking art deco National Grid building is illuminated by layers of color when the sun sets.

The former Carousel Mall has morphed into Destiny USA, a sprawling multilevel shopping, dining, and entertainment complex reputed to be the state's largest shopping destination; on historic Automobile Row (Genesee St.), a 40,000-square-foot one-hundred-year-old brick building, formerly a plumbing supply, has been dynamically renovated by the Pinckney Hugo Group advertising agency for their offices.

Clinton Square, the site of concerts and other summer events, is transformed into a skating rink in the winter, while automobile enthusiasts are being drawn into the city by such events as the Syracuse Nationals Classic Show at the Empire Expo Center.

For sports enthusiasts, there are several golf courses and parks in and around the city, with ski areas within a half-hour drive. Syracuse is not a place to drive through, but a place to stop and experience.

✳ Lodging

Most major hotel chains are represented in Syracuse, including Holiday Inn, Marriott, Embassy Suites, Comfort Suites, DoubleTree, and Crowne Plaza. The area also has a number of smaller inns and bed-and-breakfasts.

HISTORIC Good news for Syracuse is the restoration of the **Hotel Syracuse**, a city landmark since 1924, when it was the place to go see and be seen, the venue for grand balls and parties. Sadly, since the 1980s it had deteriorated and ultimately closed. Now Marriott has stepped in and is putting $57 million into the hotel's restoration, including reclaiming the grandeur of the former grand dame. The once-elegant Persian Terrace dining room is being restored, and even the original wood flooring that lay under layers of material, is being reclaimed, along with historic murals in the lobby that were obscured by huge mirrors. The ballroom, too, is being redone, and all 261 guest rooms are being updated and furnished with Stickley furniture. The **Marriott Syracuse Downtown** is expected to open to the public in 2016. 100 E. Onondaga St., Syracuse 13201; 315-474-2424; www.marriott.com

HOTELS AND INNS **The Craftsman Inn** has 93 rooms and suites furnished in the simple Arts and Crafts mode, with clean lines, rich colors, wood moldings, and Stickley tables and chairs. Rooms are equipped with the latest in communications equipment. 7300 E. Genesee St., Fayetteville 13066; 800-797-4464, 315-637-8000; www.craftsmaninn.com

Hotel Skyler in the University area, an eclectic 58-room boutique hotel where metro meets retro rendered in light, clean colors and lines, evokes Scandinavia. The city's first LEED-Platinum hotel, Hotel Skyler makes clever use of a building once used as a theater and temple. 601 S. Crouse Ave., Syracuse 13210; 800-365-4663, 315-701-2613; www.hotelskyler.com

SUITE DREAMS **CrestHill Suites** at Carrier Circle near I-81 is an all-suites hotel designed for extended-stay business travelers and frequent guests. There are studios and one- and two-bedroom suites. 6410 New Venture Gear Dr., E. Syracuse 13057; 315-463-0258, 888-723-1655; www.cresthillsuites.com

Jefferson Clinton Hotel, a 60-room all-suite hotel, offers business and leisure travelers alike comfortable, spacious accommodations in the heart of downtown's Armory Square. 416 S. Clinton St., Syracuse 13202; 315-425-0500; www.jeffersonclintonhotel.com

COMFORT AND LUXURY **Genesee Grande Hotel,** located in the heart of the city's historic University Hill section, is one of the most upscale places to stay in Syracuse. With 157 rooms, a world-class restaurant, and a casual bistro, the inn features pillow-top mattresses, marble vanities, and elegant fabrics and linens. 1060 E. Genesee St., Syracuse 13210; 800-365-4663, 315-476-4212; www.geneseegrande.com

FULL-SERVICE HOTELS **Crowne Plaza Hotel,** with 279 rooms, is the largest hotel in the city, with meeting rooms, a fitness facility, and a restaurant. 701 E. Genesee St., Syracuse 13210; 800-227-6963; www.crowneplaza.com

    Sheraton Syracuse University, a 236-room hotel with an indoor pool and fitness facility, is on the campus of Syracuse University. 801 University Ave., Syracuse 13210; 315-475-3000, 800-395-2105; www.sheratonsyracuse.com

B&BS **Bed & Breakfast Wellington** has five comfortable rooms, four with private baths. Furnished with period antiques, this Arts and Crafts-style home offers WiFi and luxury linens. 707 Danforth St., Syracuse 13208; 800-724-5006, 315-474-3641; www.bbwellington.com

    Beard Morgan House B&B in Fayetteville, a lovely white brick Italianate home built in 1830, has four rooms with baths. 120 E. Genesee St., Fayetteville 13066; 800-775-4234, 315-637-4234

✳ Dining Out

Syracuse is a magical place for people who love food. From the boom in food trucks like **Steve's Street Eats** to ethnic eateries like **Eva's,** casual brewpubs, and high-end fancy places such as the **Arad Evans Inn,** you can find something to whet your appetite and keep you craving more.

TRADITION, TRADITION **Arad Evans Inn,** in an 1840s Federal-style residence in Fayetteville, serves French American, food beautifully presented. Desserts are over the moon. 7206 E. Genesee St., Fayetteville 13066; 315-637-2020; www.aradevansinn.com

    The Inn Between Restaurant in Camillus is in a Victorian Colonial house with three fireplaces. Meals are artfully presented and feature such items as baby rack of lamb, fresh seafood, and veal dishes. 2290 W. Genesee Tpke., Camillus 13031; 315-672-3166

    Marriott Syracuse Downtown will offer elegant dining in the Persian Room along with other venues. 315-474-2424; www.marriott.com

    Phoebe's Restaurant & Coffee Lounge across from Syracuse Stage features fine dining in one of the charming, intimate dining rooms. 900 E. Genesee St., Syracuse 13210; 315-475-5154; www.phoebessyracuse.com

HIP BISTRO-STYLE **Empire Brewing Company** is a great place to enjoy good food with flair along with craft beer including Two Dragons Beer, where ancient Chinese tea meets American brewing methods. 120 Walton St., Syracuse 13202; 315-475-2337; www.empirebrew.com

    Pascale Wine Bar and Restaurant is an elegant little place in Fayetteville specializing in Continental cuisine—fabulous bakery scones. 104 Limestone Plaza, Fayetteville 13066; 315-637-8321; www.pascalerestaurant.com

    Strada Mia is fast becoming one of Syracuse's best places to eat. The cuisine, a skillful fusion of Italian and American contemporary, is fresh and delicious; service is excellent; and the low-key clubby ambiance is conducive to dining and lingering.

There is a smart bar area with high-top tables, several HDTVs, and an upstairs room for private events and dinners. When we left it was raining hard, but we were escorted to our car by a gentleman carrying an umbrella. Now that's service. $$–$$$ 313 N. Geddes St., Syracuse 13204; 315-883-5995; www.stradamia313.com

The York Restaurant & Lounge in Armory Square is a new hip bistro/bar quickly gaining a reputation for excellent, fresh food. Order charcuterie and your preferred drink, indulge in your favorite seafood from the raw bar, try the lobster-loaded chowder, or choose from their specialty meat selections—a farm-to-table winner. And did we mention the awesome presentations? 247 W. Fayette St., Syracuse 13202; 315-701-0636; www.yorkcny.com

ETHNIC TASTES **Alto Cinco**, a tiny place serving great Mexican cuisine, is the real thing. 526 Wescott St., Syracuse 13210; 315-422-6399; www.altocinco.net. A nice spin-off, **Otro Cinc**, not only serves great Mexican burritos but Spanish, Californian, and Southwestern dishes as well as tapas, crispy tofu, and various kinds of paella. 206 S. Warren St., Syracuse 13202; 315-422-6876; www.otro5cinco.com

Creole Soul Cafe rolls out that good old down South Cajun and Creole cooking with soul. 128 E. Jefferson St., Syracuse 13202; 315-530-4178; www.creolesoulcafe.com

Eva's European Sweets is where the food is authentic Polish, the décor is authentic Polish, and the owner is Polish. Fabulous. 1305 Milton Ave., Syracuse 13204; 315-487-2722; www.evaspolish.com

Heid's of Liverpool, recently featured on the Travel Channel's *Man vs. Food*, has been here for years, serving up Hoffman's hot dogs, bratwurst, and all the fixin's. 305 Oswego St., Liverpool 13088; 315-451-0786; www.heidsofliverpool.com

Ichiban, another Liverpool favorite, is your ultimate Japanese steakhouse and sushi bar with all the flair that goes along with presenting the food. 302 Old Liverpool Rd., Liverpool 13088; 315-457-0000; www.ichibanjapanesesteakhouse.com

The **Jamerican Diner** downtown cooks and serves authentic Jamaican fare and other Caribbean dishes along with some American food in simple surroundings. 415 E. Washington St., Syracuse 13202; 315-424-7090

Lemon Grass Grille in Armory Square specializes in Pacific Rim cuisine, including Thai dishes. 238 E. Jefferson St., Syracuse 13202; 315-475-1111; www.lemongrasscny.com

The Mission Restaurant is in a former church with a steeple, stained glass, and hand-painted walls, all of which add to the sense of mission. Food is south of the border and island Caribbean, with super margaritas and fajitas. 304 E. Onondaga St., Syracuse 13202; 315-475-7344; www.themissionrestaurant.com

Peppino's Neapolitan Express—for really, truly traditional Italian and award-winning pizza, come here. 409 S. Clinton St., Syracuse 13202; 315-422-8811; www.mypeppinos.com

Sakana-Ya Sushi Bar in Armory Square rolls out tempting food on a conveyor belt. 215 Walton St., Syracuse 13202; 315-475-0117; www.syracusesushi.com

PASTA AMORE **Asti** in Little Italy is operated and owned by the Tumino family, who founded the restaurant in 1987. Eat indoors in the bar area or dining room or outdoors on the sidewalk patio. Still serving great Italian specialities like Christina's homemade lasagna and pasta Milano as well as grilled smoked steaks and other meats. If you crave Italian, this is where to come. 411 N. Salina St., Syracuse 13203; 315-478-1039; www.asticaffe.com

Francesca's Cucina recalls a little part of Italy in the heart of Syracuse serving dishes from family recipes. 545 N. Salina St., Syracuse 13208; 315425-1556; www.francescas-cucina.com

Pastabilities serves wonderful pasta and homemade bread from their bakeshop in Armory Square. An intimate outdoor patio is perfect for a warm day. 311 S. Franklin St., Syracuse 13202; 315-474-1153

CASUAL FARE **Blarney Stone** in Tipp Hill gets high fives for its Blarney Burger. Order with onion rings or beer-battered fries and you're in business. 314 Avery Ave., Syracuse 13204; 315-487-9675; www.blarneystonesyr.com

Cams Pizzeria has several locations in the Finger Lakes and is the place to go if you crave a perfect pizza with a thin crust or, as they say, "love at first slice." www.camspizzeria.com

Dinosaur Bar-B-Que has been called the best place to get barbecue in the east. One thing is for sure: Portions are huge, ribs are finger-lickin' good, and décor featuring biker memorabilia is fun. The place is full all the time. Outside, Harleys are parked next to BMWs and SUVs. 246 W. Willow St., Syracuse 13202; 315-476-4937; www.dinosaurbarbeque.com

Limestone Grill in the Craftsman Inn is furnished in the simple Arts and Crafts mode—clean lines with lots of wood and Stickley tables and chairs. Food is American traditional with items like steak, brook trout, and prime rib. 7300 E. Genesee St., Fayetteville 13066; 315-637-9999; www.craftsmaninn.com

At **Modern Malt**, how can you go wrong with their Barney Rubble, a colorful fruity French toast served with strawberry ginger jam and crème anglaise? 325 S. Clinton St., Syracuse 13202; 315-471-MALT; eatdrinkmalt.com

LOCAL WATERING HOLES Blarney Stone (see above)

Coleman's Authentic Irish Pub, a super pub, with a long wooden bar and full-service restaurant, is housed in a wonderful old building on Syracuse's Tipperary Hill. Great pub fare, ales, and beer. 100 S. Lowell Ave., Syracuse 13204; 315-476-1933; www.colemansirishpub.com

DINOSAUR BAR-B-QUE IS AN INSTITUTION

MODERN MALT IS PERFECT FOR KIDS

Empire Brewing Company invites you to sip a glass of stout or Skinny Atlas Light while watching beer being brewed behind the glass wall. 120 Walton St., Syracuse 13202 (see "Hip Bistro-Style")

J. Ryan's in Hanover Square offers more than 70 craft beers to accompany their pub fare. 253 E. Water St., Syracuse 13202; 315-399-5533; jryanspub.com

Kitty Hoynes Irish Pub in Armory Square is a traditional Irish pub complete with Irish music, numerous beers on tap, and good food. 301 W. Fayette St., Syracuse 13202; 315-424-1974; www .kittyhoynes.com

Riley's Irish Bar has perfected the comfort food, pub grub niche. 312 Park St., Syracuse 13203; 315-471-7111

FUN AND FUNKY **The Gem Diner** is not your typical diner. Housed in an old trolley car, it's all about stainless steel, '50s-style décor and basic food groups. 832 Spencer St., Syracuse 13204; 315-314-7380

LoFo: Whatever you dietary preferences—gluten free, dairy free, carnivore—LoFo caters to your needs with healthy, locally sourced organic food. 214 Walton St., Syracuse 13202; 315-422-6200; www.lofosyracuse.com

ICE CREAM **Carol's Polar Parlor's** custom-made ice cream concoctions, like their ice cream pies or turtle sundaes, are truly decadent. There is a huge selection of yummy flavors, but portions are not overly large. 3800 W. Genesee St., Syracuse 13219; 315-468-3404; www.carolspolarparlor.com

Gannon's Ice Cream in the Valley in Syracuse is simply the best ice cream, according to people I know who drive miles to stock up on their favorite flavors. It's an institution with a following of fervent fans Taylor Swift could envy. Think 14% butterfat, little air, handmade, caramel cashew, chocolate raspberry truffle and, and . . . 1525 Valley Dr., Syracuse 13207; 315-469-8647. There's also Gannon's Downtown at 400 S. Salina St., Syracuse 13202; 315-214-8477; and Gannon's at 4800 McDonald Rd., Syracuse 13215; 315-299-7040. All are opened seasonally. www .gannonsicecream.com

Vicky's Tasty Treat in an iconic red-and-white building in Liverpool is known for its tried-and-true twists with sprinkles. The orange-vanilla combo is a beauty. 680 Old Liverpool Rd., Liverpool 13088; 315-457-9084

GREEN BEER IS A TRADITION AT PLACES LIKE COLEMAN'S ON ST. PATRICK'S DAY

✳ To See

LOCAL LORE **Camillus Erie Canal Park and Sims' Museum** is set on the banks of the old Erie Canal, offering both a museum and boat tours. The park is also home to the newly restored aqueduct and to the Steam Engine Exhibit. 5750 Devoe Rd., Camillus 13031; 315-488-3409; www.eriecanalcamillus.com

The **Erie Canal Museum** is housed in an original 1850s Weighlock Building and contains a lot of very cool interactive exhibits plus a full-size replica canal boat. 318 Erie Blvd. E., Syracuse 13202; 315-471-0593; eriecanalmuseum.org

Onondaga Historical Association Museum features historical information, paintings, maps, and rare artifacts spanning three hundred years of history. 321 Montgomery St., Syracuse 13202; 315-428-1864; www.cnyhistory.org

The Salt Museum covers 150 years of the salt industry in Syracuse. 106 Lake Dr., Liverpool 13088; 315-453-6715

MUSEUMS For truly fine art (and framing), go to the **Edgewood Gallery**. It's a small place, but the quality of the art is first-rate, with revolving exhibits of local artists like Margie Hughto and Jee Eun Lee. Shows take place every six weeks. 216 Tecumseh Rd., Syracuse 13224; 315-445-8111; www.edgewoodartandframe.com

Everson Museum of Art, designed by I. M. Pei, contains a fabulous collection of ceramics and other arts, revolving exhibits with 10 galleries on three levels along with special exhibitions, tours, lectures, workshops, and a film series. 401 Harrison St., Syracuse 13202; 315-474-6064; www.everson.org

MOST: **Milton J. Rubenstein Museum of Science and Technology** buzzes with activity and is filled with exhibits, many interactive. Explore the giant maze, thrill to dinosaurs, climb the rock wall, see how your lungs work as you navigate your way through the human body, stand inside a gigantic bubble, and learn about the universe at the Silverman Planetarium. The only domed IMAX theater in Upstate New York, the

SCIENCE DEMO AT THE MUSEUM OF SCIENCE AND TECHNOLOGY

Bristol Omnitheater, with its six-story screen, puts you in the middle of the action, whether climbing Mt. Everest or diving into the depths of the ocean. 500 S. Franklin St., Syracuse 13202; 315-425-9068; www.most.org

Redhouse Arts Center situated in a three-story historic building in Armory Square has hosted more than 300 programs spanning theater, film, visual arts, and music. Plans call for the center to move into the former Sibley's department store building that will be redeveloped into City Center, a mixed-use facility. 201 S. West St., Syracuse 13202; 315-425-0405; www.theredhouse.org

PERFORMING ARTS **Clinton Square** near Armory Square is the venue for a variety of outdoor musical and theatrical events in the summer such as jazz nights and blues festivals. In the winter Clinton Square becomes an ice-skating rink. 315-473-4330

The Landmark Theatre (circa 1928) in the heart of the city has been carefully restored and glitters and gleams once again with its gold leaf, chandeliers, and staircases. The theatre is the venue for a number of productions bringing in headliners like Josh Groban and Jerry Seinfeld. 362 S. Salina St., Syracuse 13202; 315-475-7979; www.landmarktheater.org

Syracuse Opera is a year-round opera company offering productions and ongoing educational programs. 411 Montgomery St., Syracuse 13202; 315-476-7372; www.syracuseopera.com,

Syracuse Stage produces seven or more main-stage plays during the season, which runs from September through May. 820 E. Genesee St., Syracuse 13210; 315-443-3275; www.syracusestage.org

Syracuse Symphoria, Syracuse's musician-owned and -operated orchestra, offers concerts at the Civic Center and at various venues around the city. 234 Harrison St., Syracuse 13202; 315-299-5598; www.experiencesymphoria.org

A new $100 million, 17,500-seat outdoor concert **Amphitheater** on Onondaga Lake replaces the aging grandstand at the New York State Fairgrounds. www.syracuse.com

✳ To Do

DISCOVERING NATURE **Beaver Lake Nature Center** in Baldwinsville has forest, meadows, and wetlands along miles of trails and boardwalks. Paddle a canoe or kayak across the lake, learn about maple sugaring, go snowshoeing, enjoy birdwatching and tour the visitor's center. 8477 E. Mud Lake Rd., Baldwinsville 13027; 315-638-2519; www.onondagacountyparks.com

Green Lakes State Park in Fayetteville has all the natural assets like canoeing, fishing, and camping plus disc golf and a super scenic golf course. 7900 Green Lakes Rd., Fayetteville 13066; www.nysparks.com

Rosamond Gifford Zoo at Burnet Park is a first-class zoo with a thousand animals and creatures living in spacious, natural-looking environments on 36 acres. See Amur tigers, Asian elephants, Humboldt penguins, seals, an aviary, and

ROSAMOND GIFFORD ZOO

a wildlife trail. Don't miss the monkey house or the baby elephants. 1 Conservation Pl., Syracuse 13204; 315-435-8511; www.rosamondgiffordzoo.org

SPORTS **Oncenter Complex**, a multipurpose facility, combines the Onondaga County Convention Center, Onondaga County War Memorial, and John H. Mulroy Civic Center. It's used as a convention center, sports arena, meeting place, banquet hall, ice rink, concert hall, showroom, and theater. 800 S. State St., Syracuse 13202; 315-435-8000; www.oncenter.org

Alliance Bank Stadium is home of the Washington Nationals–affiliated Syracuse SkyChiefs, and a venue for many events. 300 NBT Bank Pkwy., Syracuse 13208; 315-474-7833; www.ongov.net

Pole Position Raceway at Destiny ups your thrills with the fastest indoor electric karts in the country. There are karts for kids and adults, and opportunities for head-on racing. 315-423-RACE

Syracuse University Dome Box Office Carrier Dome, Syracuse University, 900 Irving Ave. (Gate B), Syracuse 13202; 888-DOMETIX; www.carrierdome.com

GOLF These courses in or near Syracuse offer enjoyable golf experiences at reasonable rates.

Foxfire at Village Green near Syracuse, a well-manicured par-72 championship, wanders through a community of homes and condos. Elevated tees, narrow fairways, water, and bunkers make it a challenge. 1 Village Blvd. N. Baldwinsville 13027; 315-638-2930; www.foxfire147.com

Green Lakes State Park Golf Course in Fayetteville, gets raves for its wildly scenic layout with two glacial lakes, plush fairways, pines, and deep bunkers. Designed by Robert Trent Jones (1936), rolling landscape guarantees many tricky lies. 7900 Green Lakes Rd., Fayetteville 13066; 315-637-4653

SYRACUSE UNIVERSITY FOOTBALL AND BASKETBALL GAMES ARE HELD IN THE DOME

Links at Erie Village is a semiprivate course bordering the Erie Canal with winding creeks. 5904 N. Burdick St., E. Syracuse 13057; 315-656-4653; www .golferielinks.com

Marcellus Golf Club (formerly the Links at Sunset Ridge) is fairly flat, with high roughs designed to resemble a links layout. Tees are gender-neutral, so where you tee off from depends on your handicap. Water comes into play on four holes, and the course is well-bunkered. 2814 W. Seneca Tpke., Marcellus 13108; 315-673-7380

Liverpool Golf & Public Country Club has an island green and six-hole short course. 7209 Morgan Rd., Liverpool 13090; 315-457-7170; www.lgpcc.com

Radisson Greens Golf Club in Baldwinsville comes with a Robert Trent Jones pedigree. With tough par fives, great greens, and fairways, this is a good bet for better players, but beware—over the years, the course has had some maintenance issues. 8055 Potter Rd., Baldwinsville 13027; 315-638-0092

Timber Banks Golf & Marina, the only Jack Nicklaus–designed course, is a welcome addition to the Syracuse golfing scene. The centerpiece for a real estate community, Timber Banks is a scenic layout winding through trees, wetlands, and meadows. 3536 Timber Banks Pkwy., Baldwinsville 13027; 315-635-8800; www .timberbanks.com

West Hill Golf Course is one of the best par-three courses in the state. A virtual arboretum, West Hill has an enormous variety of trees planted along the fairways. The front nine is much easier and less dramatic than the back nine, where a lake brings water into play on several holes. 2500 W. Genesee St., Camillus 13031; 315-672-8677; www.westhillgolfcourse.com

MINIATURE GOLF Putt your ball through a turning windmill and a red barn, around stone walls and bushes, up hills, and into the mouth of a clown. **Fairmont Glen Miniature Golf Course** near the Fairmont shopping area in Camillus has been entertaining kids of all ages since the late 1940s. Today you can carve out a good hour or two

with your kids playing 18 holes on Fairmont Glen, one of the more elaborate and well-maintained miniature golf layouts in the Finger Lakes. It's landscaped with lots of flowers, shrubs, and a creek spanned by a covered bridge. Single game $7.50; two hours unlimited $11.25; plus specials and parties. Open 10–midnight. 210 N. Onondaga Rd., Syracuse 13219; 315-685-0546; www.fairmontglen.com

FAMILY FUN Test your putting skills at **Fairmont Glen's Miniature Golf Course** (see "Golf"). After golf, grab some peanuts and a burger at **Five Guys** (315-299-7027) in the shopping center just across the road, or create your own Mexican meal at **Boom Boom Mex Mix** in Camillus (315-673-1151). If pizza is in your sights, head to **Cams Pizzeria**—you won't find any better (see "Casual Fare" in Syracuse).

FAIRMONT GLEN MINIATURE GOLF

GOLF NEARBY **Turning Stone Resort & Casino**, about a half hour east of Syracuse, has arguably three of New York State's top golf courses: Kaluhyat (ga-LU-yut), Atunyote (uh-DUNE-yote), and Shenendoah. There's also no-slouch par-three Sandstone Hollow, perfect for a gentle introduction to the game. 5218 Patrick Rd., Verona 13478; 315-361-8140, 877-748-GOLF; www.turningstone.com

✳ Shopping

Armory Square Headquarters takes in Walton St., S. Clinton St., W. Jefferson St., and S. Franklin. Armory Square is highly recommended for more intimate specialty shopping where you can get away from the mall crowds. Browse small boutiques, crafts shops, and other stores such as **Eureka Crafts, Sound Garden, Jet Black, Designer Warehouse** for killer clothing at huge discounts, and **Urban Outfitters**. Try **Bounce** for stylish clothing and accessories as well as the **MOST Gift Shop** for science-related things. Get your sugar fix at **Sweet on Chocolate**.

DESTINY USA **Destiny USA** is a destination in itself, with high-end stores like Lord & Taylor, Banana Republic, and Ann Taylor; money-saving outlets like Coach, Saks Fifth Avenue, Salvatore Ferragamo, Armani and Brooks Brothers; and family attractions such as a working antique carousel, **Glowgolf, Lazer Tag, Margaritaville, Pole Position** racing, **WonderWorks**—an indoor "amusement park" for the mind with its 4DXD Motion Theater and 360° bikes—plus the **Regal Cinemas**. 315-466-7000; www.destinyusa.com

Regional Market Commons is located in the original 1938 wholesale market structure. Find everything from boutiques to foods. 2100 Park St., Syracuse 13208; 315-422-8647; www.cnyrea.com

Northern Lights Plaza, Mattydale (close to the airport), is the go-to place for those hard-to-resist bargains at stores like the **Christmas Tree Shop, TJ Maxx**, and other bargain hunters' favorite haunts.

Sarah Kinslow

GO-KART RACING AT DESTINY

ONE CRAZY TRAFFIC LIGHT

If you happen to look up at the traffic light at the corner of Tompkins St. and Milton Ave., you'll notice something very strange: The green light is on top of the red light. Well, why not. This is the heart of the Irish neighborhood, Tipp Hill, after all. It all dates back to 1920s when the light was installed and the Irish immigrants did not want to see the British red on top. Syracuse officials eventually allowed the green light to be placed on top. So there you have it.

Syracuse Convention and Visitors Bureau

THE COUNTRY'S ONLY UPSIDE-DOWN TRAFFIC LIGHT AT TIPPERARY HILL

✳ What's Happening

SPRING **Jamesville Balloonfest**, Jamesville Beach, Syracuse. The sky fills with close to 50 colorful hot air balloons. Rides, family activities, entertainment, and food. 315-451-7275; www.syracuseballoonfest.com

Jazz Fest, Clinton and Hanover Squares, Syracuse. National and international jazz greats perform throughout the month. 315-422-8284; www.syracusejazzfest.com

St. Patrick's Day Parade: Wear green and watch the parade to celebrate this festive Irish holiday.

Taste of Syracuse in Clinton Square treats you to an impressive array of food vendors with samples from Syracuse's best restaurants. 315-471-9597; www.tasteofsyracuse.com

SUMMER **Central New York Scottish Games**, Long Branch Park, Liverpool. Scottish and Celtic music and dancing, bands, and clan genealogy. 315-463-8876; www.cnyscots.com

Great New York State Fair: Almost two weeks of fun and exhibits at the NYS Fairgrounds in late August through September, featuring car races, craft fairs, amusements, animals, horticulture, ethnic celebrations, food, and top entertainers. 800-475-FAIR; www.nysfair.org

Pops in the Park, Onondaga Park, Syracuse. Free concerts on Tuesdays in July. 315-473-4330

New York State Rhythm & Blues Festival, Clinton, Armory, and Hanover Squares and Hotel Syracuse/Radisson Plaza. Performers entertain throughout several days. 315-469-1723; www.nysbluesfest.com

Syracuse Nationals, largest hot-rod custom and classic car show in the Northeast, at the NY State Fairgrounds. 800-753-3978

US Rowing Northeast Mid-Atlantic Masters Regional Championship: More than 50 Masters events take place on the new rowing course on Onondaga Lake. www.regattacentral.com

BALLOON FUN AT THE GREAT NEW YORK STATE FAIR

FALL/WINTER Golden Harvest Festival, Beaver Lake Nature Center, Baldwinsville. More than one hundred crafters join blues, folk, jazz, and reggae musicians; puppet shows; and pony rides for this fall celebration. 315-638-2519

Great Eastern Whiteout, a vintage snowmobile show and swap meet, is held annually on a weekend in February in Fulton. There are trail rides, entertainment, racing, food, and more. www.thegreateasternwhiteout.net

Lights on the Lake, Syracuse Chamber of Commerce, Syracuse. See incredible displays of light wizardry along a two-mile drive in Onondaga Lake Park. 800-243-4797; www.lightsonthelake.com

Bald eagles can be seen nesting in the trees between Onondaga Lake and the back of the Destiny complex, especially in late winter.

Cortland

TASTES OF LOCALLY PRODUCED FOODS ARE OFFERED AT THE NEW YORK STATE FAIR

Cortland in the eastern Finger Lakes, home to the State University at Cortland, is close to three popular ski areas. Just north of Cortland around Preble are several lakes, including Tully Lake, Song Lake, Goodale Lake, and Green Lake. Little York Lake is part of Dwyer Memorial Park, where you find Little York Pavilion (a National Historical Preservation site) and the Cortland Repertory Theatre.

Just north of Cortland, the historic district of Homer Village contains dozens of lovely nineteenth-century homes in the Greek Revival and Queen Anne style. The village green is a popular venue for concerts, fairs, sporting events and ice-skating. At 26 Clinton St., there is an excellent example of an octagonal house, a popular architectural style during the mid-1800s. The Salisbury-Pratt Homestead, on Route 281 between Homer and Little York, was part of the Underground Railroad. And be sure to visit the farmers' market on Main St., East End Market on Elm St., and the Homer farmers' market on the Village Green during the growing season.

✳ Lodging

The Cortland area has a number of hotels, inns, and bed-and-breakfasts with all major hotel chains represented, including Ramada, Comfort Inn, Days Inn, Econo Lodge, Hampton Inn, Holiday Inn, and Quality Inn.

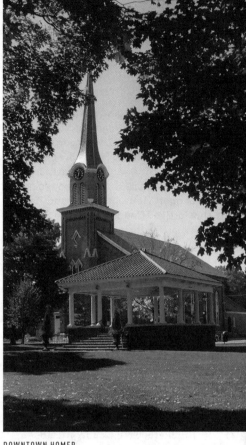

DOWNTOWN HOMER

B&B Among the B&Bs, **Alice's Dowry** has a comfortable, down-home feeling, rooms furnished with antiques, a parlor and a comfy sofa, and you can sit down to a full breakfast at your own private table. With advance notice you can also have dinner. 2789 NY Rt. 26, Cincinnatus 13040; 607-863-3934; www.alicesdowry.com

Chrysler's B&B in a renovated barn is basic, clean, and welcoming to children. There are four rooms, and rates include a full breakfast. And wait till you see the bathroom tiles! $–$$ 1344 US 11, Marathon 13803; www.chryslersbb.com

✳ Dining Out

CASUAL FARE **A&W Restaurant** is an old-fashioned carhop (without the skates). Order over a tin speaker; enjoy dogs, burgers, root beer, and shakes from a window tray; and play miniature golf next door. 281 NY Rt. 13, Cortland 13045; 607-756-2021

Brix Pubaria sells gourmet brick-oven pizza, wings and more in an environment of industrial chic. 60 Main St., Cortland 13045; 607 662-0005; www.brixpubaria.com

The Community Restaurant specializes in Greek and Italian cuisine. 10 Main St., Cortland 13046; 607-756-5441; www.thecommunityrestaurant.com

Hollywood Restaurant serves good Italian food, pizza, steaks, and seafood. 27 Groton Ave., Cortland 13045; 607-753-3242; www.hollywoodcortlandny.com

Hollenbeck's Cider Mill sells cider, apples, cheese, fudge, bakery goods, and much more in season. 1265 NY Rt. 392, Cortland 13045; 607-835-6455

✲ To See

MUSEUMS **Cortland Country Music Park Museum** has a dance hall, Hall of Fame museum, campground, and outdoor performance center. 1824 NY Rt. 13, Cortland 13045; 607-753-0377; www.cortlandmusicpark.org

The **1890 House Museum and Center for Victorian Arts**, a castle-like stone manor with a round tower, houses artifacts, furniture, and memorabilia from the Victorian era. 37 Tompkins St., Cortland 13045; 607-756-7551; www.1890house.org

Suggett House Museum and Kellogg Memorial Research Library is the home of the Cortland County Historical Society. 25 Homer Ave., Cortland 13045; 607-756-6071; www.cortlandhistory.com

PERFORMING ARTS **Center for the Arts** 72. S. Main St., Homer 13077; 607-749-4900; www.center4art.org

Cortland Repertory Theatre in Dwyer Memorial Park brings in professionals to perform year-round American theater, including comedies and musicals, June through September (the rest of the year in downtown Cortland). 24 Port Watson St., Cortland 13045; 607-756-2627; www.cortlandrep.org

✲ To Do

GOLF **Elm Tree Golf Course** 283 NY Rt. 13, Cortland 13045; 607-753-1341; www.elmtreegolfcourse.com

Knickerbocker Country Club: 5471 Telephone Rd., Cincinnatus 13041; 607-863-3800; www.knickbockercc.com

Maple Hill Golf Club: 1561 Conrad Rd., Marathon 13803; 607-849-3285; www.golfmaplehillgc.com

Walden Oaks Country Club: 3369 Walden Oaks Blvd., Cortland 13045; 607-753-9452; www.waldenoakscc.com

Willowbrook Golf Club: 3267 NY Rt. 215, Cortland 13045; 607-756-7382; www.willowbrookcortland.com

Highest rated are Maple Hill and Walden Oaks.

HIKING **Lime Hollow Nature Center for Environment and Culture** offers an interpretive center and hiking trails. 338 McLean Rd., Cortland 13045; 607-662-4632; www.limehollow.org

SPORTS **J. M. McDonald Sports Complex** has an ice rink, tennis court, batting cage, mixed martial arts, indoor turf fields, and fitness center. 4292 Fairgrounds Dr., Cortland 13045; 607-753-8100; www.jmmcomplex.com

SKIING In the eastern Finger Lakes, the best skiing can be found in and around Cortland.

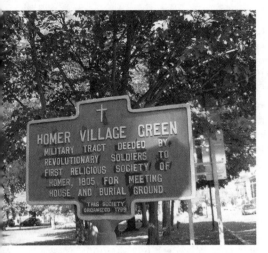

HOMER

Greek Peak Ski Resort in Cortland, site of the magic carpet lift, has close to 30 trails, seven ski lifts, a tubing center, more than two hundred instructors, night skiing, cross-country trails, slope-side accommodations, a lodge, and restaurants. There is also an indoor water park and adventure center. 2000 NY Rt. 392, Cortland 13045; 800-955-2754; www.greek peak.net

Labrador Mountain in Truxton has 22 slopes, downhill skiing, snowboarding, night skiing, three base lodges, instruction, babysitting, and ski rentals. 6935 NY Rt. 91, Truxton 13158; 607-842-6204; www.labradormtn.com

Song Mountain in Tully has 25 trails and 4 lifts. 1 Song Mountain Rd., Tully 13159; 315-696-5711; www.songmountain.com

Toggenburg Mountain Winter Sports Center in Fabius offers skiing and tubing with day and night hours on 24 trails. 1135 Toggenburg Rd., Fabius 13063; 315-683-5842; www.skitog.com

SKATING In the winter, skate in an old-fashioned ice rink on Homer's Village Green.

✻ Shopping

BOOKS The College Store, SUNY Cortland, offers books, clothing, logo items, and gifts. 607-753-4621

GIFTS AND CLOTHING Bev & Co. in Homer sells gifts, clothes, and antiques. 607-749-2149; www.bevandco.com

Homer Men & Boys' Store Inc. offers work and casual clothing for the family. 607-749-3314; www.homermensandboys.com

Olde Homer House sells traditional furnishings and gifts. 607-756-0750

✻ What's Happening

SPRING Apple Jazz Festival, Dwyer Memorial Park, Little York. Great music plus food and craft stands.

Central New York Maple Festival, Marathon. When the sugar maple sap starts running in early spring, it's time to celebrate. The weekend's activities include a parade, helicopter rides, all-you-can-eat pancakes, a charity walk/run, and a sugar shack where maple syrup is processed (free samples). www.maplefest.org

Dairy Parade, Cortland. On Tuesdays in June at 6 p.m., the county celebrates its dairy heritage with marching bands, floats, vendors, and more. 607-753-1593

Firemen's Field Days, Homer. It's games, fun, amusements, food, and a parade.

SUMMER **Concerts in Courthouse Park**, Courthouse Park/West Lawn, Cortland. Free concerts Thursday evenings through July and August on the lawn adjacent to the historic domed courthouse. 607-753-3021; www.cortlandyb.recdesk.com

Cortland Celtic Festival, Dwyer Memorial Park, Preble, features Gaelic music, foods, activities, crafts, and more. www.cortlandcelticfestival.com

Holiday in Homer, Homer. This annual crafters' festival features entertainment, refreshments, activities, and craft booths beginning at 9 a.m. the next-to-last Saturday of July. 607-749-7124

Main Street Farmers' Market, Cortland. May–October. Tuesdays and Saturdays.

National Brockway Truck Show, Cortland. August 607-753-8463; www.brockway trucks.org

Summer Concerts on the Green, Homer. Enjoy concerts under the cool trees every Wednesday night through July and August. 607-749-3322; www.homerny.org

FALL/WINTER **Cincinnatus Cornfest**, Cincinnatus (third week September), rolls out crafts, a farmers' market, hayrides, a parade, and a quilt show at Heritage Hall along with music and food (got to have their corn chowder). 607-345-0001; www .cincycornfest.org

1890 Union Fair, Marathon., celebrates small-town agricultural roots with parades and other events the first Saturday after Labor Day. 607-849-3960

The Great Cortland Pumpkinfest, Courthouse Park, Cortland. There are pumpkins everywhere, wagon rides, carving contests, and food. It's lots of fun for the whole family (October). 800-859-2227, 607-753-8463; www.cortlandpumpkinfest .org

Homer Winterfest, Homer. A village-wide two-day celebration featuring fireworks, snow sculpture, games, a craft show, entertainment, and more. 607-749-7604

Ice skating, Homer. On sunny winter days, the village green is filled with skaters of all ages. 607-753-8463; www.experiencecortland.com

New Year's Eve Fireworks & First Night Celebration, Main St., downtown Cortland, has snow sculpture, games, a craft show, entertainment, and more. 607-749-7604; www.homerwinterfest.org

Elmira

Samuel Clemens, better known as Mark Twain, spent several summers in this quiet town with his wife, Olivia Langdon, an Elmira native. Here he wrote many of his beloved novels including *The Adventures of Huckleberry Finn* and *The Adventures of Tom Sawyer*. He did much of his work in an octagonal study now located on the Elmira College campus.

Those interested in the life and work of this famous author can visit the Mark Twain Exhibit in Cowles Hall and see his grave in Woodlawn Cemetery.

Elmira is the official Soaring Capital of America. The City has hosted regional, national, and international soaring contests at Harris Hill since the 1930s. Take a glider ride at Harris Hill Soaring Corp., or tour the National Soaring Museum, home to the world's largest sailplane collection.

Other area attractions include the Clemens Center, the region's premier performing arts center; Arnot Art Museum, exhibiting contemporary work as well as old masters and nineteenth-century paintings; Tanglewood Nature Center & Museum, with extensive hiking trails through breathtaking terrain; and First Arena, home

ELMIRA CAROUSEL

to the Elmira Jackals professional hockey team and host to exciting year-round entertainment.

A restored circa 1890s Carousel with hand-carved wooden horses is greatly enjoyed by visitors to Eldridge Park in Elmira where you also find a fleet of dragon boats, dance hall, kiddy rides and The Mark Twain Miniature Golf Course featuring a ticket booth evoking the famous author's study at Quarry Farm.

✷ Lodging

Holiday Inn Riverview is convenient to Mark Twain attractions. 760 E. Water St., Elmira 14901; 607-734-4211; www.fingerlakeshotels.com

Rufus Tanner House has four guest rooms with private baths and moderate rates. Like many old houses in the area, this 1864 farmhouse sits in a grove of one-hundred-year-old sugar maples that produce maple syrup for the inn's pancake breakfasts. Furnishings are mostly antiques; one room has a queen-size bed and a fireplace. Another has a Jacuzzi. 60 Sagetown Rd., Pine City 14871; 607-732-0213; www.rufustanner.com

✷ Dining Out

Beijing Garden is one of the most elegant Chinese restaurants around, with uphol-stered dining chairs, linens, and crystal. The food is authentic—not just a tourist spot. 145 W. Gray St., Elmira 14901; 607-732-7464

Charlie's Café is a local favorite, serving up fresh cuisine in a casual yet elegant setting. 205 Hoffman St., Elmira 14901; 607-733-0440; www.charliescafeelmira.com

Hill Top Inn has been a city landmark since 1933. Dine while overlooking the same views that inspired Mark Twain while he penned his classics from his summer home just up the road. 171 Jerusalem Hill Rd., Elmira 14901; 607-732-6728; www.hill-top -inn.com

At **Turtle Leaf Café**, diners eat good to feel good! Turtle serves fresh wraps, salads, paninis, smoothies, and more in a setting that supports a green environment. 315 E. Water St., Elmira 14901; 607-767-6191; www.turtleleafcafe.com

✳ To See

MUSEUMS **Arnot Art Museum** features European and American art exhibits as well as contemporary traveling exhibits, housed in a neoclassical mansion. 235 Lake St., Elmira 14901; 607-734-3697; www.arnotartmuseum.org

Chemung Valley History Museum: Experience the stories of Mark Twain's Elmira, local immigrant life, Elmira's role in the Civil War, and more. 415 E. Water St., Elmira 14901; 607-734-4168; www.chemungvalleymuseum.org

Mark Twain Study and Exhibit on the Elmira College campus is in the octagonal study where Samuel Clemens wrote some of his best-known books while a summer resident in the town. Nearby an exhibit contains photographs and Mark Twain memorabilia. One Park Pl., Elmira 14901; 607-735-1941; www.elmira.edu

National Soaring Museum is a museum for aviation buffs. See a glider cockpit simulator, sailplane collection, and other exhibits. 51 Soaring Hill Dr., Elmira 14901; 607-734-3128; www.soaringmuseum.org

At the **Wings of Eagles Discovery Center**, military aviation history comes to life through a series of exhibits and vintage aircraft. Watch old airplanes being restored and look inside the cockpits and gunners' areas. 339 Daniel Zenker Dr., Horseheads 14845; 607-358-4247; www.wingsofeagles.com

Chemung County Commerce Center

MARK TWAIN'S STUDY IS A POPULAR TOURISM STOP

PERFORMING ARTS **The Clemens Center for the Performing Arts** is a major performing arts center offering international touring artists, fully staged Broadway musicals, concerts, jazz, rock 'n' roll, dance, stand-up comedy, and children's theater. 207 Clemens Center Pkwy., Elmira 14901; 607-733-5639; www.clemenscenter.com

✽ To Do

Trolley into Twain Country Tours. Hop aboard a trolley at the Chemung Valley History Museum for a tour of Twain's Elmira. The summer tours include a visit inside the Mark Twain Study, and the last tour of the each day includes at stop at the author's gravesite at Woodlawn Cemetery. 607-734-4167; www.marktwaincountry.com

Harris Hill Soaring in Horseheads takes you soaring above the countryside with FAA-certified pilots. 62 Soaring Hill Dr., Elmira 14901; 607-796-2988, 607-734-0641; www.harrishillsoaring.org

GOLF Mark Twain State Park is the home of **Soaring Eagles Golf Course,** a scenic, challenging course with a unique design: Only two holes run parallel. Water-filled depressions or "kettle ponds" are a reminder of the glaciers that melted here thousands of years ago. 201 Middle Rd., Horseheads 14845; 607-739-0551; www.nysparks.com

Mark Twain Golf Course is a classic 18-hole Donald Ross–designed course with a large clubhouse and snack bar. 2275 Corning Rd., Elmira 14903; 607-737-5770; www.marktwaingolf.com

Willowcreek Golf Club is located in a picturesque valley and offers 27 holes of challenging tree-lined golf as well as extensive practice facilities. 3069 NY Rt. 352, Big Flats 14814; 607-562-8898; www.willowcreekgolfclub.com

✽ Shopping

Arnot Mall, Horseheads, is a major mall complex with more than one hundred stores, several theaters, a food court, and restaurants. 3300 Chambers Rd., Horseheads 14845; 607-739-8704; www.arnotmall.com

Antique Revival is arguably New York State's largest antique store with more than 10,000 square feet of Victorian-era antiques and decorative arts. The elegant setting is a destination for both shoppers and browsers. 26 Palmer Rd. N., Big Flats 14814; 607-562-2202; www.antiquerevival.com

The Christmas House in an 1894 Queen Anne mansion features six rooms full of holiday ornaments and gifts—Santas, nutcrackers, decorated trees, and much more. Also visit their outlet in the Arnot Mall in Horseheads. 361 Maple Ave., Elmira 14901; 607-734-9547; www.christmas-house.com

Oldies but Goodies provides a delightful shopping experience with more than 35 rooms of treasures and good old-fashioned hospitality. 10 Carpenter Rd., Elmira 14901; 607-562-7416; www.oldiesbutgoodiesinc.com

✽ What's Happening

Community Soaring Day, Harris Hill Soaring & the National Soaring Museum. 607-734-4211; www.soaringmuseum.org

A BIRD'S EYE-VIEW OF THE COUNTRYSIDE FROM A HARRIS HILL GLIDER

Chemung County Fair, Chemung County Fairgrounds. 607-737-2843

Elmira Street Painting Festival, a fun-filled, family-friendly weekend where artists create giant chalk masterpieces on the streets throughout downtown. 607-734-0341; www.elmirastreetpaintingfestival.org

Corning

Hundreds of thousands come to Corning each year to visit the **Corning Museum of Glass**, home of the largest collection of glass in the world and one of New York State's most popular attractions. Recently the museum doubled in size with a 100,000-square-foot addition: the new Contemporary Art + Design Wing.

The **Steuben Glass Factory** and the **Rockwell Museum** are also here, as well as historic **Market Street**, with more than one hundred craft shops, artists' studios, gift stores, boutiques, cafés, and restaurants. This tree-shaded street and **Centerway Square** are listed on the National Register of Historic Places and are graced by period lighting, hanging baskets of flowers, brick walkways, and restored nineteenth-century buildings. Market Street's successful restoration has been cited as a benchmark for Main Street America, a national downtown restoration program. New breweries and bistro-style restaurants like **Hand + Foot** are serving fresh local produce, handcrafted beer, and Finger Lakes wines, adding to Corning's upbeat nature.

Corning's **Gaffer District** is the venue for many special events, including art and crafts fairs, street parties, jazz festivals, a festival of lights parade, and seasonal celebrations. Streets are closed for the annual Sparkle of Christmas so you can shop, take buggy rides, and enjoy the ice carving and live entertainment. If art is your passion, be sure to take Corning's self-guided fire arts trail, **Tiffany and Treasures**.

Complimentary shuttle bus service carries passengers from Market Street to the Corning Museum of Glass and the Rockwell Museum. A visitor-friendly town, Corning offers two free hours of parking. No wonder it was voted the "Most Fun" small town in America (Rand McNally's "Best of the Road" contest).

Corning Museum of Glass

INNOVATION CENTER AT THE
CORNING MUSEUM OF GLASS

✳ Lodging

In addition to a number of chain hotels, including **Fairfield Inn Corning**, **Holiday Inn**, **Radisson Hotel Corning** at the end of Market Street, **Best Western**, and other chain properties, there are several inns and bed-and-breakfasts.

Inn at the Gaffer Grille, a four-room boutique hotel on Market Street in the middle of everything and only a 10-minute walk to the Corning Museum of Glass, is smartly decorated with soft chocolate walls accented by natural brick, polished dark wood floors, and wood and leather upholstered furniture. Corning's shops, pubs, and cafés are just out the door. $$–$$$ 60 W. Market St., Corning 14830; 607-962-4649; www .innatthegaffnergrille.com

Rosewood Inn B&B, Suzanne and Stewart Sanders's lovely blush-pink Tudor house, is within walking distance of Market Street. The seven rooms have private baths and are elaborately furnished with period antiques and memorabilia. All rooms are air-conditioned and feature luxurious 300-thread-count linens. A full breakfast is served in the formal dining room. $$–$$$ 134 First St., Corning 14830; 607-962-3253; www.rosewoodinn.com

Villa Bernese has four guest rooms with European-style amenities in a secluded Tudor-style villa overlooking the Chemung River valley. Enjoy the pool table, ping-pong, patios, gardens, and delicious breakfasts. $$–$$$ 11881 Overlook Dr., Corning 14830; 607-936-2633; www.bedbreakfastcorning.com

VACATION RENTAL PROPERTY **Marsh Creek Cabin**: Experience the serenity of country living just minutes from the Corning's Gaffer District. Tucked among the trees on over 70 acres of land, Marsh Creek Cabin has two newly furnished bedrooms, hand-crafted décor, an outdoor grill and fire pit, washer and dryer, fully stocked kitchen-ware, and it is oh so peaceful and quiet. 980 Marsh Rd., Corning 14830; 607-857-1185; www.corningvacationrentals.com

✳ Dining Out

FAMILY FAVORITES **Cap'n Morgan's Sports & Seafood** is a great place to bring the family, with a full menu including wraps, BBQ, crab cakes, Paradise burgers, steaks, fish dinners, raw bar, seafood, and arguably the best wings in town. There are more than 10 televisions for sports viewing. 36 South Bridge St.,

Corning 14830; 607-962-1616; www.capn morgan.com

R&M Restaurant has some of the best burgers and fries in the Finger Lakes. Want real gut-warming grease? Dat's the place. 101 W. Market St., Corning 14830; 607-936-9679

Sorge's Restaurant, a family-owned and -operated Italian American restaurant, is known among the locals for its homemade pasta dishes and friendly service. A staple of the community, it was recently renovated and is more spacious than ever. 68 W. Market St., Corning 14830; 607-937-5422; www.sorges .com

Another great spot for food in Corning is **The Source**. This eclectic and popular eatery and gift shop offers dishes for vegans, vegetarians, meat lovers, and those seeking gluten-free options. 85 W. Market St., Corning 14830; 607-936-1663; www.sassy source.com

HAND + FOOT OFFERS AN ECLECTIC MENU AND GREAT SELECTION OF BEER

HIP BISTRO-STYLE **The Cellar** is known for its small plates, tapas, and great martinis. Love their lamb lollipops. 21 W. Market St., Corning 14830; 607-377-5552; www .corningwinebar.com

The Gaffer Grille & Tap Room offers superb contemporary cuisine in a Victorian atmosphere surrounded by artwork and glassblown sculptures by local artists. The taproom features casual dining, international brews, wine, spirits, specialty coffees, and late-night dining. For overnight guests, there are four well-appointed rooms upstairs. 58 W. Market St., Corning 14830; 607-962-4649; www .gaffergrilleandtaproom.com

Hand + Foot has a huge selection of beer from around the world along with an eclectic menu, with items like a "Hippie be Good" sandwich containing goat cheese, mango, and other good things, and amaro, the Italian digestif to cure everything. It's a creative bar serving very good food in an environment focused on craft and community. 69 W. Market St., Corning 14830; 607-973-2547; www.handandfoot .com

Market Street Brewing Company embodies the essence of the microbrew revolution, serving fresh beer brewed on premises as well as a diverse luncheon and dinner menu—hot stuffed banana peppers, loaded chips, appetizers, and tempting entrées. The vibe is upscale with etched glass mirrors and antique woods. Also find rooftop seating, a biergarten, and a dining room. 63 W. Market St., Corning 14830; 607-936-2337; www.936-beer.com

CASUAL FARE **DeClemente's Deli** is one of the area's best delis. Eat inside in a warm, intimate dining room or outside at wrought-iron tables. 30 W. Market St., Corning 14830; 607-937-5657

Jim's Texas Hots has no sign on the building, but look for the line of customers outside waiting to buy ice cream, hot dogs, and sandwiches. Texas Hots are hot. 8 W. Market St., Corning 14830; 607-936-1820

Poppleton Bakery and Café is a wonderful spot for crepes, breakfasts, lunches, awesome baked goods, and more. 23 W. Market St. #104, Corning 14830; 607-937-3311; www.poppletonbakery.com

ICE CREAM At **Dippity Do Dahs**, even in the winter, there can be a line to order a handmade waffle cone filled with the most delicious homemade ice cream and hot fudge sauce. And wait until you see all the flavors. Bacon-flavored ice cream? Really? Dippity is becoming a cult! 58 E. Market St., Corning 14830; 607-542-9416; www.dippitydodahs.com

Old World Café and Ice Cream at Centerway Square evokes the spirit of years gone by with a soda fountain counter, marble-topped round tables, tile floor, and pressed metal ceiling. Most of the fixtures and furnishings, including the hand-carved mahogany woodwork, come from a circa-1800s ice cream parlor. In addition to ice cream, there are salads, sandwiches, wraps, soup, and other items. 1 W. Market St., Corning 14830; 607-936-1953; www.oldworldcafe.com

✻ To See & Do

ATTRACTIONS The **Corning Museum of Glass** is the place to learn about the history of glassmaking. Check out the Glass Innovation Center, where the mysteries of creating windows, optical glass, and vessels are revealed. Examine space shuttle windows and mirrors for telescopes and flight simulators. One gallery displays a stunning array of contemporary glass sculptures, from minute to towering; while a glass sculpture by Dale Chihuly, a 13-foot-high tower of green flame-like blown glass pieces, livens up the reception area.

Watch Hot Glass Shows, where master craftspeople transform gobs of molten glass into exquisite objects. Then make your own glass art at The Studio, where you can try your hand at hot glassblowing, flame-working, fusing, and sandblasting. Make a glass flower, a glass bead, or create an original design on a drinking glass. It's a joyful experience for the whole family, and there are projects for children as young as two. The

AN EXHIBIT IN THE NEW WING OF THE CORNING MUSEUM OF GLASS

Studio also offers glass-working classes—for a day, a weekend, or weeklong (schedule ahead if possible).

Pure white curved walls and an expansive glass ceiling set the background for the amazing new Contemporary Art + Design wing. It's like walking through a cloud. Exhibits like *Constellation* by Kiki Smith feature 26 hot-sculpted glass animals, and in another exhibit, three giant glass trees emerge from perfectly placed glasses on tiers of glass in *Forest Glass*.

Finally, browse one of the largest museum shops in the country and perhaps purchase a giant light bulb lamp, a glass putter, or Christmas ornaments. 1 Museum Way, Corning 14830; 800-732-6845; www.cmog.org

The Fun Park near the intersection of Gorton Rd. and E. Corning Rd. occupies a 32-acre site where you can enjoy indoor and outdoor 18-hole miniature golf courses, a 32-foot hydraulically operated climbing rock wall, roller racer track, bumper boat ride, video game arcade, a 250-yard golf driving range, trampoline basketball, and a concession stand. Sure, the park could use some TLC, but there is still plenty to do here. 11233 E. Corning Rd., Corning 14830; 607-936-1888; www.thefunparkofcorning.com

Experience glassmaking at the **Hands-On Glass Studio**. Make your own paperweight or blow your own Christmas ornament or glass Easter egg in their workshops. Call for the schedule. 124 Crystal Lane, Corning 14830; 607-962-3044; www.handsonglass.com

Heritage Village of the Southern Finger Lakes features guides in period costume who show you through a restored 1796 inn, a 1784 log cabin, an 1878 one-room schoolhouse, a working blacksmith shop, and a nineteenth-century agricultural exhibit. 73 W. Pulteney St., Corning 14830; 607-937-5281; heritagevillagesfl.org

Park Ave. Sports Center has something fun for the entire family including mini golf, batting cages, a driving range, rock climbing, water wars (opponents, man your battle stations), and bungee jumping. 412 Park Ave., Corning 14830; 607-936-4820; www.parkavesportscenter.com

HERITAGE VILLAGE DEMONSTRATES HEARTH COOKING

Steuben County Conference & Visitors Bureau

The **Rockwell Museum** showcases the largest collection of Western and Native American art east of the Mississippi, hence the moniker "The Best of the West in the East." Exhibits include a mix of traditional and contemporary art, ranging from paintings and sculptures to leatherwork and pottery. Artists represented include Frederic Remington, Thomas Moran, C. M. Russell, N. C. Wyeth, and painters from the Taos Society of Artists. The museum's current focus is on art about America, or art that conveys the American experience. There is a great kids program called Art Packs designed to help children understand, interpret, and experience art. It utilizes a backpack filled with activities, puzzles, and creative challenges related to the exhibits. 111 Cedar St., Corning 14830; 607-937-5386; www.rockwellmuseum.org

Tiffany and Treasures is a self-guided fire arts trail visiting working potter and glass artists' studios, museums and buildings designed by Tiffany, The Glass Menagerie Gallery, the Hands-on Glass Studio, Vitrix Hot Glass Studio, and other "firey" places. 866-946-3386; www.corningfingerlakes.com

Follow Corning's Gaffer District's **Chocolate Trail** to sweet indulgences like Connors Mercantile for handmade chocolates, the Palace Theatre for chocolate crispy critters, the Glass Market Café for double chocolate brownies, and many more places in the Gaffer District. www.gafferdistrict.com/chocolate-trail

KAYAKING **Kim's Kayaks** operating out of Kinselle Park offers self-guided kayak tours along four miles of scenic riverbeds and wildlife areas. 1 W. Market St., Corning 14830; 607-481-3925; www.corningfingerlakes.com/outdoors/kims-kayaks-llc

✳ Shopping

Bacalles Glass Shop offers everything glass—oil lamps, crystal, jewelry, and other items. 607-962-3339

For customized gift baskets with a variety of arts and crafts made by regional artisans go to **Beyond Baskets.** 607-936-1663

Connors Market Street Mercantile presents a unique shopping experience featuring Crabtree and Evelyn, Portmeiron, Boyds Collection, Mary Englebreit, the Cat's Meow, and more. The interior has been restored to its original early 1900s splendor. 607-937-GIFT; www.connorsmercantile.com

The Glass Menagerie features hundreds of kaleidoscopes and paperweights along with crystal ornaments, jewelry, stained glass, bottles, animals, and other interesting things. There is also a specialty shop/gallery across the street with more unique works of art. 607-962-6300

Imagine That sells amazing games, dance wear, young children's clothing, and toys for kids to encourage creative play—or, as they say, "We stock imagination and specialize in fun." 607-937-4242; www.imaginethatkids.com

The Schoolhouse Country Store has some great collectibles, country goods, primitives, candles, old-fashioned candy, a baby corner, and antiques. 607-962-4374

Glass artist Thomas Kelly works and sells his glass creations to collectors all over the world from his **Vitrix Hot Glass Studio.** 607-936-8707

West End Gallery is a fine-art gallery selling paintings, prints, and contemporary work by nationally acclaimed regional artists like G. C. Myers, Tom Gardner, Martin Poole, and the late Thomas Buechner. 607-936-2011

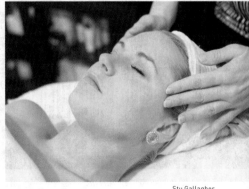

SPA Services at the **AgeLess Spa** at Hotel Radisson Corning balance scientific and time-honored natural medicine practices. The spa offers massages, facials, steam therapies, and other treatments. 130 E. Tioga Ave., Corning 14830; 607-684-6121; www.ageless llc.com

AGELESS SPA

Stu Gallagher

✳ What's Happening

Arts in Bloom, a county-wide art trail in Steuben County usually held last weekend in April. www.artsinbloom.net

GlassFest celebrates glass with a four-day fest featuring glassblowing demos, art exhibits, wine and beer tastings, sports events, and music (end of May). 607-937-6292; www.glassfest.org

Crystal City Christmas, Gaffer District, Corning. 607-936-6544

Spring Antique Show and Sale. Vendors show and sell a wide assortment of furniture, glassware, memorabilia, and other things (March). 607-937-5281

Rochester

The greater Rochester area, with about a million people, offers all the cultural attractions and facilities you'd expect from a major urban area but without the hassle. It has its own international airport, and its attractive suburbs are considered highly desirable places to live.

Education plays a strong role in Rochester, with St. John Fisher College, Monroe Community College, Nazareth College, Roberts Wesleyan College, Rochester Institute of Technology, and the University of Rochester.

HISTORY As early as the mid-1800s, Rochester's thriving horticulture industry and gardens led to its being called the "Flower City." It is one of just four cities in the country having an entire park system designed by Frederick Law Olmsted, known as the

Visit Rochester

THE DAZZLING ROCHESTER SKYLINE

father of American landscape design. At Maplewood Park, an important station on the Underground Railroad, slaves boarded boats headed across Lake Ontario to Canada—and freedom.

Commerce was framed by the Erie Canal, which meanders through Fairport, Bushnell's Basin, Pittsford, the southern rim of metro Rochester, Greece, and Spencerport on to Buffalo. Today it is a valuable recreational asset.

Famous residents include Frederick Douglass, African-American orator, reformer, abolitionist, and publisher of the *North Star* newspaper; and George Eastman, who founded the Eastman Dry Plate Company, precursor to the Eastman Kodak Company. In 1888, the easy-to-use Kodak camera was introduced as well as a flexible film that would help launch the motion picture industry. Another famous Rochester citizen, Susan B. Anthony, founded the Women's Educational and Industrial Union. Anthony worked all her life to secure rights for women.

✳ Lodging

Most of the major hotel chains can be found in and around Rochester, along with small inns, bed-and-breakfasts, and midsize boutique hotels.

Del Monte Lodge Renaissance Hotel & Spa, a boutique gem in Pittsford overlooking the Erie Canal, is polished and honed to appeal to guests willing to pay for a full cadre of services and amenities including top-drawer beds and linens. Famous guests have included Bill and Hillary Clinton. 41 N. Main St., Pittsford 14534; 585-381-9900

Strathallan Doubletree by Hilton, at the hub of Rochester's cultural and business districts, is within walking distance of the Memorial Art Gallery, the George Eastman House, and the Rochester Museum and Science Center. All 155 guest rooms have WiFi and two telephones. A free shuttle takes you to other area attractions. Dine on the roof at Hattie's with its Japanese-centered cuisine and 360-degree view of the city. Or pitch into a steak, homemade pasta, or fresh seafood from the Char Steak and Lounge. $$$ 550 East Ave., Rochester 14607; 585-461-5010; info@strathallan.com

The **Woodcliff Hotel & Spa** is low-key modern with understated elegance and knockout views looking down and out to the countryside from the bar, dining room, pool and gazebo. On the property is a nine-hole golf course and the Spa Elan. Honeymooners love the whirlpool suites. 199 Woodcliff Dr., Fairport 14450; 585-381-4000; www.woodcliffhotelspa.com

The Irish manor–style B&B, **428 Mt. Vernon** is a gracious Victorian home set on two acres. All rooms have private baths, phones, televisions and WiFi. Known for made-to-order breakfasts, they offer delicious scones, homemade jams, and French toast. 428 Mount Vernon Ave., Rochester 14620; 800-836-3159

✳ Dining Out

TRADITION, TRADITION **Richardson's Canal House** in Pittsford is on the roster of the National Registry of Historic Places. This restored Erie Canal tavern offers an a la carte menu featuring French and American regional food and boasts a great location on the canal. Eat inside or on the outdoor patio. 1474 Marsh Rd., Pittsford 14534; 585-248-5000; www.richardsonscanalhouse.com

PASTA AMORE Bacco's Ristorante serves Northern-style Italian cuisine, homemade bread and desserts. Delicious. 263 Park Ave., Rochester 14607; 585-442-5090; www.baccosristorante.com

HIP BISTRO-STYLE 2 Vine Restaurant dishes out French and Italian fare in cozy, intimate surroundings and specializes in small plates. Everything is homemade using fresh, local ingredients. No out-of-season tomatoes or swordfish (yes, migratory fish have seasons when they can be legally caught). 24 Winthrop St., Rochester 14607; 585-454-6020; www.2vine.com

ETHNIC TASTES Tapas 177 offers an eclectic fusion of Mediterranean and Asian food and cocktails including homemade sangria and freshly muddled mojitos. The atmosphere is candlelit Spanish. Open for dinner seven nights a week. Free salsa dancing lessons every Thursday and live music on some weekends. $$ 177 Saint Paul St., Rochester 14607; 585-262-2090; www.tapas177.com

Tokyo Japanese Restaurant & Steak House has excellent sushi, hibachi table, tempura, and other Japanese specialties. 2930 W. Henrietta Rd., Rochester 14623; 585-424-4166; www.tokyorestaurantrochester.com

CASUAL FARE Char Steak & Lounge in the Strathallan Rochester Hotel is a fine-dining restaurant popular for business lunches and dinners. Its cuisine is good, dependable, its bar and wine list even better. 550 East Ave., Rochester 14607; 585-241-7100; www.strathallan.com

Dinosaur Bar-B-Que is known for its super ribs, while Cajun and Cuban food have gained Dinosaur a solid reputation for great meals and value. It's the real deal. 99 Court St., Rochester 14604; 585-325-7090; www.dinosaurbarbque.com

The Frog Pond (or "Charlie's Frog Pond") serves breakfast all day, lunch, and dinner from an extensive menu in a pint-size setting. Check out their daily blackboard specials. 652 Park Ave., Rochester 14607; 585-271-1970

Java's Cafe uses fine loose tea, hand squeezes its lemons, roasts its own coffee, and makes sandwiches on fresh bread. It now features vegan and flourless cakes, cupcakes, and cookies. $ 16 Gibbs St., Rochester 14604; 585-232-4820; www.javascafe.com

Jines Restaurant on Park Ave. serves family fare and breakfast, lunch, and dinner seven days a week. They also serve some Greek specialities. Eat inside or out. 658 Park Ave., Rochester 14607; 585-461-1280; www.jinesrestaurant.com

Magnolia's Deli & Café serves exceptional, fresh food with flair including paninis wraps, salads, and pizza. All sandwiches are from scratch and they're worth the half-hour (sometimes) wait. Sit inside or outside. 366 Park Ave., Rochester 14607; 585-271-7380; www.magnoliascafe.com

Murphy's Law at the corner of East and Alexander, an Irish pub with a fabulous mahogany bar, is a social hub. Serves great hearty fare and a mean brunch on Sundays. $$ 370 East Ave., Rochester 14604; 585-232-7115; www.murphyslawrochester.com

Ristorante Lucano is where locals in the know come for home-cooked Italian dinners. The façade may be nondescript, but the food prepared from authentic recipes is fine dining Italian style, and patrons enjoy the full bar. 1815 East Ave., Rochester 14610; 585-244-3460; www.ristorantelucano.com

ICE CREAM No trip to Rochester would be complete without a creamy frozen custard fix at **Abbott's Frozen Custard**. It's been around since 1902, treating customers to flavors like chocolate almond and black raspberry. Simply the best. Several locations. 585-865-7400; www.abbottscustard.com

ABBOTT'S FROZEN CUSTARD HAS SEVERAL LOCATIONS IN THE CITY

✳ To See

Rochester has a huge cultural base, with just about every aspect of the arts repre-sented, including the Geva Theatre Center, the Rochester Philharmonic Orchestra, the George Eastman House International Museum of Photography and Film, the Memo-rial Art Gallery, and Strong National Museum of Play—the second-largest children's museum in the country and home to the National Toy Hall of Fame. Also visit the Susan B. Anthony House and see wild animals at the Seneca Park Zoo.

MUSEUMS AND HISTORIC SITES **The High Falls Center and Interpretive Museum**, built on the banks of the Genesee River, is a fascinating cultural park with interactive 3-D exhibits—a room-size "supermap," taxi tour, flour mill, 30-foot waterwheel, and talking camera. There is also the Triphammer Forge, with multilevel views of 1816 fac-tory ruins. 74 Browns Race, Rochester 14614; 585-325-2030; www.cityofrochester.gov /highfallsmuseum

Genesee Country Village & Museum has more than 60 restored historic structures with costumed villagers and artisans portraying life in western New York from the 1790s to the 1920s. Visit houses, schools, farms, blacksmiths, an opera house, stores, a working nineteenth-century brewery, and a historic bakery. There are restaurants and picnic areas. Open seasonally. 1410 Flint Hill Rd., Mumford 14511; 585-538-6822; www.gcv.org

National Warplane Museum features aircraft of the past with a focus on World War II and Korean War aviation. Watch for the Geneseo Airshow. 3489 Big Tree Ln., Geneseo 14454; 585-243-2100; www.1941hag.org

Courtesy of George Eastman House

GEORGE EASTMAN HOUSE

George Eastman House, a 50-room turn-of-the-twentieth-century National Historic Landmark, is what George Eastman called home. Site of the **International Museum of Photography and Film,** it is filled with important collections of films, cameras, books, and photography in changing exhibits as well as many of the original pieces in the house. The mansion and gardens have been restored to their early 1900s appearance. 900 East Ave., Rochester 14607; 585-271-3361; www.eastmanhouse.org

Museums of the Landmark Society showcases the Stone-Tolan House, an early 1800s farmhouse and tavern. 133 Fitzhugh St. S., Rochester 14608; 585-546-7029; www .landmarksociety.org

The **New York Museum of Transportation** in West Henrietta is open all year on Sundays only. The museum contains many exhibits, including historic trolley cars, a steam locomotive, horse-drawn and highway vehicles, and two large model railroads. Trolley rides are included in the admission mid-May through October and during the Christmas holidays. 6393 E. River Rd., West Henrietta 14586; 585-533-1113; www .nymtmuseum.org

The **Rochester & Genesee Valley Railroad Museum,** Rush (20 minutes south of Rochester), invites you to board an authentically restored freight train caboose at a 1909 passenger station, ride a mile and a half, disembark to tour a collection of vintage trains and equipment, then return by caboose to explore the museum display. 282 Rush Scottsville Rd., Rush 14543; 585-533-1431; www.rochestertrainrides.com

Susan B. Anthony House, home of women's rights champion Susan B. Anthony from 1866 until her death in 1906, is a National Historic Landmark and museum filled with memorabilia from Anthony's life and the women's suffrage movement. 17 Madison St., Rochester 14608; 585-235-6124; www.susanbanthonyhouse.org

MUSIC **The Eastman School of Music of the University of Rochester** presents more than 700 student concerts during the year, in the school's Kodak Hall, Kilbourn Hall, and Hatch Recital Hall. 26 Gibbs St., Rochester 14604; 585-274-1000, 585-274-1400; 585-454-2100; www.esm.rochester.edu

Rochester Philharmonic Orchestra, a critically acclaimed orchestra, offers classical, pops, and special children's concerts, including traditional favorites like *The Nutcracker*, a fully staged ballet in collaboration with Rochester City Ballet. 60 Gibbs St., Rochester 14604; 585-454-2100; www.rpo.org

PERFORMING ARTS **Garth Fagan Dance** has been performing for more than 40 years. 50 Chestnut St., Rochester 14604; 585-454-3260; www.garthfagandance.org

Geva Theatre Center, a highly popular professional regional theater, produces a variety of performances, including comedies, musicals, and world premieres. 75 Woodbury Blvd., Rochester 14607; 585-232-GEVA; www.gevatheatre.org

Rochester City Ballet, rated as one of the best regional companies in the country, presents classic and contemporary ballets. 1326 University Ave., Rochester 14607; 585-461-5850; www.rochestercityballet.com

FINE ARTS **Memorial Art Gallery** contains an enormous collection of artwork spanning five thousand years including works by Edgar Degas, Mary Cassatt, Henry Moore, Jacob Lawrence, Hans Hofmann, the French impressionists, and many others. See revolving exhibits from the gallery's permanent collection and the new Helen H. Berkeley Gallery of Ancient Art, plus exceptional art from leading contemporary and regional artists. The new Centennial Sculpture Park adds punch to the campus. 500 University Ave., Rochester 14607; 585-276-8900; www.mag.rochester.edu

SCIENCE AND MORE **Rochester Museum and Science Center** comprising the Strasenburgh Planetarium, the Science Museum, and the 900-acre Cumming Nature Center offers multilevel hands-on learning at every turn: 200 interactive exhibits,

MEMORIAL ART GALLERY

Rochester Museum and Science Center

FASCINATION WITH EXHIBITS AT THE
SCIENCE CENTER

computerized laser star shows in the planetarium, six miles of trails through wetlands and forests, and a walk through Rochester's rich history of innovation. It's a place to spend many hours, totally absorbed. 657 East Ave., Rochester 14607; 585-271-4320; www.rmsc.org

FAMILY FUN **Jell-O Gallery Museum** in LeRoy, just west of Rochester, invites you to find out all the things you never knew about this famous dessert. And while you're there visit the historic LeRoy House (circa early 1800s). 23 E. Main St., LeRoy 14482; 585-768-7433; www .jellogallery.org

Seabreeze Amusement Park and Raging Rivers Waterpark rolls out all kinds of fun: rides, slides, games, soak zone, carousel, bumper cars, water park, giant Jack Rabbit roller coaster, food, entertainment, and more roller coasters. Open seasonally. 4600 Culver Rd., Rochester 14622; 585-323-1900; www.seabreeze.com

Seneca Park Zoo: Open all year long, Monroe County's Seneca Park Zoo is easy walking for all ages. Highlights are the herd of African elephants, the penguin-breeding program, Bella the baby Bornean orangutan and her parents, and other endangered species the zoo is working to conserve through its Special Survival Programs. A place for serious fun. 2222 Saint Paul St., Rochester 14621; 585-336-7200; www .senecaparkzoo.org

Seabreeze Amusement Park

ONE GREAT WAY TO COOL OFF

FACE-TO-FACE

The Strong Museum (National Museum of Play) is simply one of the best places you'll ever take your kids. Home to the National Toy Hall of Fame and the world's most comprehensive collection of toys, miniatures, and dolls, the museum has many hands-on exhibits. Step onto Sesame Street, pilot a giant helicopter, walk into a butterfly garden, shop for food in a king-size supermarket, ride a 1918 Herschell carousel, walk through favorite books in Reading Adventureland, and board a whaling ship. See a 1950s diner and an old-fashioned ice-cream fountain. Play some of the blinking, beeping, bonging games in the Broadway Arcade. 1 Manhattan Square Dr., Rochester 14607; 585-263-2700; www.museumofplay.org

✳ To Do

BOATING With Lake Ontario on the northern border, the Genesee River on the west, Irondequoit Bay to the northeast, and the Erie Canal, running east to west on the south, Rochester offers plenty of options for boaters. Kayaking and canoeing on the Genesee River is quite accessible thanks to the Corn Hill Landing, and you can paddle along the Erie Canal as well.

Genesee Waterways Center in Genesee Valley Park has 600 feet of accessible docks plus boat rentals, seasonal kayak and canoe rentals, and year-round rowing and training opportunities. 149 Elmwood Ave., Rochester 14611; 585-0328-3960; www.geneseewaterways.org

CRUISES The *Colonial Belle*, a 149-passenger double-deck boat, departs from Fairport to cruise the Erie Canal with three trips daily (mid-May through the end of October). 400 Packetts Lndg., Fairport 14450; 585-223-9470; www.colonialbelle.com

Corn Hill Navigation offers cruises on the *Sam Patch*, a replica of an Erie Canal packet boat, three times daily in season. Each cruise goes through a century-old canal lock. They also offer lunch cruises, happy hour and wine-tasting cruises, and private charters. 290 Exchange Blvd., Rochester 14608; 585-662-5748 www.sampatch.org

GOLF There are more than 80 courses within a 45-minute drive of Rochester (www.rochestergolfcourses.com) including **Greystone Golf Club**, a links-style

LYDIA KO, TOP LPGA GOLFER, PLAYS AT A MAJOR TOURNAMENT AT MONROE GOLF CLUB

layout and one of the best public courses in the state. 1400 Atlantic Ave., Walworth 14568; 315-524-0022

Highly rated are the private courses **Locust Hill Country Club** and **Monroe Golf Club**, both in Pittsford, two of Rochester's prettiest courses and coveted by the pros as the site of former Wegman's LPGA Championships. Another treasure, the private **Oak Hill Country Club**'s West and East courses, originally designed by Donald Ross in the 1920s, have been the venue for the Ryder Cup, the United States Open, the United States Amateur, the United States Senior Open, and the Senior PGA Championship!

Walter Hagen, captain of America's first Ryder Cup Team, and Robert Trent Jones, one of the world's best-known course architects, are natives of the city. RTJ's area designs include **Midvale Golf & Country Club** in Penfield, the course at **Bristol Harbour** in Canandaigua, and the second nine at **Durand-Eastman Golf Course**, a public track in Rochester. (585-266-0110).

Whispering Pines (1929) in Seabreeze is the country's oldest, miniature golf course. Renovated in 2012, it's got everything—the windmill, the two-tiered holes, and more. www.parksidediner.com/miniature-golf

GOLF IS A FAMILY AFFAIR AT COURSES IN THE FINGER LAKES

HIKING AND BIKING For hikers and bikers, Rochester has miles of trails, off-road and urban. Pedal along the shores of Lake Ontario, follow the Genesee River from Rochester to Letchworth State Park, and travel along the Erie Canalway Trail. Many of the parks have trails for hiking including Mendons Ponds Park; Durand-Eastman Park; and Genesee Valley Greenway, where trails follow a route once used by boats and trains.

PRO SPORTS Among the six minor league sports teams in Rochester are the **Rochester Redwings**, a AAA baseball team; the **Rochester Raging Rhinos**, a champion soccer team; and the **Rochester Americans** hockey team, winner of several Calder Cups. With Lake Ontario on its northern boundaries and the many rivers and lakes in the region, Rochester offers a plethora of water sports.

SKIING **Bristol Mountain** offers good downhill skiing, with a vertical drop of 1,200 feet, 22 trails, and five lifts. www.bristolmountain.com

❋ Shopping

Trendy **Park Avenue**, running from Alexander St. to Culver Rd., contains a number of stylish shops, boutiques, and cafés. In the summer months, the street is a lively place with sidewalk cafés in full swing.

Rochester's three major malls house more than 500 stores and services. **EastView Mall** is upscale enough to have valet parking yet it's the place you can find L.L.Bean; other malls include **The Mall at Greece Ridge Center** and **Marketplace Mall**.

Some speciality shops include **The Shops on West Ridge** for antiques (3200 W. Ridge Rd., Rochester 14626; 585-368-0670; www.theshopsonwestridge.net); **Stever's Candies** for homemade candy made on the premises including chocolates, brittles, truffles, jellies, and sugar-free candy since 1946 (623 Park Ave., Rochester 14607; 585-473-2098; www.steverscandy.com); and **Parkleigh** loaded with colorful and interesting items, from the goofy and funky to sublime, including MacKenzie-Childs, Vera Bradley, charms, original glass crafts, coffee—you name it. 215 Park Ave., Rochester 14607; 585-244-4842; www.parkleigh.com

FOR MORE INFORMATION **Chemung County Commerce Center**: 607-734-5137, 800-MARK-TWAIN; www.chemungchamber.org

Corning Area Chamber of Commerce: 607-936-4686, 866-463-6264; www.corning ny.com

Cortland County Convention and Visitors Bureau: 607-753-8463, 800-859-2227; www.experiencecortland.com

Finger Lakes Tourism Alliance: 315-536-7488; www.fingerlakes.org

Greater Rochester Bed and Breakfast: www.grbaba.com

Steuben County Conference & Visitors Bureau: 607-936-6544, 866-946-3386; www.corningfingerlakes.com

Visit Syracuse: 315-470-1910, 800-234-4797; www.visitsyracuse.org

Visit Rochester: 800-677-7282, 585-279-8300; www.visitrochester.com

❋ What's Happening

SPRING **Fairport Canal Days:** More than 300 artisan booths, food, music, and fun make this one of the biggest festivals on the historic Erie Canal. www.fairportcanaldays.com

Lilac Festival, Highland Park. A brilliant spring display of lilacs plus a parade, races, arts and crafts, activities, entertainment, and horticultural exhibits. 585-473-4482; www.lilacfestival.com

The **Xerox Rochester International Jazz Festival**, second only to Newport, brings more than 1,500 musicians to perform in more than 325 concerts in June. 585-454-2060; www.rochesterjazz.com

SUMMER **Corn Hill Arts Festival**, streets of Corn Hill neighborhood. An eclectic variety of arts and crafts, live music, food, and entertainment featuring more than 375 vendors. 585-262-3142; www.cornhill.org

The **Finger Lakes Fiber Festival** at the Hemlock Fairground, is devoted to everything connected with the fiber arts—hand spinning, weaving, knitting, felting, and much more. 607-522-4374; www.gvhg.org

GELL CENTER

At the Gell Center about 30 miles south of Rochester, Writers & Books offers peaceful, quiet accommodations for writers and artists looking for creative solitude. 585-473-2590; www.wab.org

First Fridays/Wide Open Mic, sponsored by Writers & Books in their Verb Café and Performance Space, welcomes poets, performers, and writers. 585-473-2590

Monroe County Fair, Northampton Park. A good old country-style fair, with agricultural exhibits, rides, games, and entertainment. 585-334-4000; www.mcfair.com

Park Ave. Summer Art Fest, running along the 1-mile stretch of Park Avenue in Rochester, draws more than 300 artists and exhibitors from 20 states and Canada. There are three music stages, juried arts and crafts exhibits, outdoor dining, and shopping (August) www.rochesterevents.com

The Rochester Summer Fest: A two-day festival of American music, featuring a variety of internationally known R&B musicians (July). 917-771-3197; www.rochestersummerfest.com

Sterling Renaissance Festival, Sterling. Live jousting, food, period music and dance, knights in shining armor, stage and street performances, games, and marketplace, weekends July through August. 800-879-4446; www.sterlingfestival.com

Taste of Rochester, Main St., Rochester, showcases the city's best restaurants, wineries, breweries, and music (June). www.tasteofrochester.net

FALL/WINTER Clothesline Festival, Memorial Art Gallery. Hundreds of local and statewide artists sell and show their goods at one of the oldest and largest outdoor art shows in the country. 585-276-8900; www.mag.rochester.edu/clothesline

Harvest Jamboree & Country Fair, Rochester Public Market. Local produce plus wagon and pony rides, pumpkin decorating, and country line dancing.

Oktoberfest, Irondequoit. Two weekends in September (yes, in September) of fun, music, food, and entertainment. 585-336-6070; www.irondequoit.org

Xerox Rochester International Jazz Festival

ROCHESTER HOLDS MANY MUSIC FESTIVALS AND CONCERTS

SUNFLOWERS GROW IN ABUNDANCE OVERLOOKING THE LAKES

Purple Foot Festival, Fairport. Casa Larga Vineyards sponsors grape stomping along with live music, beer and wine tastings, hayrides, winery tours, grape pies, and more (September). 585-223-4210; www.casalarga.com

Rochester River Romance Weekend: A celebration of the Genesee River, this weekend party includes hiking, boating, gorge tours, regatta, entertainment, and children's activities. 585-428-5990; www.cityofrochester.gov

Yuletide in the Country at Genesee Country Village & Museum features day and nighttime tours of the historic village, with costumed period guides showing how the holiday would have been celebrated in the mid-nineteenth century. 585-538-6822; www.gcv.org

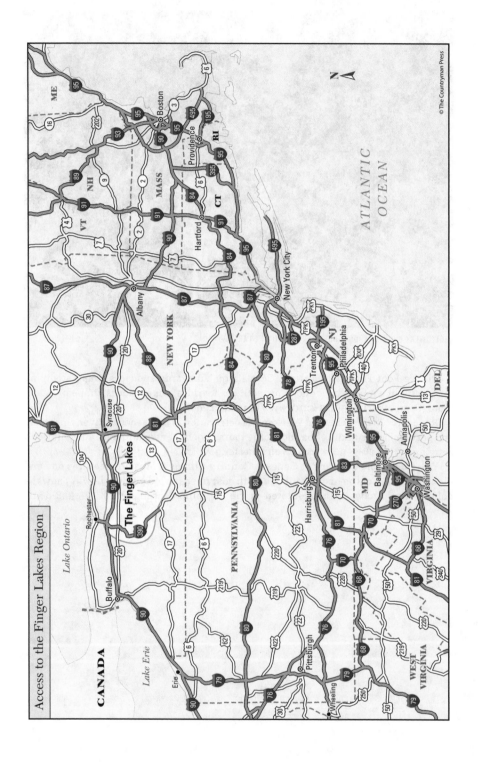

Access to the Finger Lakes Region

CANADA

Lake Ontario

Lake Erie

The Finger Lakes

ATLANTIC OCEAN

N

© The Countryman Press

INFORMATION: FINGER LAKES FACTS AND FIGURES

Ambulance/Fire/Police

Cayuga County Sheriff's Office 315-253-1222
Seneca County Sheriff's Office 315-539-9241
Steuben County Emergency Services/Control Center 607-776-4099
Tompkins County Sheriff's Office 607-272-2444
Tompkins County Ambulance/Fire 607-273-8000
Tompkins County City Police 607-272-3245
All other counties 911

Lake Facts and Figures

Each Finger Lake is unique; all but one are named after a Native American word or phrase. The list below goes from east to west.

OTISCO

Length: 6 miles
Depth: 76 feet
Elevation: 788 feet
Characteristics: Ringed by small lakeside camps and homes
Meaning: "Waters much dried away"
Largest town: Amber

SKANEATELES

Length: 15 miles
Depth: 315 feet
Elevation: 868 feet
Characteristics: Cold and clean water, shale base, steep hillsides at southern end; large homes and mansions hug northern shores
Meaning: "Long lake"
Largest town: Skaneateles

OWASCO

Length: 11 miles
Depth: 177 feet
Elevation: 710 feet
Characteristics: Smaller than Skaneateles and not quite so hectic.
Meaning: "Floating bridge" or "crossing place"
Largest town: Auburn

CAYUGA

Length: 40 miles
Depth: 435 feet
Elevation: 382 feet
Characteristics: Long and wide, can get very rough on windy days; large stretches of open rolling land between towns; many vineyards
Meaning: "Boat landing"
Largest town: Ithaca

SENECA

Length: 36 miles
Depth: 618 feet
Elevation: 444 feet
Characteristics: Deepest of the Finger Lakes and second deepest in the country; ringed by hills and vineyards
Meaning: "Place of the stone"
Largest town: Geneva

KEUKA

Length: 19.6 miles
Depth: 183 feet
Elevation: 715 feet
Characteristics: Branches into a Y shape; many vineyards
Meaning: "Canoe landing"
Largest town: Penn Yan

CANANDAIGUA

Length: 16 miles
Depth: 276 feet
Elevation: 686 feet
Characteristics: Mostly lined by homes
Meaning: "Chosen spot"
Largest town: Canandaigua

HONEOYE

Length: 5 miles
Depth: 30 feet

Elevation: 804 feet
Characteristics: Small; some nice houses
Meaning: "Finger lying"
Largest town: Honeoye

CANADICE

Length: 3 miles
Depth: 95 feet
Elevation: 1,099 feet
Characteristics: Highest elevation, yet the smallest lake
Meaning: "Long lake"
Largest town: Canadice

HEMLOCK

Length: 7 miles
Depth: 91 feet
Elevation: 905 feet
Characteristics: No motorized craft allowed on this pristine reservoir
Meaning: Only lake named by white man; it refers to the Native American word *Onehda*
Largest town: Hemlock

CONESUS

Length: 9 miles
Depth: 59 feet
Elevation: 818 feet
Characteristics: Small, quiet, and pretty; surrounded by meadows and woodlands
Meaning: "Always beautiful"
Largest townn: Lakeville

FINGER LAKES CULINARY BOUNTY

Finger Lakes Culinary Bounty has identified restaurants that use high-quality, fresh food from local producers. To find out which restaurants are doing this, email info@flcb.org

Medical Facilities

AUBURN

Auburn Memorial Hospital 315-255-7011

CLIFTON

Clifton Springs Hospital & Clinic 315-462-9561

CORTLAND

Cortland Memorial Hospital 607-756-3500

GENEVA

Geneva General Hospital 315-462-9561

ITHACA

Cayuga Medical Center at Ithaca 607-274-4011

ROCHESTER

Highland Hospital 585-341-8097
Park Ridge Hospital 585-723-7000
Rochester General Hospital 585-922-4000
Strong Memorial Hospital 585-275-2100

SYRACUSE

Crouse Hospital 315-470-7111 **St. Joseph's Hospital Health Center** 315-448-5111
Syracuse VA Medical Center 315-425-4400
Upstate Medical University Hospital 315-464-5540
Upstate Medical University Hospital Community Campus 315-492-5011

Recreation Facts and Figures

HIKING The Finger Lakes Trail, maintained by the Finger Lakes Trail Conference, covers more than 559 miles, running south of the lakes from Allegheny State Park in southwestern New York State to the Catskill Mountains. Six spurs run from the main trail north, with a total of 238 miles. Motorized vehicles are not allowed. Longer-term hikers can take advantage of the well-maintained footpath, lean-tos, and camping areas spread out along the trail. 585-658-9320; www.fingerlakestrail.org

BIKING Cyclists have an excellent network of well-paved back roads as well as roads ringing the lakes. The terrain in the northern part of the lakes is generally easier, more level, less rugged than the southern part. And cycling in the direction that the lakes run—north and south—is for the most part less strenuous than riding in an east–west direction.

FISHING Fed by underground streams and rivers that flow from Lake Ontario, the Finger Lakes host a variety of fish including rainbow trout, rock bass, sunfish, lake trout, perch, panfish, bluegills, pickerel, smelt, and other species.

Other Useful Numbers

NEW YORK STATE

Empire State Bed & Breakfast Association of New York State www.esbba.com
I Love New York NY Thruway conditions, vacation planning, etc. 1-800-225-5697; www.iloveny.com
NYS Canal Information Center 1-800-4-CANAL-4; www.canals.ny.gov
NYS Department of Environmental Conservation 518-457-3521 (hunting and fishing information), 315-426-7400; www.dec/ny.gov
NYS Office of Parks, Recreation, and Historic Preservation 518-474-0456; www.ny parks.com

NYS Parks Reservation Center 800-456-CAMPS (for camping and cabin reservations); www.reserveamerica.com

ROCHESTER

Cinemark Tinseltown USA and IMAX 585-247-0042; www.cinemark.com

City of Rochester Events Hotline 585-428-6697; www.cityofrochester.gov

Greater Rochester International Airport 585-753-7000; www.rocairport.com

Information for the Deaf www.urmc.rochester.edu/ncdhr/resourcedirectory

Rochester Broadway Theatre League 585-222-5000; www.rbtl.org

Rochester Riverside Convention Center (Joseph A. Floreano Rochester Riverside Convention Center) 585-232-7200, 800-856-1678; www.rrcc.com

Visit Rochester 800-677-7282; www.visitrochester.com

SYRACUSE

NYS Fairgrounds 315-487-7711, 800-475-FAIR; www.nysfair.org

Fishing Information 315-472-2111, ext. 2645

Oncenter Complex , 315-435-8000; www.oncenter.org

Onondaga County Parks 315-451-PARK; www.onondagacountyparks.com

Syracuse Hancock International Airport 315-454-4330; www.syrairport.org

Syracuse University Information 315-443-5500; www.cuse.com; **Carrier Dome Box Office** 315-443-2121; www.carrierdome.com

Tourism Organizations

COUNTY TOURISM BOARDS

Cayuga County Office of Tourism 315-255-1658, 800-499-9615; www.tourcayuga.com

Chemung County Chamber of Commerce 607-734-5137, 800-MARK-TWAIN; www.chemungchamber.org; www.marktwaincountry.com

Cortland County Convention and Visitors Bureau 607-753-8463, 800-859-2227; www.cortlandtourism.com

Ithaca and Tompkins County Convention and Visitors Bureau 800-28-ITHACA; www.visitithaca.com

Ontario County/Finger Lakes Visitors Connection 877-386-4669; www.visitfingerlakes.com

Schuyler County Chamber of Commerce 800-607-4552; www.watkinsglenchamber.com

Seneca County Tourism 800-732-1848; www.fingerlakescentral.com

Steuben County Conference & Visitors Bureau 866-946-3386, www.corningfingerlakes.com

Visit Rochester 585-546-3070, 800-677-7282; www.visitrochester.com

Visit Syracuse 315-470-1910, 800-234-4797; www.visitsyracuse.com

Yates County Chamber of Commerce 800-868-9283, 585-536-3111; www.yatesny.com

Other Tourism Organizations

Camillus Chamber of Commerce 315-247-5992; www.camilluschamber.com

Canandaigua Area Chamber of Commerce Visitors Center 585-394-4400; www
.canandaiguachamber.com

Central Steuben Chamber of Commerce 607-776-7122; www.centralsteubenchamber
.com

Corning Area Chamber of Commerce 866-463-6264; www.corningny.com

Finger Lakes Tourism Alliance 800-548-4386; www.fingerlakes.org

Finger Lakes Visitors Connection/Ontario County Tourism Office 877-FUN-IN-NY
(877-386-4669); www.visitfingerlakes.com

Geneva Area Chamber of Commerce Information Center 315-789-1776; www.genevany
.com

Greater Rochester Chamber of Commerce 585-244-180; www.rochesterbusinessalliance
.com

Information Center of Corning 607-962-8997; www.corningny.com

Hammondsport Chamber of Commerce 607-569-2989; www.hammondsport.org

Honeoye Chamber of Commerce www.honeoye.com

Skaneateles Chamber of Commerce 315-685-0552; www.skaneateles.com

Trumansburg Area Chamber of Commerce 607-387-9254; www.trumansburgchamber
.com

Watkins Glen Area Chamber of Commerce 607-535-4300, 800-607-4552; www.watkins
glenchamber.com

INDEX